T0294983

THE GREATER SAN RAFAEL SWELL

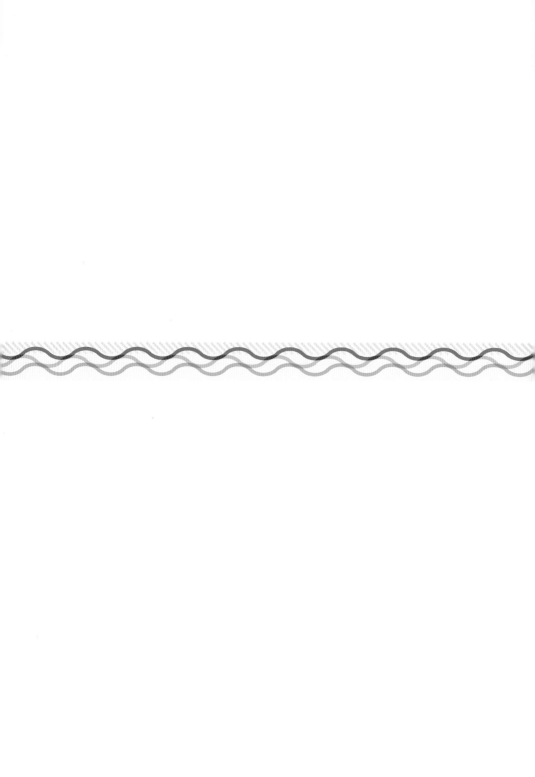

THE GREATER SAN RAFAEL SWELL

Honoring Tradition and Preserving Storied Lands

STEPHEN E. STROM | JONATHAN T. BAILEY

THE UNIVERSITY OF ARIZONA PRESS
TUCSON

The University of Arizona Press
www.uapress.arizona.edu

ISBN-13: 978-0-8165-4392-2 (paperback)

Cover design by Leigh McDonald
Cover photo by Jonathan T. Bailey
Designed and typeset by Sara Thaxton in 10/14 Warnock Pro
with Acumin Pro and Ehrhardt MT Std

Library of Congress Cataloging-in-Publication Data
Names: Strom, Stephen, author. | Bailey, Jonathan T., 1995– author.
Title: The Greater San Rafael Swell : honoring tradition and preserving storied lands / Stephen E. Strom and Jonathan T. Bailey.
Description: Tucson : University of Arizona Press, 2022. | Includes bibliographical references and index.
Identifiers: LCCN 2021027319 | ISBN 9780816543922 (paperback)
Subjects: LCSH: Landscape protection—Utah—Emery County. | Natural resources—Multiple use—Utah—Emery County. | Environmental management—Utah—Emery County. | San Rafael Swell (Utah)
Classification: LCC F832.S415 S77 2022 | DDC 979.2/57—dc23
LC record available at https://lccn.loc.gov/2021027319

Printed in the United States of America
♾ This paper meets the requirements of ANSI/NISO Z39.48-1992 (Permanence of Paper).

CONTENTS

Landscape west of Temple Mountain. Aerial photo by Stephen E. Strom.

PREFACE

> One cannot be pessimistic about the West. This is the native home of hope. When it fully learns that cooperation, not rugged individualism, is the quality that most characterizes and preserves it, then it will have achieved itself and outlived its origins. Then it has a chance to create a society to match its scenery.
>
> — WALLACE STEGNER, *THE SOUND OF MOUNTAIN WATER*

For the past twenty years, politics in America has been suffused with a toxic combination of economic and cultural anxiety. Ideology often overwhelms reason, and a sense of shared citizenship on a shared land seems a distant memory.

This book chronicles a more hopeful story for our times: how citizens of a small county in the rural West resolved perhaps the most volatile issue in the region—the future of public lands. Told through the voices of more than forty individuals, *The Greater San Rafael Swell: Honoring Tradition and Preserving Storied Lands* relates how citizens of Emery County, Utah, forged a shared vision for public land use among ranchers, miners, off-highway vehicle (OHV) enthusiasts, conservationists, recreationists, and Native American tribal nations. Emery's success finds resonance in the accomplishments of three other western counties: Custer and Owyhee in Idaho, and Washington in Utah.

These counties, along with Emery, reached agreements that protected almost two million acres as wilderness, national conservation areas, and recreation areas, while also taking into account the economic interests and cultural values of local citizens. Both their successes and the processes by which they found common ground serve as beacons in today's uncertain landscape—beacons that can illuminate paths toward rebuilding our democracy from the ground up.

Our journey begins with an introduction to a landscape of great natural beauty: Emery County, a place where the passage from deep time to the present is revealed in dramatically sculpted and colorful geological strata that span 350 million years of Earth's history. We follow the history revealed in these strata, as the land underlying Emery County inched its way northward from the equator; as climate changed from arid to tropical and back; as oceans, inland seas, lakes, and rivers inundated and traversed the lands; and as deserts and marshlands appeared and disappeared over the eons. The marvel of life and its adaptability to these radical changes is recorded in these strata, with geological layers, one by one, uncovering how flora and fauna evolved and perished in response to an ever-changing environment.

Emery's now-arid climate has preserved artifacts and art dating back more than twelve millennia, keeping safe the history of Indigenous peoples from the Pleistocene to the historic period. The rock art from the Archaic period onward represents a significant window into the daily and spiritual lives of the people who once found shelter in the eroded alcoves and the tortuous canyons of the greater San Rafael Swell.

Two hundred years ago, Europeans and Americans arrived in Emery County, first as fur trappers, later as explorers charting its geography, natural features, and wildlife and assessing its economic potential. Later we follow the story of Mormon pioneers, who first came to Emery County in the late 1870s, called by Brigham Young to settle these achingly beautiful but unforgiving lands. Faith and perseverance helped them farm, raise livestock, and extract mineral wealth. The traits passed down from the first settlers have served Emery County's families well for over 150 years, as they adapted to the boom and bust of coal and uranium mining, and the vicissitudes of drought, depression, and war.

The lives of Emery County's residents are intimately intertwined with these lands—lands that provide both economic sustenance and a place to recreate and find spiritual renewal. But most land in the county is not theirs alone. It is public land, administered by two federal agencies, the U.S. Forest Service and the Bureau of Land Management, to serve multiple uses: mining, ranching, agriculture, timber harvesting, recreation, and conservation. Finding a balance among sometimes conflicting visions for how public lands should be managed can be challenging. Some believe that the economic needs of local residents and their freedom to continue traditional uses should be paramount considerations, while others advocate for policies that restrict those uses and instead favor protection of the unique geological, paleontological, and cultural histories of Emery County's lands.

How these conflicting visions of public land use were harmonized is the focus of the next chapters in the book. Groups of citizens who held radically different political and ideological views met for years, in conference rooms, over dinner tables, in the landscape, and in Washington, D.C. Over time—lots of time—they developed a level of trust and mutual understanding that allowed them to discover what they shared, and how they could reconcile their differences with civility and grace. In the end, they were able to discover not only common interests, but common values. Their efforts resulted in the passage of the Emery County Public Land Management Act, part of the John D. Dingell Jr. Conservation, Management, and Recreation Act. When signed in March 2019, the Dingell Act designated 663,000 acres as wilderness, and protected another 217,000 acres as the San Rafael Swell Recreation Area.

We next examine how three other counties in the rural West—Washington County in Utah, and Custer and Owyhee Counties in Idaho—addressed similarly vexing public land issues. While their approaches differed due to political climate, stakeholder interests, and economic needs, the lessons learned from their successful efforts to protect public lands parallel those drawn from Emery County's experiences. As a result of the land use compromises reached in these counties, Americans can now enjoy in perpetuity the grandeur and cultural history of Boulder–White Clouds Wilderness, Owyhee Canyonlands Wilderness, Zion National Wilderness, and several national conservation areas.

In the final chapters of *The Greater San Rafael Swell*, we summarize elements common to efforts to balance the economic needs and cultural values of rural communities adjacent to public lands, and the desire to protect lands of scenic, scientific, cultural, and historical value. Based on the experiences of these four rural counties, we offer thoughts regarding how to catalyze constructive discussion regarding the future of public lands, and how to address the economic challenges facing similar rural communities.

Citizens of these rural counties look at themselves as the frontline stewards of public land. In their own ways, they love these lands, which are part of their lives, their histories, and their aspirations. Successful conservation efforts in the future will depend in considerable measure on recognizing their voices, honoring them, and working in collaboration with them to meet both their economic needs and the goal of protecting lands of priceless value for future generations of Americans.

THE GREATER SAN RAFAEL SWELL

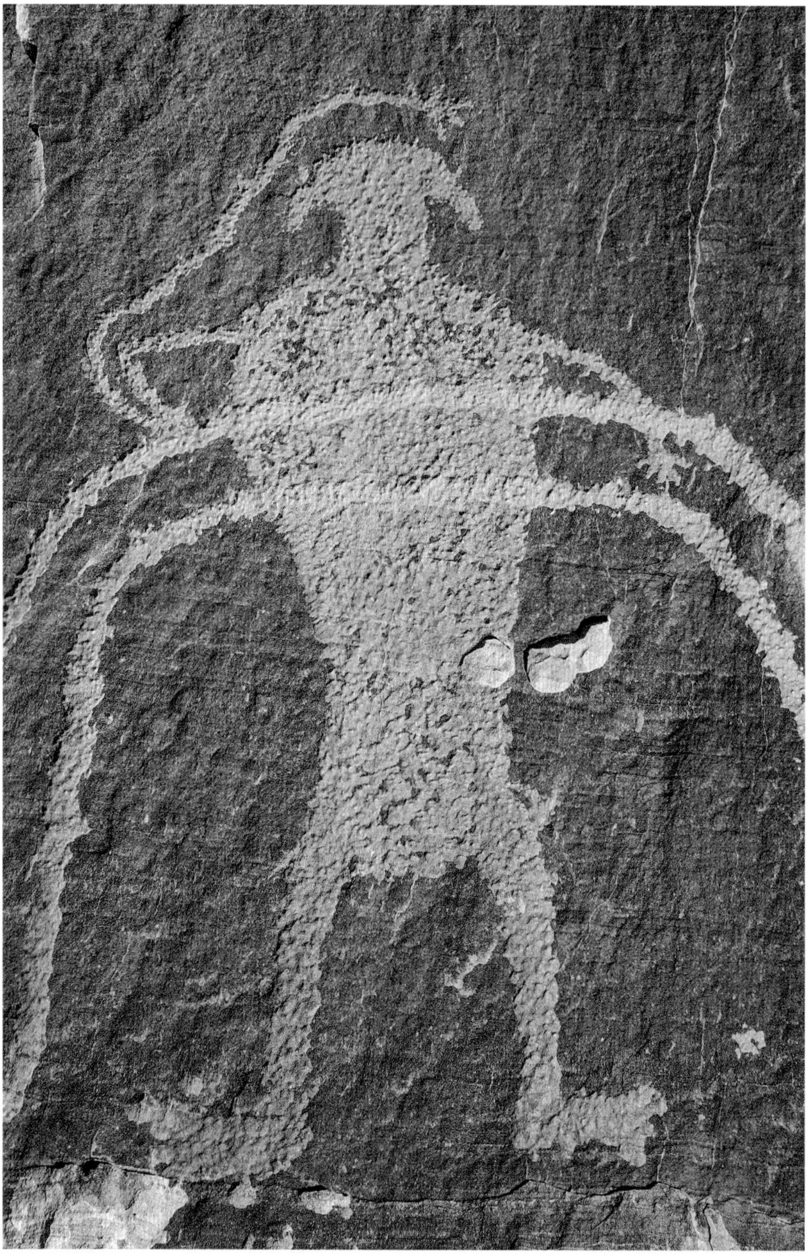

Petroglyphs possibly attributed to the Archaic period to Fremont transition. Fremont rainbow image overlaid. Photo by Jonathan T. Bailey.

Emery County

Its Land and People

Everybody needs beauty . . . places to play in and pray in where nature may heal and cheer and give strength to the body and soul alike.

— JOHN MUIR, *THE YOSEMITE*

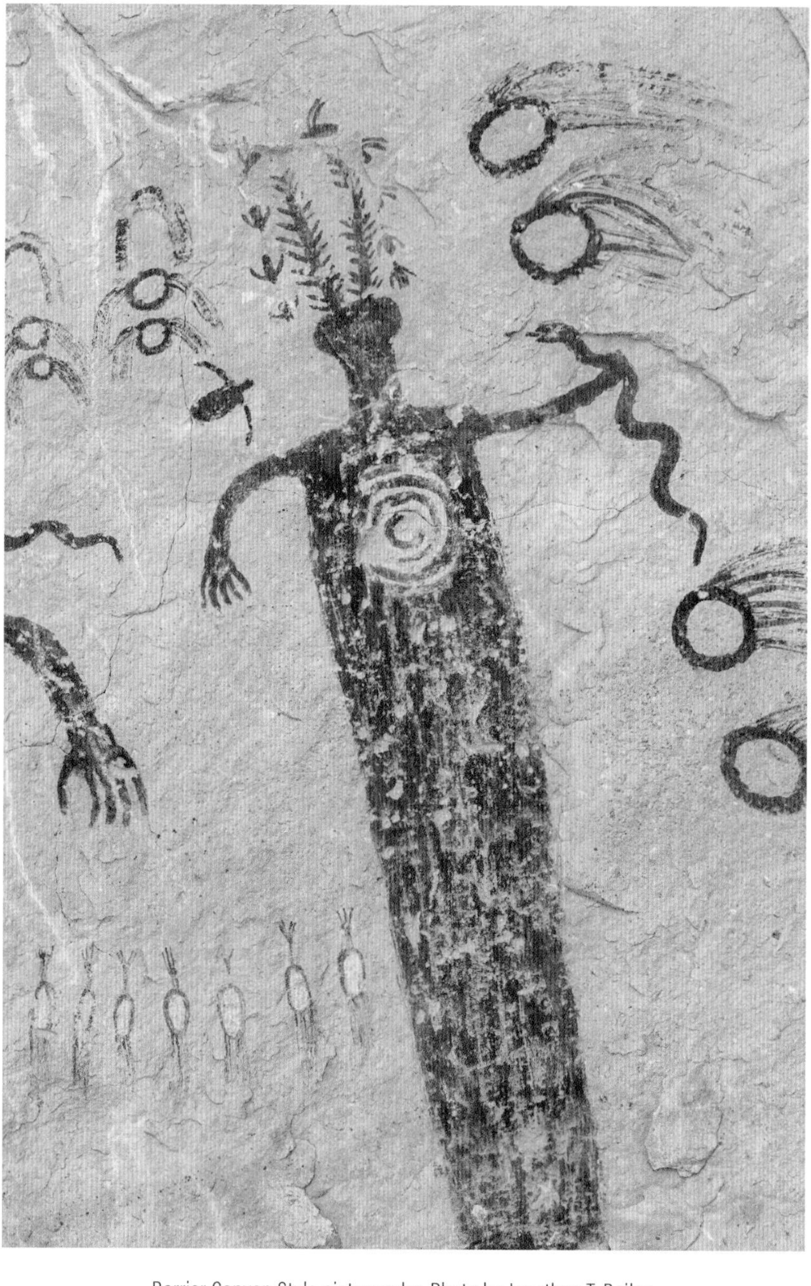

Barrier Canyon Style pictographs. Photo by Jonathan T. Bailey.

A Land of Rugged Beauty

Emery County, Utah, is located in east-central Utah, near the western edge of the Colorado Plateau, the 130,000-square-mile uplift that lies a mile and more above sea level and spans the region between the Rocky Mountains of Colorado and the Great Basin, covering parts of Colorado, New Mexico, Arizona, and Utah. The plateau's vividly colored rocks, mesas, canyons, towers, badland hills, and hoodoos compel the eye and move the soul. Millions are drawn to explore its world-renowned national parks and monuments, while others seek solitude and inspiration in the rugged wilderness of red rock country.

Emery County—four-fifths the size of Connecticut—exhibits all the stark beauty of the Colorado Plateau in microcosm.

Major Regions

Wasatch Plateau

On the county's western boundary lies the Wasatch Plateau. At its highest, the plateau stands more than ten thousand feet above sea level. During the winter, it captures moisture from Pacific storms and stores it as snow. Snowmelt in spring and summer feed four major creeks—Huntington, Cottonwood, Ferron, and Muddy—which flow eastward, irrigating the arid Castle Valley, which lies three thousand to four thousand feet below. Over the years, multiple reservoirs have been built to capture water crucial to sustaining agriculture and industry in western Emery County.

While the highest ridges of the plateau are lightly forested, moisture and more moderate temperatures at lower altitudes combine to support dense evergreen forests and one of the largest aspen forests in the United States. Vibrantly colored aspens in the fall, meadows filled with wildflowers in spring, and the plateau's streams and lakes draw visitors from throughout Utah and beyond. Timber from its forests and forage for livestock grazing in the plateau's high, cool meadows have served as important resources for Emery County's residents for nearly 150 years. Rich coal deposits on the eastern slopes of the Wasatch Plateau have been mined since the mid-1870s. Over most of Emery County's history, coal has been a major source of jobs and income.

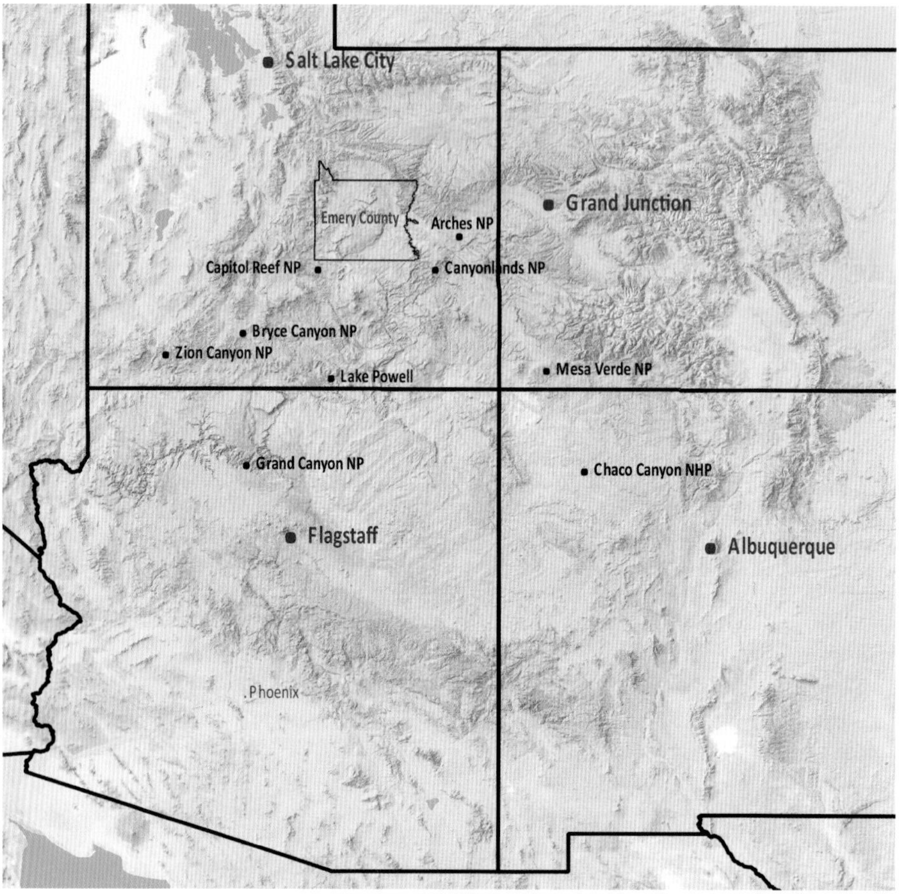

Emery County, located within the Colorado Plateau (the kidney-shaped feature near the map center). The Rocky Mountains (blue-green) lie east of the plateau, while the Great Basin extends westward of Salt Lake City.

Castle Valley

Located between the Wasatch Plateau to the west and the San Rafael Swell to the east, Castle Valley is home to 90 percent of the ten thousand citizens of Emery County. Water flows down from the plateau through Huntington, Cottonwood, Muddy, and Ferron Creeks, among other small perennial waterways. That natural gift enabled Mormon settlers and their descendants to farm this otherwise arid land and, before that, nourished Native peoples for more than ten millennia. The pride of settlers in their ability to establish

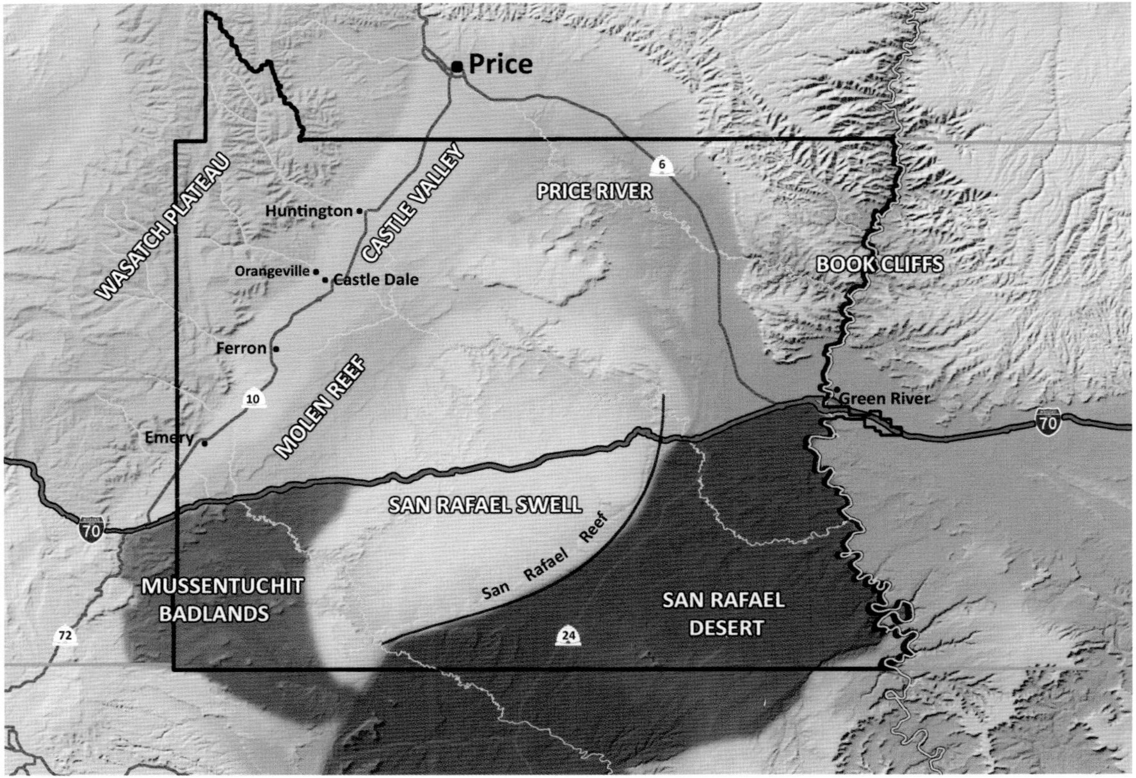

The major regions of Emery County.

A view of Cottonwood Creek as it flows downward through the rugged landscape of the Wasatch Plateau toward Castle Dale. Aerial photo by Stephen E. Strom.

farms and raise livestock in an arid region (with annual rainfall below ten inches) is palpable, and informs their deep cultural connection to the land and a powerfully held belief that they have stewarded resources responsibly. Similarly, present-day tribes feel a great sense of pride in returning to their ancestral lands in the San Rafael Swell, seeing firsthand the petroglyphs, habitation sites, and places of burial that confirm their strong cultural and spiritual ties with this landscape.

Towns from Huntington on the north, and southward through Castle Dale, Orangeville, Ferron, Molen, and Emery, still depend on the waters stored in reservoirs on the Wasatch Plateau, in addition to the spring and summer runoffs that fill Huntington, Cottonwood, and Ferron Creeks. Just beyond these towns, the creeks merge to feed the San Rafael River, which flows eastward across the county and joins the Green River, Emery County's eastern boundary.

Castle Valley, east of Ferron, Utah, in spring. Photo by Stephen E. Strom.

To the north of the San Rafael River lies the Cleveland-Lloyd Dinosaur Quarry, now part of the Jurassic National Monument, created legislatively in the Dingell Act. The quarry contains the highest known concentration of dinosaur fossils found to date. More than twelve thousand fossil bones have been discovered in this area, which once served as home to carnivorous and herbivorous dinosaurs as well as crocodiles, turtles, and snails. The well-earned renown of the quarry as a repository of prehistory from the Jurassic period (201–145 million years ago) is but one indicator of the richness of the more than 300 million years of paleontological history revealed in strata throughout Emery County.

Molen Reef

East of Castle Valley lies the Molen Reef, a twenty-five-mile-long shale ridge topped with hardened sandstone. The rock layers exposed on the ridge's face span the most recent 100 million years of geological time. The reef's strata reveal traces from mollusks, oysters, and now-extinct creatures including ammonites. Thousands of dinosaur bones are scattered across the expanse of its badlands territory. Footprints of these behemoths are found in both the Jurassic and the Cretaceous (145–66 million years ago) strata.

The reef is rich not only in fossils dating back to the time when dinosaurs roamed the region, but in artifacts: stoneworking sites, vessels, and rock art

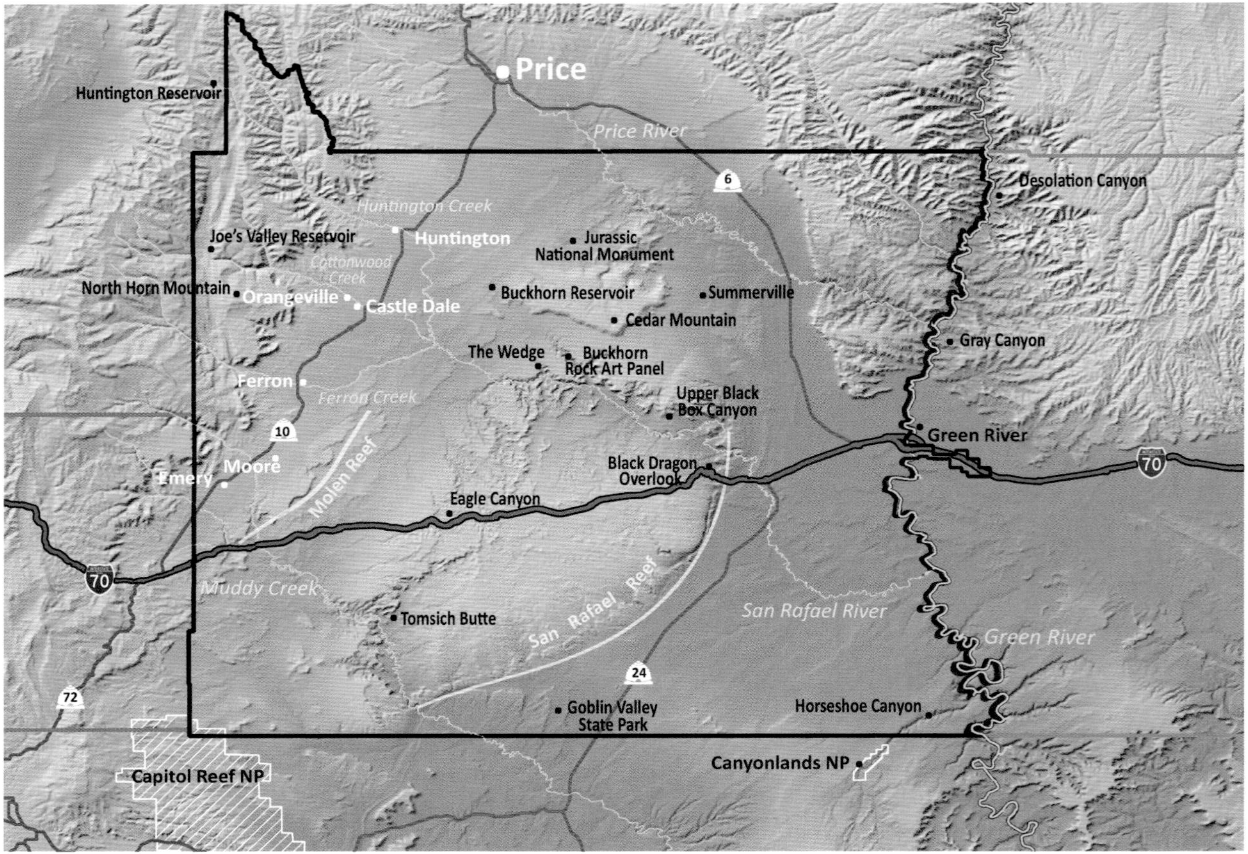

Place names in Emery County referred to in the text.

Molen Reef: A Reflection

In the desert, there are few things as alluring as *huecos*, or small hollows, carved into canyon walls. Within them, wonders await the persistent and perceptive—disheveled bird's nests, abandoned river cobbles, or tiny pools of blue-gray water.

From where we are standing, huecos pockmark the cliffs ahead, separated by the occasional aperture opening into little-known caves. To my right, investigating on her hands and knees, is Diane Orr, a close friend and fellow member of the Utah Rock Art Research Association's preservation committee.

It doesn't take long before she locates several geometric designs painted on the ceiling. One, toward the entrance, is marked with two intersecting lines that form a cross. Farther inside, numerous cryptic patterns interlock and curve toward the exterior. At the very back, tucked within a hueco, is a cavity filled with iron-rich minerals—a source of fine, powdery pigment—still imprinted by ancient fingertips. Within these walls, one can almost imagine the act of creation, the processing of pigment, the moment when thought became physical.

The Molen Reef contains hundreds of such sacred places: haunting apparitions painted in crimson, stone tools manufactured of translucent chalcedony, and granaries (storage structures for grain and corn) located on high, seemingly inaccessible cliff walls.

The reef has been occupied for at least twelve millennia. From plants used for food, medicine, and religious purposes, to culturally saturated topography marked by rivers, intermittent water sources, migratory routes, and overlooks, the depth of cultural history is evident throughout this region.

The dramatic landscapes of the Molen Reef rise just east of Castle Valley. Farther, two additional sandstone ridges are separated by varicolored badlands and brightly hued blocks of agate. Throughout the region, gravity-defying balanced rocks, ghostly withered towers, and jet-black concretions are scattered across expanses of red sand, creating landscapes more fitting for Mars than our own planet.

And yet, in this beautifully austere and haunting landscape, plant life is just as remarkable. The federally listed endangered Winkler's pincushion cactus (*Pediocactus winkleri*) lives largely below ground, rising above the desert floor solely to produce flowers and fruit. Species of *Allium* are also abundant, producing small, edible onions.

Other plants—utilized by Native Americans for millennia—include Indian ricegrass (*Oryzopsis hymenoides*) for meal and flour; two-needle piñon pine (*Pinus edulis*) for calorically valuable nuts; Utah serviceberry (*Amelanchier utahensis*) for fruits, jams, and bows; skunkbush sumac (*Rhus trilobata*) for fruit and jams, remedies for toothaches, cold symptoms, and gastrointestinal issues, and basketry; and plants such as Indian paintbrush (*Castilleja*), yellow beeplant (*Cleome lutea*), and Fremont cottonwood (*Populus fremontii*) for pigments to create rock art and decorate pottery.

The Molen Reef is both a geological wonder and a rich cultural landscape. It is a place of sacred contemplation, where memory is tightly woven to its topography. In all its strangeness, in the inexplicable wonder of its underpinnings, is a semblance of the divine.

JONATHAN T. BAILEY

left by Indigenous people that preceded European arrival. The region paints a vivid picture of the First Americans, from the plants they used for food, medicine, and religious purposes, to their rock art, habitation sites, stoneworking sites, burial sites, and granaries. Rock art of the Molen Reef—pecked, carved, and painted—displays scenes ranging from daily life to powerful rituals among Archaic period and Fremont peoples, whose history spanned 8000 to 2500 BCE, and 300 to 1300 CE, respectively.

Before and after contact with Spanish explorers in the sixteenth century, Numic cultures (Ute, Paiute, and possibly Shoshone) occupied the Molen Reef area. Evidence of their presence is found in rock art, which is occasionally carved but is usually painted with crayon-like blocks of ocher, charcoal, or other minerals applied directly to the rock. These paintings display images of horses, bison, and human figures, and are frequently found within caverns, in niches, or on the underside of boulders. Other sites of possible Numic origin are found scattered throughout the region: stone circles, Shoshone brownware ceramics, possible lumber procurement sites, and worked-glass tools.

Present-day tribes feel deeply connected to these areas, remembering traditions and oral stories evoked by images beautifully carved into and painted

Panoramic view of the Molen Reef. Photo by Stephen E. Strom.

on sandstone canvases, and by fingerprints still pressed within granary walls. The traces of distant mothers, fathers, and children that once occupied—and many believe still occupy—these sacred places create a living landscape cherished by Native peoples.

Mussentuchit Badlands

To the south of the Molen Reef lie the Mussentuchit Badlands. The landscape in the badlands varies dramatically. On the west, the Limestone Cliffs rise above the slowly undulating Blue Flats. Farther east lie labyrinthine and brightly colored badlands, inundated by hundreds of washes and gullies. To the south, 7,100-foot-high Cedar Mountain elevates more than a thousand feet above the desert. The panoramic view from its peak reveals a mesmerizing blend of chromatic and sculptural rhythms spanning sixty miles in all directions.

Signs of vulcanism abound. Thin volcanic dikes protrude above the desert floor, and volcanic rocks and boulders cover hills and valleys. These otherworldly regions are interwoven by pallid clays and dunes of sand. Livestock

Sawtooth-like volcanic dikes in the Mussentuchit Badlands (*center to center-right*) stretch across the landscape. Photo by Stephen E. Strom.

Mesa Butte, located in the northwest corner of the Mussentuchit Badlands. Aerial photo by Stephen E. Strom.

Mussentuchit Badlands: A Reflection

Welcome to the end of the world, where obsidian-black fins of volcanic rock emerge from smoldering flames of crimson-red mudstone. At its base, variegated fritillary butterflies (*Euptoieta claudia*) hover over pale white blossoms of poison milkweed (*Asclepias labriformis*), alighting before spiraling back up into the air.

This is no place for the meek: early settlers discovered that its inviting waters were alkaline and toxic, surrounded by lands permeated with basalt and volcanic intrusions—its violent beginnings written in the landscape. To the north, softer shades of the desert are observed: chalk-white slopes, brightly banded clays, and, if your timing is right, a sea of low-growing plants that bathe its floor in verdant green.

When I visit the badlands, I am reminded of a quote from Georgia O'Keeffe as she reflected on the beauty of bones: "To me, they are as beautiful as anything I know. To me, they are strangely more living than the animals walking around. The bones seem to cut sharply to the center of something that is keenly alive on the desert even though it is vast and empty and untouchable and knows no kindness with all its beauty."[a]

The Mussentuchit Badlands are bewitchingly skeletal, a hidden topography just beneath the flesh. Perhaps the people who once occupied these spaces, like me, sensed that in the expanse was something untellable that brought them closer to a central point, to a heartbeat beneath its ragged bones.

JONATHAN T. BAILEY

[a] Georgia O'Keeffe, "About Myself," *Georgia O'Keeffe: Exhibition of Oils and Pastels* (New York: An American Place, 1939), n.p.

Volcanic boulders (black rocks, sometimes called cannonballs, *foreground center to right*) dot the landscape of the upper Mussentuchit Badlands east of the Limestone Cliffs. Photo by Stephen E. Strom.

Cathedral-like structures in the southern part of the Mussentuchit Badlands region. The appearance of these sandstone spires foretells the landscape of spectacular towers in the Cathedral Valley region of Capitol Reef National Park, just to the south of the Mussentuchit Badlands. Aerial photo by Stephen E. Strom.

graze among the boulders, foraging on sparse desert grasses and shrubs. They can often be seen assembling around small reservoirs and stock tanks constructed over the decades by intrepid ranchers to store water—critical in a landscape where annual precipitation rarely exceeds eight inches.

There is ample evidence of early Indigenous people populating the badlands. Unfortunately, archaeological surveys in the region have been limited, and the extent of occupation is not well established. However, vast stone-working sites can be observed among areas containing rock art, habitation sites, and other cultural features. The geological resources found within the vibrantly exposed Morrison Formation provided a rich source of raw materials for projectile points, scrapers, and knives.

In the centuries that followed, Mormon settlers found their way to the region, some of them moving south to Wayne County after experiencing devastating losses to their livestock during winter. Their names—marked on canyon walls—detail their voyages through tortuous terrain. Other historical places are found throughout the region: ranch sites, stock tanks, and small clay, selenite, and gypsum mines.

San Rafael Swell

To the east of Castle Valley lies perhaps the best-known area of Emery County: the San Rafael Swell, a kidney-shaped uplift, extending approximately seventy-five miles from southwest to northeast, and forty miles across from east to west. At its highest, the swell rises 1,500 feet above Castle Valley. The swell, along with the Colorado Plateau, was formed between seventy million and forty million years ago during a geological event that elevated the land comprising the plateau and the swell from near sea level to its current four thousand to seven thousand feet. Over time, flash floods have carved the geological strata that make up the swell into gorges, canyons, mesas, buttes, and towers within and around taller "reefs" comprising rock that proved most able to resist the erosive force of water.

Most prominent among these reefs is the San Rafael Reef, which forms the eastern edge of the swell. The seventy-five-mile-long reef rises between 800 and 1,500 feet above the desert floor. Its surface reveals tilted layers of sandstone that have been shaped by water and wind into triangular "fins" and jagged peaks. Canyons—some a quarter-mile wide, others "slots," no wider than a few feet—have been carved through the reef, revealing within

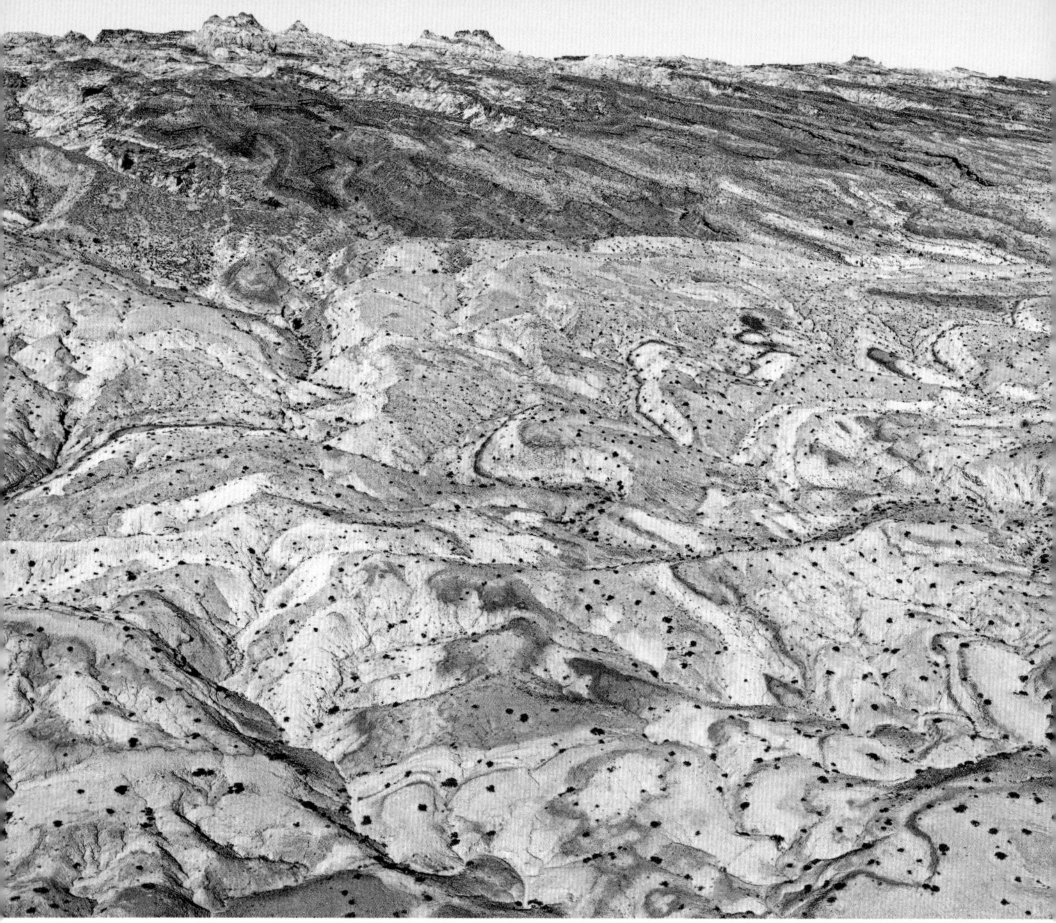

San Rafael Reef, near Little White Horse Canyon. Aerial photo by Stephen E. Strom.

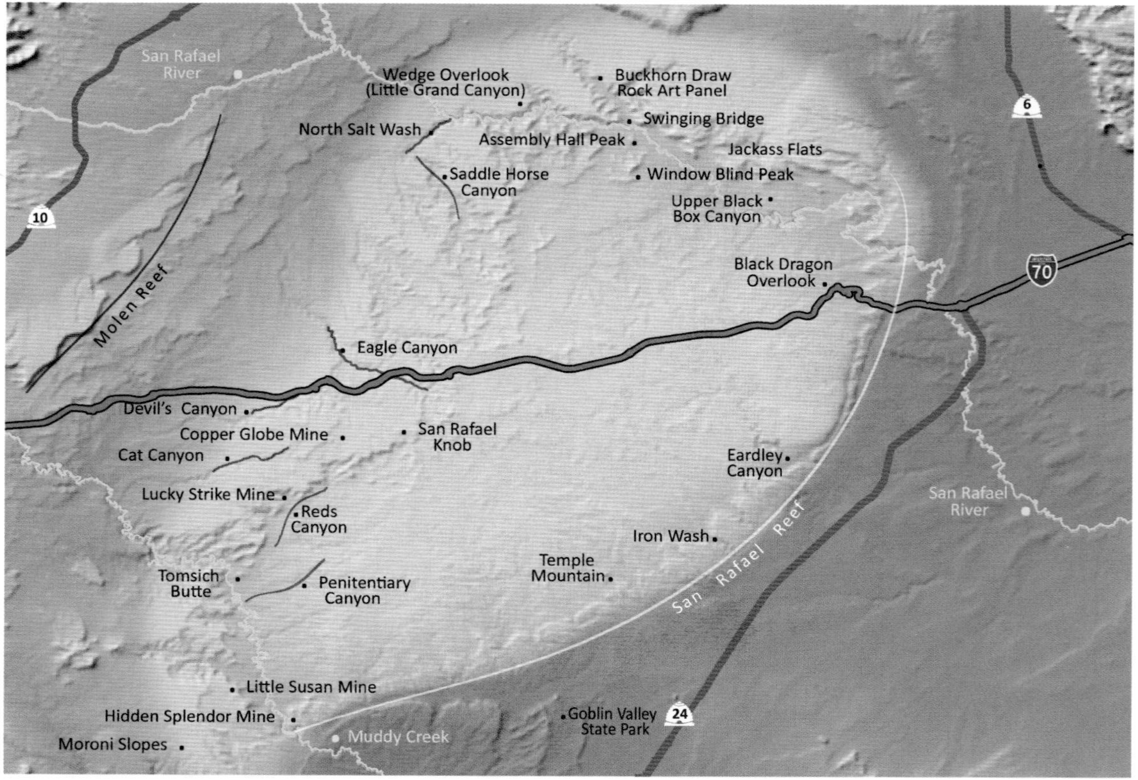

Prominent features and historical sites within the San Rafael Swell.

their walls multicolored strata carved into sinuous forms by water and wind. It is a place deeply rewarding to those willing to embrace its rugged beauty.

Inside the Swell

Nestled within the swell's canyons are signs of human occupation dating back perhaps ten thousand years: lithic scatters, hunting tools, and the evocative forms carved into and painted on canyon walls. One of the most well-known rock art panels in the swell is found along Buckhorn Wash. The panel, populated by a series of red hominid and animal figures, was painted during the Archaic period by hunter-gatherers, perhaps two thousand or more years ago.

Petroglyph panel (*top*) and pictographs, Buckhorn Wash. Photos by Karen Strom.

Fremont petroglyphs (*top*) depicting hands with bulbous fingers; and Fremont shield figure. Photos by Jonathan T. Bailey.

Seasonal pond near Head of Sinbad, east of the San Rafael Knob, west of Eardley Canyon, and south of Interstate 70. Photo by Stephen E. Strom.

Landscape north of Upper Black Box Canyon. Aerial photo by Stephen E. Strom.

Near the geographic center of the swell is the Wedge, a plateau encompassing a sinuous, 1,200-foot-deep gorge, eroded over eons by the San Rafael River and popularly known as the Little Grand Canyon. The view from the Wedge into the gorge reveals layers of multicolored sandstone, the deepest of which dates back 200–250 million years.

To the east of the Wedge lie a series of peaks that have held tall against the erosive forces of wind and water: Window Blind Peak, Assembly Hall Peak, and the San Rafael Knob are among the most prominent. Viewed from a distance, these peaks appeared to early settlers as "castles" towering above the landscape, giving rise to the name Castle Valley.

To its south lie a wealth of canyons: Eagle, Saddle Horse, Devil's, and Red's among them. In the 1950s and early 1960s, during the height of the Cold War, output from uranium mines—Lucky Strike, Hidden Splendor, Little Susan, Tomsich Butte, and Copper Globe—located in and to the south of Red's Canyon, along with those near Temple Mountain on the eastern edge of the San Rafael Swell, made Emery County the largest producer of uranium in the United States. Today, the boom is long over, but the histories of those mines, and the tens of mom-and-pop operations staked out by intrepid individual miners, remain deeply significant to residents of Emery County.

The "Little Grand Canyon" carved by the San Rafael River, as viewed from the Wedge. Aerial photo by Stephen E. Strom.

Approaching the Swinging Bridge from the east. Assembly Hall Peak is located to the far left.
Photo by Stephen E. Strom.

Limestone Bench (*foreground*) and Window Blind Peak (*background, upper left*). Aerial photo by Jonathan T. Bailey.

Penitentiary Canyon, Hondu Country. Photo by Stephen E. Strom.

Just south of Red's Canyon, Muddy Creek, a tributary of the Dirty Devil River, courses through a landscape filled with dozens of remote twisting canyons, mesas, badlands, sandstone domes, and igneous intrusions. One of the most dramatic of these canyons is the wild and twisting Cat Canyon, which winds below six-hundred-foot-high walls. Near the Emery-Wayne county border lie the Moroni Slopes and the sensuous blue-gray badlands just north of Factory Butte. Nearly 208,000 acres of this remarkable region was set aside as wilderness in the Emery County bill, thereby protecting a landscape that reveals two hundred million years of geological history in its strata (see appendix B for descriptions of various public land designations).

San Rafael Desert

Between the San Rafael Reef—the edge of the swell—and the Green River lies the San Rafael Desert, an area of windblown sand plains, the occasional butte, and little vegetation. The Green River, which defines the eastern boundary of Emery County, wends its way through the northern part of the desert after emerging from the Book Cliffs and Desolation Canyon to the north of the eponymous town of Green River. The Emery County Public Land Management Act protects 172,000 acres of Desolation Canyon.

The first people likely to have migrated through this region were hunter-gathers, who arrived over ten thousand years ago, leaving behind stone tools and stoneworking sites. They were followed by individuals in the Archaic period (which extended from 8,000 to 2,500 years ago). Enigmatic, abstract

Area near Assembly Hall Peak and the Swinging Bridge. Aerial photo by Stephen E. Strom.

The southern part of the San Rafael Reef, west of Muddy Creek. The blue-gray badlands lie just north of Factory Butte in adjacent Wayne County. Aerial photo by Stephen E. Strom.

Blue-gray badlands, just north of Factory Butte near the Caineville Reef. Aerial photo by Stephen E. Strom.

The San Rafael Desert south of Goblin Valley State Park. The San Rafael Reef spans the full frame of the photograph (light, sawtooth feature at the top of the image). The peak behind the reef leaning to the right is Temple Mountain. Aerial photo by Stephen E. Strom.

rock art images—depicting grids, animal tracks, and disembodied vulvas—are possibly some of the earliest panels in the region. Later, humanlike (anthropomorphic) characters were decorated on rock surfaces accompanied by animal forms known as zoomorphs and other images. During this time, people sporadically occupied deep alcoves eroded from sandstone canyon walls, adjacent to grinding slicks used to process gathered grains.

The Fremont (300–1300 CE) were also drawn to the San Rafael Desert, creating large spirals, serpentine patterns, and triangular-bodied to stick-like human characters. During this time, agriculture, ceramics, and the bow and arrow were introduced. In overhangs and alcoves of the region, these changes are evident in habitation sites that were occupied longer in response to crop growing. Dried corn cobs produced from these agricultural activities are occasionally also seen, either in dry alcoves or in granaries used to store grains and goods.

Although traces of highly mobile Numic-speaking individuals are fleeting, Ute rock art is expressed in panels depicting horseback riders and bison. Other panels feature elaborate hunting scenes marked in dark red pigment. Most Ute rock art dates to between 1300 and 1880 CE.

The river provides water to a large number of farms along its banks, some of which have produced sweet Green River melons for more than one hundred years. Despite the arid conditions, the San Rafael Desert is home to ranching activities that have persisted to the present. As the Green flows southward toward the confluence with the Colorado River in Canyonlands

Green River emerging from Gray Canyon, north of the town of Green River, Utah. Photo by Stephen E. Strom.

San Rafael Desert Region: A Reflection

There is no point closer to the earth than within the chambers of a slot canyon. Through its water-swept walls—each close enough to touch—you feel as if you had been dropped within the source, injected directly within the desert's sinuous bloodstream. Here, beyond the reach of daybreak, you are left in striking darkness, relieved only by thin slivers of light.

If you were to follow this canyon, it would lead you to the edge of the San Rafael River, flowing through a grassy plain lined with cottonwoods, surrounded by rolling alabaster cliffs of the Navajo Sandstone. Appropriately, the San Rafael Swell is named after this river that bisects its heartland, coursing through the Little Grand Canyon (San Rafael Gorge), down the Black Box, through the San Rafael Reef, and eventually to its confluence with the Green River.

The waterway now known as the San Rafael River was not the original river to have the name. The Don Bernardo de Miera map of the 1776 Dominguez-Escalante Expedition designated today's Colorado River as the Rio de San Rafael. But in John C. Fremont's 1845 and 1848 maps, a tributary to the Green River was falsely identified as the San Rafael River. The error has persisted, with that tributary now established as the San Rafael.

Near to this place, to the south of the San Rafael River, a vast sea of windblown sand was deposited beginning around the middle Pleistocene. Extending toward Horseshoe Canyon in Canyonlands National Park, this parched and arid desert—the San Rafael Desert—is marked with few natural springs or sources of water. People have nonetheless traveled through this landscape for over thirteen thousand years, their presence revealed by petroglyphs, pictographs, places of habitation, metates, and seemingly endless masses of worked stone.

JONATHAN T. BAILEY

Mushroom-shaped eroded sandstone in Goblin Valley State Park. Photo by Stephen E. Strom.

National Park, the surrounding land rises, forming the walls of Labyrinth Canyon, fifty-five thousand acres of which is protected as wilderness in the Emery County bill. The southeasternmost area of the San Rafael Desert in Emery County borders a remote area known as Robbers Roost Country, where Matt Warner, Butch Cassidy, and other outlaws once hid from the law.

Perhaps the best-known area within the San Rafael Desert is Goblin Valley State Park, located just east of the San Rafael Reef about two-thirds of the way from the town of Green River to Hanksville in Wayne County. The park was created in 1964 in order to preserve a mesmerizing landscape populated by unusual, deep-red-brown mushroom or goblin-shaped rock formations, sometimes called hoodoos. The hoodoos reflect weathering and sculpting of sandstone by water and wind that took place at the edge of an ancient sea. The state park tripled in size following passage of the Emery County legislation.

Book Cliffs

North and west of the town of Green River lie Gray and Desolation Canyons. Both Gray Canyon to the south and Desolation to the north (the latter now protected as wilderness by the Emery County bill) are carved into the Book Cliffs, one- to ten-mile-wide bluffs that loom two thousand to four thousand feet above the desert floor, and whose bases comprise lead- to blue-gray Mancos Shale. The cliffs extend north and west toward the Wasatch Plateau. The strata in the Book Cliffs range were largely deposited between one hundred million and fifty million years ago. The marine fossils found in the area reflect a time when parts of Utah were inundated by an inland sea. Horse Canyon, which intrudes into the Book Cliffs just south of the Emery-Carbon county line, was home to the once-productive Geneva Mine, which from the mid-1940s to the early 1980s produced at peak more than three thousand tons of coal per day.

Price River Corridor

Entering Emery County from Carbon County to the north, the Price River wends its way through three of the seven major regions within Emery County: the Wasatch Plateau, Castle Valley, and the Book Cliffs. After passing through the cities of Price and Wellington, it cuts through the Mounds area, where it becomes nearly inaccessible. With few access roads and abundant overgrowth adjacent to the river, the area is understandably poorly explored.

Blue Castle Canyon, Book Cliffs, north of Green River, Utah. Aerial photo by Stephen E. Strom.

The landscape within the Price River corridor ranges from purple to green mudstone descending into deeply patinated sandstones. The region surrounding Price River and its tributaries is cluttered with broken masses of pallid rock that extend nearly as far as the eye can see. Patches of green junipers and pinyons speckle the horizon on the rims of its canyons.

Owing to the river's inaccessibility, the full extent of its cultural history is barely known. Little can be said at present about the Indigenous history of the Price River drainage, although this isolated source of perennial water was almost certainly occupied for millennia. Much more exploration and research in this region is needed.

About a thousand years after Indigenous farmers occupied the corridor, an intrepid Mormon family constructed a residence, Marsing Ranch, along the river. The family came to this remote territory from the town of Desert Lake—a present-day ghost town northeast of Huntington—with 150 head of cattle.

An essay from the daughter recounts the struggle of living in this area:

> We raised a big garden [at Marsing Ranch]. We had about 2 acres of ground broken up that year. The river wasn't more than 30 feet wide at that time. . . . The water was clear, and full of fish. It was only about 2 feet deep.

Book Cliffs, north of Green River, Utah. Aerial photo by Stephen E. Strom.

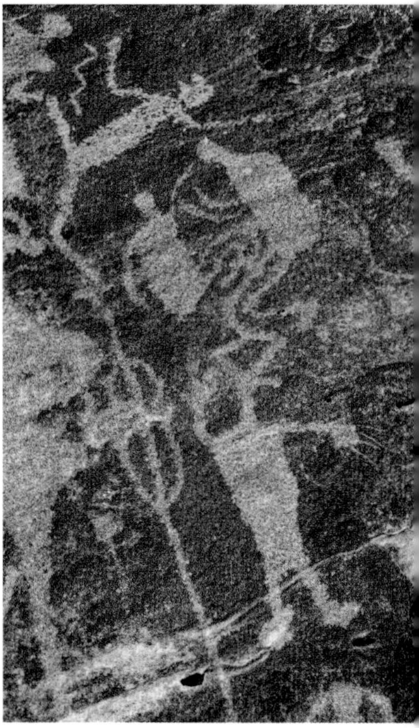

Rock art and architecture in the Mussentuchit Badlands, San Rafael Desert, and Price River Basin. The upper-left panel and the lower-left structure are Fremont. The other two images are possibly from the Archaic period / Fremont transition. Photos by Jonathan T. Bailey. Locations omitted to protect the sites.

Price River / Cedar Mountain Region: A Reflection

The Price River / Cedar Mountain region is a landscape shaped by erosion wrought by the inexorable working of water against rock. Cliffs rise above the cottonwood-lined river, broken into red clays, conglomeratic knobs, and mirrorlike sheens of purple-brown patina on the surfaces of fractured walls. Stalks of yucca erupt from its shale-rich soils. Between them, the imprinted tracks of horned lizards, *Shicheii*, grandfathers to the Diné people, fill the empty space.

This was the last place I visited with my dear friend Jim Keele—a former high school teacher of mine, who quickly became one of my closest hiking companions—before his untimely death. Since then, I have returned to the Price River on many occasions, seeking the macabre quality inherent to this space, a sadness draped just below its surface.

To remember Jim, I sat off a cliff's edge to the north, where the Price River burrows beneath conglomeratic, weather-beaten walls scattered with petroglyphs. I opened my notebook and recalled the words of Virginia Woolf: "The melancholy river bears us on. When the moon comes through the trailing willow boughs, I see your face, I hear your voice and the bird singing as we pass the osier bed. What are you whispering? Sorrow, sorrow. Joy, joy. Woven together, like reeds in moonlight."[a]

Shortly after I first met Jim, he offered his classroom as an escape. After my sexuality became known to my schoolmates, any sense of personal security vanished along with hope of my surviving unscarred. Yet, Jim was always in the back of his office, prepared to discuss anything from the wonder of plants to the understated beauty of ancient pigment scrawled on canyon walls.

In our lives, peace and safety are often woven from the fear and insecurities that drive us to seek shelter. These spaces hold ground for sharing difficult emotions with special people. Like sadness, like grief, this landscape knows beauty first and walks us through.

JONATHAN T. BAILEY

[a] Virginia Woolf, *The Complete Shorter Fiction of Virginia Woolf*, ed. Susan Dick, 2nd ed. (San Diego: Harcourt, 1989), 140.

[A] flood came in the Fall of 1908. . . . That flood ran over the banks, and we had to get out of the house. We took the kids, and ran for the side hill. There was three feet of water inside the cabin. I don't think the water ever went down any for three days, and it washed a channel 15 feet deep, and 100 feet wide. . . . All we had to live on was milk, and a little squash that mother gathered up.[1]

1. "1875 - October 31 - Alma Marsing was born . . . ," Family Search, accessed July 10, 2021, https://www.familysearch.org/service/records/storage/das-mem/patron/v2/TH-904-66976-1706-88/dist.txt.

A few years later, the mother, Annabella, passed away from health complications and was buried at the ranch. Both the ranch and her burial site are still preserved, weathering in a field above the Price River.

Scattered elsewhere along the Price River are historical small-scale mining sites, sections of the abandoned railroad grade, other cabin sites, and a campsite of explorer John W. Gunnison.

Ranching activities, while rare, are still carried out along the Price River, particularly in the southeast, nearer to the ghost town of Woodside. Off-road vehicle and hunting activities take place on the distant mesas above the canyons.

Today's Citizens and the Challenges They Face

Emery County's residents number just over ten thousand, of whom 91 percent are white, non-Latino, while the remainder comprises individuals of Hispanic or Latino background (7 percent), Native Americans (1 percent), and small numbers of other ethnic groups.[2] Members of the Church of Jesus Christ of Latter-day Saints represent nearly 80 percent of the population, reflecting the dominance of Mormons among the groups that established significant permanent settlements in the late 1870s and the very modest level of in-migration.[3]

More than 90 percent of the county's citizens live in the towns of Huntington, Castle Dale, Orangeville, Ferron, and Emery, spread out below the Wasatch Plateau; the remainder are located in Green River.

As has been true in much of the West, the employment profile in the county reflects the growth of service, tourism, and government jobs (60 percent) relative to the "traditional" agriculture, ranching, and mining jobs (40 percent) that dominated the economy for much of the twentieth century.[4] However, the loss of coal mining jobs—reflecting the diminishing role of coal in the country's energy portfolio—along with the impending closure of large coal-fired power plants in the county has stressed its economy.

2. "Quick Facts: Emery County, Utah," U.S. Census Bureau, July 1, 2019, https://www.census.gov/quickfacts/emerycountyutah.

3. "County Membership Report: Emery County, Utah," Association of Religion Data Archives, accessed June 1, 2021, https://www.thearda.com/rcms2010/rcms2010.asp?U=49015&T=county&Y=2010&S=Name.

4. "Emery County, UT," Economic Profile System, Headwaters Economics, accessed June 1, 2021, https://headwaterseconomics.org/apps/economic-profile-system/49015.

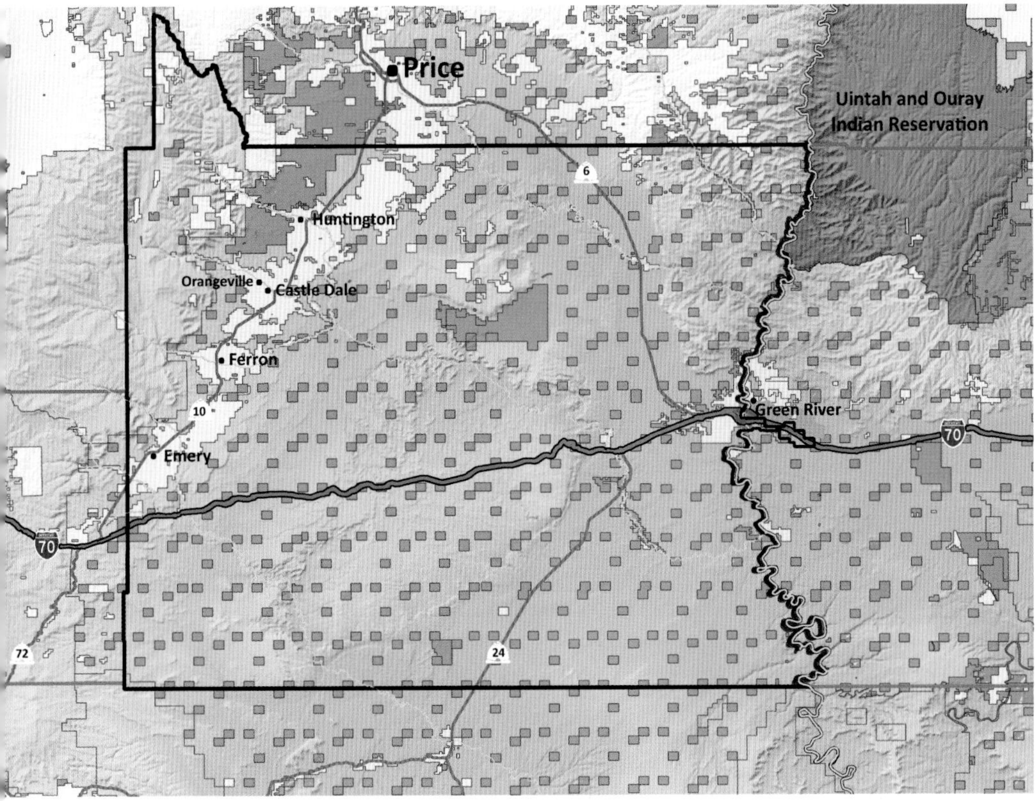

Map of Emery County's public land (*all shades of green*); school trust land, administered by the Utah School and Institutional Trust Lands Administration (SITLA, *purple*); and private land (*off-white*). Public land, administered by the U.S. Forest Service (USFS, *bright green*) and the Bureau of Land Management (BLM, *brownish green*), together with SITLA land, accounts for 95 percent of Emery County's land area. To the northwest of Emery County lies the southwestern part of the Uintah and Ouray Reservation of the Ute Indian Tribe (*red*). Map adapted from the Utah Automated Geographic Reference Center, https://gis.utah.gov/.

Moreover, the loss of "traditional" jobs affects not only the county's economy, but essential cultural assumptions about what represents a "real" job. The impending need to develop a new economic model has motivated county leadership to explore options for diversifying Emery's economic base in ways that ensure the viability of careers that offer both security and satisfaction.

Imagining a successful transition to a multifaceted economic base is intimately tied to how public lands in the county are managed and what fraction of those lands is available for economic sustenance. Of Emery County's 2.7 million acres, only 5 percent is held in private hands, while 83 percent is "public land" (75 percent managed by the Bureau of Land Management and 8 percent by the U.S. Forest Service), and 12 percent is state land (including school trust land).[5]

Ranchers depend on access to public land to graze livestock. The ability to extract mineral and energy resources requires opening selected areas of public land to development. Attracting tourists and recreationists may require limiting access to mineral extraction, while protecting cultural and historical resources can demand even more stringent regulation. And finally, preserving wild and pristine landscapes for their beauty and spiritual value necessitates balancing present needs against those of future generations, for whom open spaces and solitude are likely to become ever more precious resources.

The relationship of Emery County's residents to the public lands that surround them goes well beyond the practicalities of finding a path toward a sustainable economy. The large majority have lived on, worked on, recreated in, and sought spiritual sustenance in this land for five or six generations. They believe that they have been good stewards of the land, and they can at times be offended by "outsiders" who in their zeal to protect public lands intentionally or not belittle locals' culture and ignore their economic needs.

The tensions inherent in finding a balanced approach among multiple demands on public land have loomed large in the minds of Emery County's leadership since the mid-1990s. Resolving those tensions required a twenty-five-year effort by Emery County's citizens, their elected county commissioners, a Public Lands Council that reached out to stakeholders within the county and across the country, and political leadership in Utah and in Washington, D.C.

In what follows, we try to capture the combination of imagination, persistence, personal courage, and commitment to civility and common good that led to passage of the landmark Emery County Public Land Management Act. But first, we look more closely at the geological, paleontological, and human history that makes Emery County such an extraordinary place.

5. "Emery County Pre-Disaster Hazard Mitigation Plan, 2018," Utah Hazard Mitigation, accessed June 1, 2021, https://hazards.utah.gov/wp-content/uploads/Emery-County-Plan.pdf.

Fremont characters beneath the Milky Way. Photo by Jonathan T. Bailey.

Fish fossil found in Emery County. Photo by Jonathan T. Bailey.

Memory of Deep Time

To encounter the sacred is to be alive at the deepest center of human existence. Sacred places are the truest definitions of the earth; they stand for the earth immediately and forever; they are its flags and shields. If you would know the earth for what it really is, learn it through its sacred places. At Devil's Tower or Canyon de Chelly or the Cahokia Mounds, you touch the pulse of the living planet; you feel its breath upon you. You become one with a spirit that pervades geologic time and space.

— N. SCOTT MOMADAY, ADDRESS TO THE UNITED NATIONS

Emery County is a place where beauty abounds in a wild landscape of hoodoos, badland hills, mesas, and towers. Memory of deep time is carved in its canyons and encoded in shelves of steeply tilted sandstone, and brightly colored clays that bear silent witness to ever-changing winds, the appearance and disappearance of ancient oceans, lakes, and rivers, and the vicissitudes of an always changing climate. Other memories, more recent, reveal the ebb and flow of life in Emery County during the past 350 million years: fossilized plants and animals who once dominated, then disappeared, to be replaced by new species.

Origin

The land now underlying Emery County originated billions of years ago when oceans still dominated Earth. About 2.5 billion years into Earth's 4.5-billion-year history, continents began to form as individual solid plates of rock known as continental crust moved slowly above a roiling mantle of hot, liquid rock—traveling at a rate of mere inches per year—occasionally colliding with one another, sometimes gaining, sometimes losing material.[1]

Remarkably, the continental plate on which Emery County now lies was originally located near the equator. Over 2.2 billion years, the plate moved northward under the relentless push and pull of currents of molten rock, not reaching its current location in the mid-latitude northern hemisphere until between 150 and 100 million years ago.[2]

During most of its 2,500-mile journey northward from the equator, the land that makes up Emery County was located not much above sea level. As the land inched northward, it experienced inundations by oceans and inland seas, tidal flats, and lakes as Earth's climate warmed and cooled, melting or reforming the ice caps at the North and South Poles and, as a consequence, raising or lowering sea levels. In response to global temperature changes, the climate of what would become Emery County varied between desert and tropical. At times, marshes and junglelike forests covered the land, and during others, endless miles of sand dunes predominated. The multicolored sediments now revealed in its canyons are a reflection of the ever-changing

1. Bruno Dhuime, Andreas Wuestefeld, and Chris J. Hawkesworth, "Emergence of Modern Continental Crust About 3 Billion Years Ago," *Nature Geoscience* 8 (2015): 552–55.

2. Ron Blakey and Wayne Ranney, *Ancient Landscapes of the Colorado Plateau* (Grand Canyon, Ariz.: Grand Canyon Association, 2008).

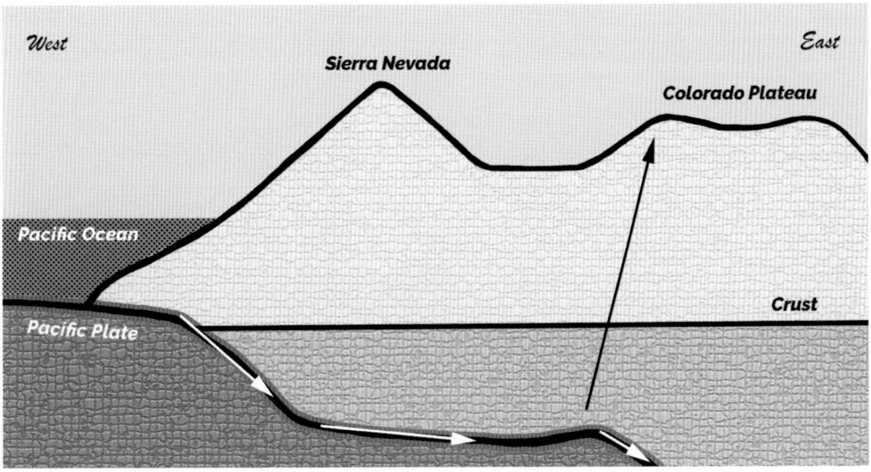

Uplift of the Colorado Plateau. The plateau was uplifted approximately sixty million years ago as the Pacific continental plate slid under the North American continental plate. Illustration by Jonathan T. Bailey.

environment as silt, mudstone, limestone, salt, sand, and volcanic ash were deposited by water and dispersed by wind over millions of years.

The Great Uplift

All these strata and the history they reveal were carried upward from sea level to their current mile-high perch about sixty million years ago, when a ridge of ocean crust known as the Pacific continental plate slid under the North American continental plate.

During the resulting violent upheaval, which geologists call the Laramide orogeny, Emery County, along with the surrounding Colorado Plateau, was lifted upward from sea level by more than a mile.[3] Near the center of Emery County, at the western edge of the Colorado Plateau, a dome forty miles wide and seventy-five miles long rose above the plateau, thrust upward by rocks deep below the swell's strata. To the east, the Laramide orogeny led to an even more dramatic episode: the rise of the current-day Rocky Mountains.

3. Chad Trexler, "Tectonic and Landscape Evolution of the Colorado Plateau" (paper, Grand Canyon Ecogeomorphology graduate class, Center for Watershed Sciences, University of California, Davis, 2014), https://watershed.ucdavis.edu/education/classes/ecogeomorphology-grand-canyon-2014/pages/final-student-reports.

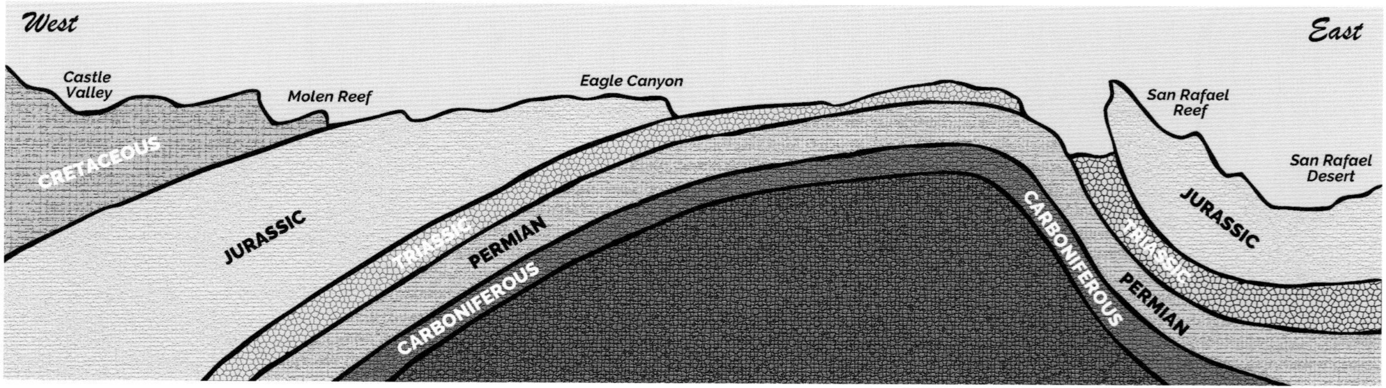

Geological strata uplifted in the event that created the San Rafael Swell. Illustration by Jonathan T. Bailey.

From canyon bottoms to the top of the Wasatch Plateau, the strata revealed in Emery County remained coherent as they were lifted upward by more than a mile—testimony both to chance, and to the unusually thick crust and strong rocks underlying the region. It is rare to find such ordered geological history so well preserved in the face of such cataclysmic tectonic events.

At the time that Emery County, the Colorado Plateau, and the Rocky Mountains began to rise, waters on the surface of the ancestral plateau wandered in gentle meanders fed from the snowpack in mountain ranges situated in Colorado and Wyoming. As the land rose, waters began to flow briskly downhill, from the Colorado Plateau southwestward toward Arizona. The drainages of the Price, Muddy, and San Rafael Rivers were captured by the Green River, which in turn merged with the Colorado near the center of what now is Canyonlands National Park.

The Great Stretching

At first, the path of the Colorado River toward the southwest was blocked by the Mogollon Mountains in Arizona. Soon (in geological time) after the uplift of the plateau, the continental crust in the western United States began to stretch, and in the process created the structure of alternating wide valley basins and mountain ranges characteristic of the American West. The Great Basin—perhaps the most dramatic example of basin-range geology—begins just to the west of Emery County's Wasatch Plateau and extends through western Utah and all of Nevada, ending at the eastern side of the Sierra Nevada.[4] During that stretching event, the Mogollon Mountains collapsed, allowing the waters of the Colorado to flow farther to the southwest.[5]

Following the great stretching event, the relative motions of the North American and adjacent Pacific plates changed. Rather than riding over the Pacific plate, the North American plate started to slide along the edge of its continental neighbor, creating crustal faults. About six million years ago, movement of crustal layers along the most well-known of those faults, the San Andreas, ripped open the boundary between present-day Baja California

4. Ron Blakey and Wayne Ranney, *Ancient Landscapes of the Colorado Plateau.*

5. Mary Gavin and Dave Wegner, "The Evolution of the Colorado Plateau and Colorado River," *Medium*, June 26, 2017, https://medium.com/river-talk/the-evolution-of-the-colorado-plateau-and-colorado-river-ac159791b73c.

and Mexico, creating an opening for the Colorado to flow unimpeded from Utah to the Gulf of California—the path it follows today.

Sculpting the Land

Even as the Colorado Plateau rose by more than a mile, the San Rafael, Green, and other rivers and streams still followed meanders channeled when the Colorado Plateau and Emery County rested near sea level some sixty million years ago. As they flowed through Emery County, the rivers carved and chiseled deep canyons, cutting through Desolation and Gray Canyons, past Labyrinth, to their junction with the Colorado River near the center of today's Canyonlands National Park. Once uncovered, canyon walls revealed in their strata the events that shaped Emery County. Atop the landscape, wind and water served as the rasps and rifflers that removed softer rocks and sculpted finer-scale structures—spires and hoodoos, flat irons and hogbacks—that add a surreal quality to the arresting drama of the county's landscape.

Were these sculpted features merely monochromatic, they would stand as impressive monuments to the shaping hands of plate tectonics, wind, and water. The interplay of the sculptural with chromatic rhythms speaks to the history of Emery County and the Colorado Plateau in yet another language. Looking eastward across the landscape from the Molen Reef, one finds the view transformed from the merely mesmerizing to something transcendent: the sense of witnessing the passage of eons. From the deep past to the near present, climbing through Emery County from its canyon bottoms to the crest of the Wasatch Plateau is a sacred procession, a story that begins at its bedrock.

Layers of Deep Time

Carboniferous Period (359–299 Million Years Ago)

The geological and biological stories revealed in the uplifted layers of Emery County begin with Redwall Limestone, which formed between 359 and 323 million years ago during the early Carboniferous period.[6] Corals, bra-

6. Hellmut H. Doelling et al., *Geologic Map of the San Rafael Desert 30′ × 60′ Quadrangle, Emery and Grand Counties, Utah*, map 267DM (Salt Lake City: Utah Geological Survey, 2015).

Period	Epoch	Formation	Time (millions of years ago)
Carboniferous		Redwall Limestone	359–299
Permian		Elephant Canyon Formation White Rim Sandstone Kaibab Formation	299–252
Triassic		Moenkopi Formation Chinle Formation	252–201
Jurassic		Wingate Sandstone Kayenta Formation Navajo Sandstone Carmel Formation Entrada Sandstone Curtis Formation Summerville Formation Morrison Formation	201–145
Cretaceous		Cedar Mountain Formation Naturita Formation Mancos Shale Star Point Sandstone Blackhawk Formation Castlegate Sandstone Price River Formation North Horn Formation	145–66
Paleogene	Paleocene Eocene Oligocene		66–23
Neogene	Miocene Pliocene		23–2
Quaternary	Pleistocene Holocene		2–0

Geological periods and epochs of the most prominent strata in Emery County. Adapted from Peter J. Vrolijk et al., "Anatomy of Reservoir-Scale Normal Faults in Central Utah: Stratigraphic Controls and Implications for Fault Zone Evolution and Fluid Flow," *Geological Society of America Field Guide* 6 (2005): 261–82.

chiopods, bryozoans (filter feeders comparable to coral), clams, and other marine organisms occupied these shallow waters of an inland sea that once covered the land. Their calcium carbonate–rich shells and skeletons would condense into rock and, over time, build limestone cliffs, examples of which are seen exposed deep within Eardley Canyon, carved through the San Rafael Reef by ancient tributaries of the San Rafael River.

Eardley Canyon as it cuts through the San Rafael Swell. On its rim, White Rim Sandstone is exposed above Elephant Canyon Formation within the canyon. Exposures of Redwall Limestone are visible at its floor (*out of frame*). Photo by Jonathan T. Bailey.

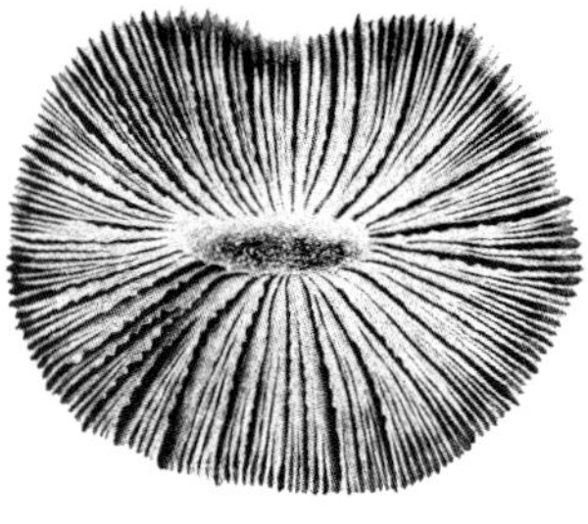

Example of fossilized coral.

Permian Period (299–252 Million Years Ago)

With the onset of the Permian period, an event known as the Uncompahgre uplift deposited thousands of feet of debris into the Paradox Basin (running southeast of the San Rafael Swell toward Moab) and the Oquirrh Basin (in midwest Utah), while much of Utah was still submerged under an inland sea.[7]

7. Steven M. Condon, *Geology of the Pennsylvanian and Permian Cutler Group and Permian Kaibab Limestone in the Paradox Basin, Southeastern Utah and Southwestern Colorado*, U.S. Geological Survey Bulletin 2000-P (Washington, D.C.: Government Printing Office, 1997).

Crinoid, Ammonite, and Trilobite. Illustrations by Jonathan T. Bailey.

Later in the Permian period, on the coasts of the inland sea, windblown sands were deposited, forming White Rim Sandstone 285–245 million years ago. Seen on the rim of Eardley Canyon and in pockets throughout the eastern San Rafael Swell, White Rim Sandstone from the Permian—white to beige, speckled with rust-orange patches—has been carved into dramatic canyons; Upper Chute Canyon and Upper Iron Wash provide good examples.

Within the coastal flats and shallow marine environments surrounding the inland sea, light gray to light brown Kaibab Formation was laid down approximately 280 to 270 million years ago. During the time of Kaibab Formation, these seas would have been occupied by otherworldly aquatic creatures such as ammonites, trilobites, and organisms with a cup-shaped body and feathery arms known as crinoids. These layers are primarily exposed in the south and east of the San Rafael Swell, not far from the San Rafael Reef.

At the end of the Permian period, upward of about 95 percent of aquatic life and 70 percent of land-dwelling vertebrates became extinct. The cause of this extinction event is still poorly understood. Some researchers have suggested that widespread acid rain produced by massive volcanic eruptions might be responsible.[8] Others have pointed to asteroid impacts or climate

8. Darcy E. Ogden and Norman H. Sleep, "Explosive Eruption of Coal and Basalt and the End-Permian Mass Extinction," *Proceedings of the National Academy of Sciences* 109, no. 1 (2012): 59–62.

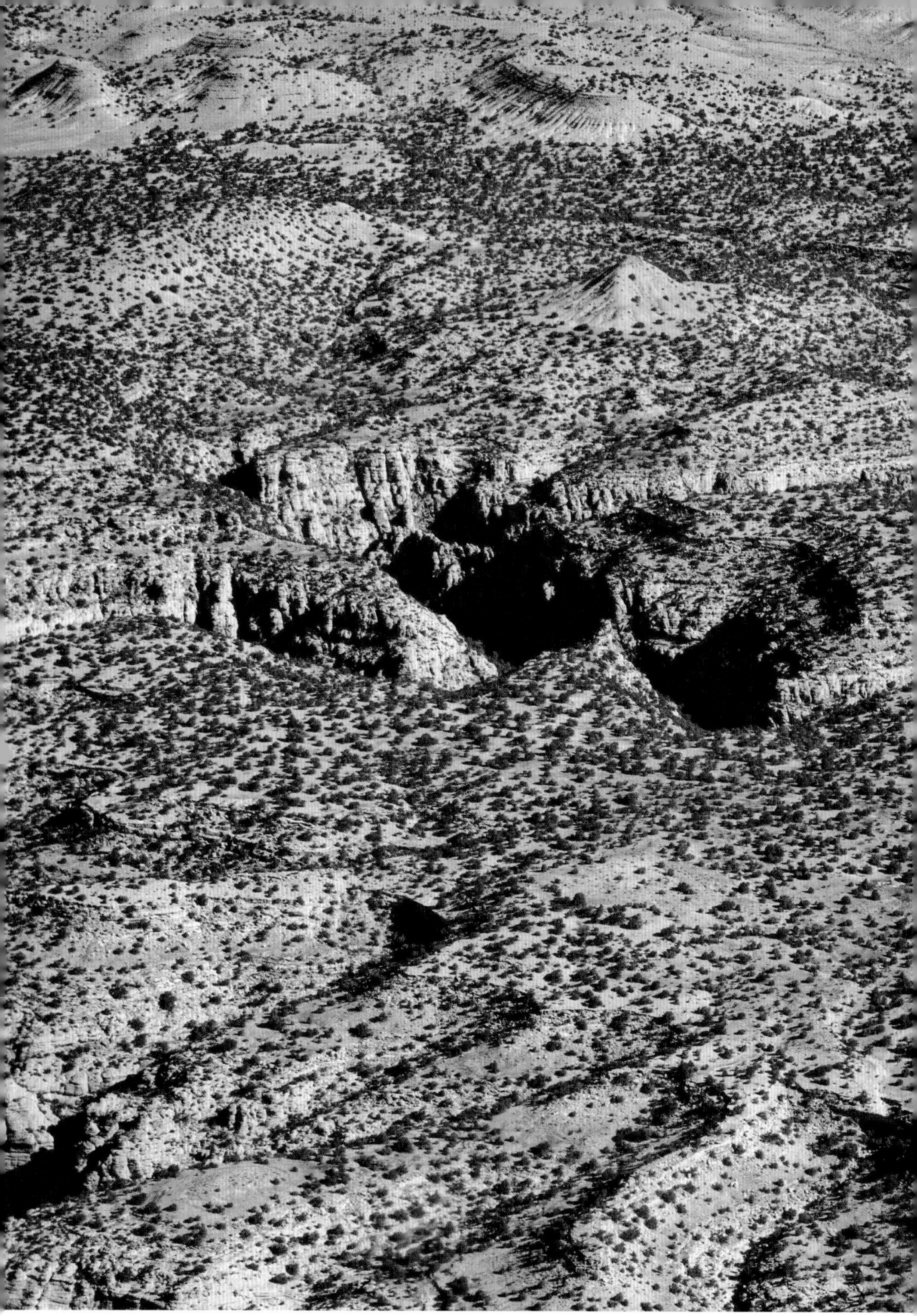

The football-shaped hill in the foreground belongs to the Moenkopi Formation. The lower, whitish slopes are the Black Dragon Member of the Moenkopi Formation. The cap of the hill is the Sinbad Limestone Member of the

Moenkopi Formation. The flat areas beneath the hill are Kaibab Formation, which pours down into the canyon (Upper Chute), which is composed of White Rim Sandstone. Aerial photo by Jonathan T. Bailey.

change triggered by a super bloom of methane-producing microbes within the ocean.[9]

Triassic Period (252–201 Million Years Ago)

In tidal flats along the coastline of a supercontinent, Pangaea—precursor to the continents of the modern world—the Moenkopi Formation was deposited following the End-Permian extinction event, during a period of extremely elevated temperatures. The Moenkopi Formation contains few fossils, a result of both the dramatic drop in biodiversity following the extinction event, and a biological recovery slowed by extreme heat. Nevertheless, reptile trackways and the remains of *Parotosuchus*, a scaly amphibian that can exceed six feet in length, have been reported in Moenkopi strata in Utah.[10]

The Moenkopi Formation is clearly revealed in layers visible from the Black Dragon Canyon viewpoint accessible to westbound travelers on Interstate 70 after it passes through the San Rafael Reef, and abundantly exposed elsewhere throughout the interior of the San Rafael Swell.

During the deposition of the ensuing Chinle Formation, about 237–201 million years ago, the land that would become Emery County was host to lakes, rivers, swamps, and floodplains. Flowerless plants—including ferns, mosses, and horsetails—and some of the earliest dinosaurs emerged during this period, along with open forests of conifers, fossilized remains of which are found in petrified wood deposits throughout the region. The Chinle Formation manifests in deep red mudstones that underlie many of the towering formations and cliff walls throughout the San Rafael Swell's "inner ring," including sections immediately below the San Rafael Reef, Tomsich Butte, and areas around Eagle Canyon.[11]

---

9. NASA, "Did an Impact Trigger the Permian-Triassic Extinction?," news release, May 17, 2004, https://astrobiology.nasa.gov/news/did-an-impact-trigger-the-permian-triassic-extinction/; Daniel H. Rothman et al., "Methanogenic Burst in the End-Permian Carbon Cycle," *Proceedings of the National Academy of Sciences* 111, no. 15 (2014): 5462–67.

10. Spencer G. Lucas and Rainer R. Schoch, "Triassic Temnospondyl Biostratigraphy, Biochronology and Correlation of the German Buntsandstein and North American Moenkopi Formation," *Lethaia* 35 (2002): 97–106, https://doi.org/10.1111/j.1502-3931.2002.tb00071.x.

11. Uranium, which is prevalent in the Chinle Formation, was profusely mined in Emery County during the mid-1900s. This "inner ring" of the San Rafael Swell is dotted with abandoned uranium mines and related ghost towns—including the Hidden Splendor, Lucky Strike, Little Susan, and Temple Mountain mines.

View toward Jackass Flats, just east of the San Rafael Reef. From bottom to top, Kaibab Formation is seen in grayish "valleys" beneath small flat-topped hills of Moenkopi Formation. Toward the San Rafael Reef on the right, deep red Chinle Formation is visible beneath dramatic cliffs of Wingate Sandstone. Aerial photo by Stephen E. Strom.

View up Red's Canyon. On the right, brown-red Moenkopi Formation. To the left, deep red Chinle Formation is exposed beneath vertical cliffs of Wingate Sandstone. Yellowish to purple Kayenta Formation caps the cliffs. Aerial photo by Stephen E. Strom.

The Glen Canyon Group: A Reflection

Navajo Sandstone. Wingate Sandstone. Kayenta Formation. These are three of the four formations that make up the Glen Canyon Group. The fourth—the Moenave Formation—is not visible in the San Rafael Swell. This geological group is exposed in the towering sandstone teeth of the San Rafael Reef, each formation measuring up to about three miles from base to summit.

Jim Keele and I have decided to take the day to travel through the center of these teeth, in the little-visited uplifts between canyons, where giant fins, knobs, and buttes meet, creating in the gaps between them an endless labyrinth of tightly packed drainages—many occupied by springs that feed deep, emerald pools that rarely see the sun.

In one of these drainages, we come across an alcove carved into a sandstone wall, nearly obscured by the flora that abounds within. Desert "hanging gardens" like this one are fed by aquifers that seep slowly through Navajo Sandstone. When these aquifers reach denser strata of rock in the Kayenta Formation, water is forced outward. Over time, water erodes the cliff into alcoves that provide well-watered, fertile, and protected habitats for rare species.

Above the alcove, our eyes are drawn to southern maidenhair ferns (*Adiantum capillus-veneris*) that drape from canyon walls. Below, patches of bone-white columbines (*Aquilegia micrantha*) descend the cliffs. Nearer to the alcove, we find alcove bog orchids (*Platanthera zothecina*), which—according to Jim—look like dancers with upraised arms, draped with the finest of green dresses.

Hanging gardens sustain a wide diversity of wetland, riparian (water-adjacent), and desert species. A surprising number of birds, amphibians, reptiles, and mammals depend on these shaded, wet, and verdant places to survive. One species—the regionally rare Great Plains toad (*Anaxyrus cognatus*)—seems to gravitate toward the swell's hanging gardens. While some researchers claim that the species is no longer found in Utah, Jim and I have been fortunate enough to find the toads hidden in these rare environments: testimony to nature's ability to find ecological niches in what, at a distance, appears to be lifeless and forbidding.

JONATHAN T. BAILEY

Jurassic Period (201–145 Million Years Ago)

By the end of the Triassic period, climate in the region turned increasingly dry and arid. As the environment became hyperarid at the beginning of the Jurassic period, vast seas of sand, reminiscent of the present-day Sahara Desert, overlaid Emery County. About 208–144 million years ago, Wingate Sandstone formed from these eolian (or windblown) sand deposits.[12] Evidence of pale orange to red Wingate can be seen among many cliffs in

12. Felicie Williams, Lucy Chronic, and Halka Chronic, *Roadside Geology of Utah*, 2nd ed. (Missoula, Mont.: Mountain Press, 2014).

San Rafael Reef. At its base, Carmel Formation rises in brown, tooth-shaped prongs, leading to steeply raised, yellowish-white Navajo Sandstone. Wingate Sandstone emerges about midway up the reef, beneath cliff-forming layers of Kayenta Formation. Aerial photo by Stephen E. Strom.

Emery County, including Assembly Hall Peak, Buckhorn Wash, and the San Rafael Reef.

Later, spanning a period between 185 and 95 million years ago, variegated sandstones, mudstones, and siltstones were deposited along ephemeral rivers, creating the Kayenta Formation, which is visible throughout the San Rafael Swell's "outer ring" in reddish outcrops. Particularly striking examples are found above Eagle Canyon along Interstate 70 and in the uplifted topography of the San Rafael Reef.

Overlying the Kayenta Formation, Navajo Sandstone forms immense cliffs, domes, and bluffs that enclose much of the San Rafael Swell's present-day boundaries, from the base of the San Rafael Reef, around Jackass Flats, through areas near the San Rafael Gorge, to the Eagle Canyon overlook on Interstate 70, and extending southward.[13]

About 185–180 million years ago, windblown sand covered most of the planet, including the land that now makes up Emery County. Compressed

13. Doelling et al., *Geologic Map of the San Rafael Desert.*

Limestone Bench, with Assembly Hall Peak on the right. Photo by Karen Strom.

Exposures of the Glen Canyon Group in Buckhorn Wash. Wingate Sandstone is the lowest, beneath steep cliffs of Kayenta Formation. Navajo Sandstone caps the canyon with its characteristically smooth, off-white sandstone. Aerial photo by Stephen E. Strom.

over time, these sands solidified into a layer of white and pink Navajo Sandstone that is visible near the top of canyon walls in Buckhorn Draw, and that tops many other mesas throughout the region.

Later in the Jurassic period, a shallow sea would enter the area—this time sweeping inland from the present-day Arctic Ocean through western Canada and south through Utah.[14] Named the Sundance Sea, this inland body of water was surrounded by desert or near-desert lands. Throughout the Jurassic, the sea would experience repeated cycles of receding and flooding.[15]

Within its shallow waters, and near its shores, mollusks, snails, corals, and other marine life abounded. In the pink-gray Carmel Formation deposited about 170–164 million years ago, their skeletons are found in large fossiliferous outcrops skirting the San Rafael Swell.[16] Noteworthy examples can be seen near the rim of North Salt Wash and along north Muddy Creek, south of Interstate 70.

---

14. Annaka M. Clement, "The Sequence Stratigraphy of the Middle Jurassic Gypsum Spring and Piper Formations in the Eastern Bighorn Basin of Wyoming, U.S.A." (MS thesis, University of Georgia, 2015).

15. This is evident in the geological record. See Marjorie Chan, *Capitol Reef National Park and Surrounding Areas: Geological Tour Guide* (Salt Lake City: University of Utah, Sedimentary and Terrestrial Analog Research, 2010).

16. This is also visible in exposures to the north, extending toward the Price River.

Fossiliferous rock of the Carmel Formation, dating to the Jurassic period. Photo by Jonathan T. Bailey.

About 160 million years ago, windblown sands formed a new layer: vibrantly crimson Entrada Sandstone. Over time, wind and water erosion shaped Entrada into unearthly formations that have been mythologized as fins, ghouls, and goblins. Examples are found throughout the area, most notably in aptly named Goblin Valley State Park and along the Red Ledges of the eastern Molen Reef.

The next youngest feature, the Curtis Formation, was deposited in shallow marine environments, forming sandstone, shale, and—as oceanic waters high in calcium and sulfate evaporated—gypsum.[17] Gray-green layers of Curtis Formation abound in Emery County. Two notable examples include the eastern parts of the Molen Reef (above the Red Ledges) and the prominent white "belt" layered within the red cliffs towering over Goblin Valley.

17. Gypsum is industrially mined in Emery County. It is used for a variety of purposes, including plasters, cement, wallboard, and agriculture.

Layers of the Summerville Formation, west of Hanksville, Utah. Photo by Karen Strom.

Just above the Curtis Formation lies the Summerville Formation, a layer comprising thinly bedded, burnished-brown sandstone and chestnut-colored shales that formed in shallow tidal flats.

Near the end of the Jurassic period, one of Emery County's most iconic strata—the Morrison Formation—formed from beds of mudstones, sandstones, and siltstones deposited in rivers and floodplains 155–148 million years ago. The light gray, greenish-gray, or muted red Morrison layer is best known for its abundance of fossilized dinosaur remains, including *Allosaurus*, *Apatosaurus*, and *Diplodocus*.

The Morrison Formation is also abundantly exposed within the Molen Reef and Mussentuchit Badlands. Serious amateurs as well as paleontologists have discovered thousands of fossilized bones primarily in its Brushy Basin Member. Many of these remains are deeply embedded within whitish outcroppings of conglomeratic rocks that formed in streams that coursed through Emery County during the late Jurassic period.

One of the richest concentrations of Jurassic-era dinosaur fossils is located within the newly designated Jurassic National Monument at the site of the Cleveland-Lloyd Dinosaur Quarry, where bones belonging to at least

The Morrison and Cedar Mountain Formations: A Reflection

If you were looking for the underworld, you would find the entrance here, embedded with the jagged bones of an armored ankylosaurid deposited about a hundred million years ago. Overhead, a great horned owl (*Bubo virginianus*) peers from the hollow suspended below the rim, then suddenly dives back to her owlets, tucked away from view. Far below, spring water seeps beneath jade-colored bladderferns (*Cystopteris utahensis*) and branched white flowers of chokecherries (*Prunus virginiana*).

In the darkness at the pit's bottom, basins of water shimmer, reflecting the pale sky before dawn, draped with the last few stars that linger in daybreak. It was no coincidence that this was the place I visited when the area was first threatened by development, nor was it a coincidence when I brought my beloved to this location. *Place*, in some sense, becomes sacred for the memory that it holds. On the scale of a landscape, memories are held in *deep time*, in bottomless histories. Each layer is ancient beyond comprehension.

As the Emery County Public Land Management Act was being considered, my mind was once again drawn to this sacred place. Writing in the *Salt Lake Tribune*, I reflected on the elements that make this space so powerful:

> *"Not long ago, I entered a canyon with Diane Orr, the head of preservation at the Utah Rock Art Research Association. The walls were tortuous and scarred, marked with serpentine breaks where rock gave way to underground springs that seeped from beneath the bedrock. This was a desert landscape that went against conventions, a sheen of emerald enveloped in a bottomless dark, trees looming, light all but swallowed by canopies of leaves and stalks of chalky white flowers. . . .*

View of the Morrison Formation through the Molen Reef. Aerial photo by Stephen E. Strom.

"Nearby, dark strands of pigment were scrawled, revealing faces with hollow eyes and sharp, carnivorous teeth. Overhead, painted insect-like beings escaped into the cracks, flanked by humanesque figures not much larger than the nail on my thumb. Birds were incorporated throughout, some migrating through the porous folds in stone, others firmly clutched in the hands of the teethed characters.

"These rock art images have remained in this space for several thousand years, haunting visitors with their unspeakable power, suspending a thin veil between the realm of dreams and our physical reality. As I continue to listen to elders and storytellers from various tribes, I find that rock art—spaces much like this—are often described as places in which living spirits reside, perhaps, in part, as a culmination of a person's thoughts and experiences—their memories."[a]

Like the strata preserved in cliff walls, this is a place where history is deeply experienced. As Indigenous people encountered the rocks of the Cedar Mountain Formation, they gifted us with a glimpse into their own beliefs and memories of deep time.

It is too often forgotten that Indigenous people discovered fragments from a time millions of years in the past, long before British fossil hunter William Buckland described the "first" dinosaur—*Megalosaurus*—in 1819. They recorded their discoveries, not in scientific journals, but in their art: dinosaur tracks depicted in vibrant pigment on canyon walls; trilobites etched into stone and fashioned into pieces of jewelry; *Pycnodonte* fossils (a genus of extinct oysters) moved from geological contexts and later found among artifacts in Fremont archaeological sites; and images like those in this canyon, many seemingly inspired by fossilized remains found among surrounding conglomerate rocks and underlying layers of Morrison Formation. Some rock art sites in Emery County and environs depict colossal beasts with sprawling wings, frightful claws, and teeth. Perhaps these fossils vivified or inspired characters in oral stories, or maybe, in the creation of art, Indigenous people imagined how these ancient creatures may have once looked—a process that continues today in paleontological studies.

JONATHAN T. BAILEY

[a] Jonathan Bailey, "Commentary: Losing Utah Rock Art Would Be Like Burning Family Photos," *Salt Lake Tribune*, May 19, 2018.

Illustration of *Allosaurus* skull. Painting by Jonathan T. Bailey.

seventy-four individuals have been identified. Examples of *Allosaurus fragilis*, a theropod (hollow-boned, bipedal dinosaur) that grew up to thirty feet in height and ate meat, are particularly abundant in the Quarry. A number of algae, freshwater mollusks, and one extinct species of turtle have been identified in the monument, along with fossilized remains of sequoia and other large trees.[18]

Cretaceous Period (145–66 Million Years Ago)

Immediately above the Morrison Formation and very similar in appearance, the Cedar Mountain Formation—a layer comprising conglomerate rocks and sandstone—was deposited by rivers about 125–94 million years ago. Much like Morrison Formation, the multicolored gray, green, and red Cedar Mountain Formation is densely fossiliferous, containing dinosaur fossils belonging to *Ankylosaurus*, *Utahraptor*, *Iguanadon*, and others.

The fossil deposits of the Cedar Mountain Formation were not well studied until the 1990s, and as a result, new discoveries are still being made. In 2019, a previously unidentified species of dinosaur, discovered in the Cedar Mountain Formation of the Mussentuchit Badlands, was announced to the public: *Moros intrepidus* ("the harbinger of doom"), a tiny tyrannosauroid, measuring only about three to four feet in height.[19] Interestingly, *M. intrepidus* may indicate a second invasion of a tyrannosauroid species from Asia that would become the notorious giants of the late Cretaceous.[20] Examples of the Cedar Mountain Formation can be found in the area around Buckhorn Reservoir and on the western slopes of Cedar Mountain, east of Castle Dale.

After the deposition of the Cedar Mountain Formation, an inland sea known as the Western Interior Seaway—connecting what would become

---

18. Hannah Osborne, "Mystery of Cleveland Dinosaur Graveyard Finally Solved by Scientists," *Newsweek*, June 6, 2017; "Cleveland-Lloyd Dinosaur Quarry," Utah State University Eastern Prehistoric Museum, accessed June 1, 2021, http://usueastern.edu/museum/paleontology/cleveland-lloyd/index.

19. Lindsay E. Zanno, "Diminutive Fleet-Footed Tyrannosauroid Narrows the 70-Million-Year Gap in the North American Fossil Record," *Communications Biology* 2 (2019), article 64, https://doi.org/10.1038/s42003-019-0308-7.

20. Michael Greshko, "New Tiny Tyrannosaur Helps Show How *T. rex* Got Big," *National Geographic*, February 21, 2019, https://www.nationalgeographic.com/science/article/new-tiny-t-rex-relative-moros-fills-north-american-fossil-gap. These species would have arrived from a land bridge that connected Asia to North America. Humans migrated into present-day Alaska by utilizing a similar path millions of years later.

Ankylosaurus tail, armor, and hip area in Cretaceous Cedar Mountain Formation. Photo by Jonathan T. Bailey.

Artistic rendition of *Utahraptor*. Courtesy of Emily Willoughby, http://www.emilywilloughby.com.

the Arctic Sea to the Gulf of Mexico —advanced slowly across present-day Utah. The seaway eventually reached Emery County, depositing the dark gray Naturita Formation (formerly Dakota Formation) in the process.

As the seaway continued its advance into Emery County and environs, it next deposited gray to blue sediments of mudrock, shale, sandstone, and siltstone, forming Mancos Shale in near-shore and marine environments. Dinosaur tracks can sometimes be seen in these Mancos layers. In the Molen Reef, where the Ferron Sandstone Member of Mancos Shale abounds, the prints of a particularly rare four-toed therizinosaur were recently discovered.[21]

21. Therizinosaur is a probable identification. See Gerard Dariusz Gierlinski and Martin Lockley, "First Report of Probable Therizinosaur (cf. *Macropodosaurus*) Tracks from North America, with Notes on the Neglected Vertebrate Ichnofauna of the Ferron Sandstone (Late Cretaceous) of Central Utah," in *At the Top of the Grand Staircase: The Late Cretaceous of Southern Utah*, ed. Alan L. Titus and Mark A. Loewen (Bloomington: Indiana University Press, 2013), 530–35.

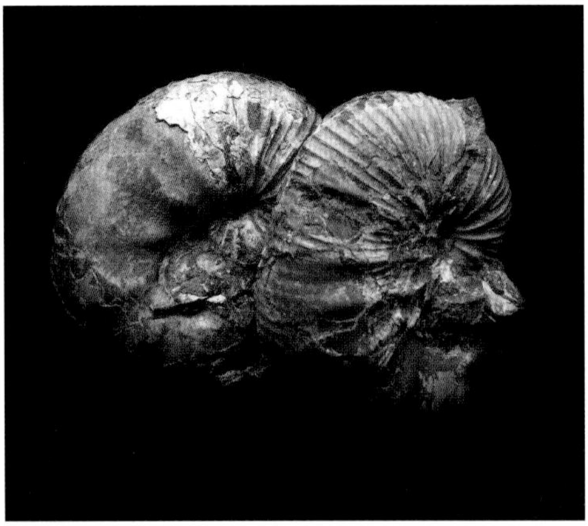

Scaphites fossils (*top left*) and *Inoceramus* fossil (*top right*) in the Mancos Shale of the Molen Reef. Photos by Jonathan T. Bailey. *Bottom*: View of Mancos Shale through the Molen Reef. Ferron Sandstone is visible on the ridge to the left. Aerial photo by Stephen E. Strom.

At the well-known "Big Snake" archaeological site near the town of Moore, a large block of Ferron Sandstone is pocked with the tracks of an ornithopod (a bipedal herbivore). In the overlying Blue Gate Member of the Mancos Shale, aquatic fossils are abundant, including those of *Scaphites* (a type of ammonite), mollusks, and *Inoceramus* (related to oysters).

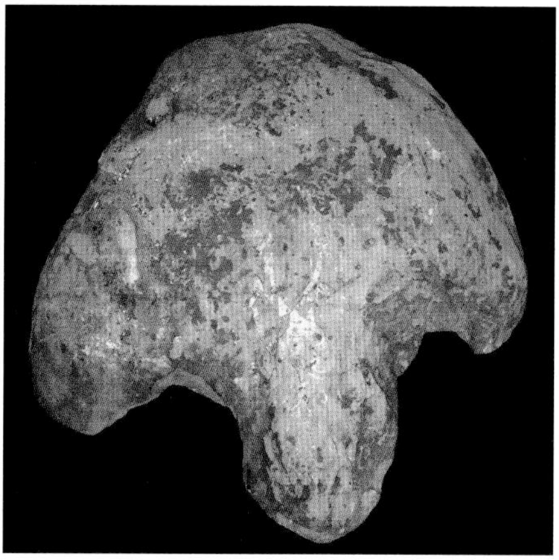

Dinosaur tracks were discovered in numerous coal mines within the Blackhawk Formation. This specimen is from a duck-billed ornithopod. Photo by Jonathan T. Bailey.

A few late Cretaceous geological formations are found toward the Wasatch Plateau and Book Cliffs. They include the Star Point Sandstone, composed of brownish sandstone and shale, frequently seen in the canyons of the Wasatch Plateau (e.g., those cut by Ferron Creek, Muddy Creek, and Quitchupah Creek) and in Price River Canyon below Woodside.

Visible above Star Point Sandstone is the Blackhawk Formation, found in canyons of the Wasatch Plateau and Book Cliffs. Star Point is composed of gray to brown sandstone, siltstone, and shale, deposited in warm, wet, tropical environments during a time when Emery County was still located on a low-lying coastal plain, and great forests and a rich ecosystem of plants filled river deltas and nearby swamps.

Advancing waters later buried the abundant organic material under deposits of sand and mud, and over time, the weight of these deposits compressed the organic material into coal. Layers of Star Point Sandstone stand out along the Wasatch Plateau and serve as a signpost for geologists searching for rich coal seams in the Blackhawk layers above. Historically, the rich coal layers deposited during the Cretaceous period have served as the lifeblood of Emery County's economy, with a large number of residents depending on coal-mining jobs, or employment in one of the county's coal-fired power plants.

Seventy million years ago, what is now the Wasatch Plateau was located in a basin, surrounded by higher lands to the east and west. During the time between the late Cretaceous and early Paleocene periods, a lake fed by rivers filled the basin. The sediments carried by the rivers formed the North Horn Formation, comprising layers of mudstone, sandstone, claystone, and limestone. Examples of the formation appear prominently on North Horn Mountain, west of Castle Dale. Fossils in the North Horn provide an essential record of a time extending from the period when dinosaurs (such as the large,

Artistic rendition of *Tyrannosaurus rex.* Courtesy of Steve O'Connor.

long-necked *Alamosaurus sanjuanensis* and the infamous *Tyrannosaurus rex*) prevailed, to the subsequent period of mammal-dominated ecosystems.[22]

At the end of the Cretaceous, about three-quarters of plant and animal species would once again become extinct. Every mammal over fifty-five pounds disappeared, as did nonavian dinosaurs. It is generally accepted that this extinction event was caused by the worldwide effects of a massive asteroid impact that radically altered Earth's climate.[23]

Early Tertiary Period (66–2.6 Million Years Ago)

During the early Tertiary period, an oceanic plate off the coast of present-day California slipped beneath the North American continent, lifting mountains upward during what geologists call the Laramide orogeny.[24] Simultaneously, the land under Emery County rose from near sea level to between five thousand and seven thousand feet. Remarkably, the strata laid down over more than three hundred million years were pushed directly upward, with only minimal tilting—each layer unveiling a slice of time.

---

22. David B. Weishampel et al., "Dinosaur Distribution," in *The Dinosauria*, ed. David B. Weishampel, Peter Dodson, and Halszka Osmólska, 2nd ed. (Berkeley: University of California Press, 2004), 517–606; Scott D. Sampson and Mark A. Loewen, "*Tyrannosaurus rex* from the Upper Cretaceous (Maastrichtian) North Horn Formation of Utah: Biogeographic and Paleoecologic Implications," *Journal of Vertebrate Paleontology* 25, no. 2 (2005): 469–72.

23. Norman H. Sleep and Donald R. Lowe, "Scientists Reconstruct Ancient Impact That Dwarfs Dinosaur-Extinction Blast," American Geophysical Union, news release, April 9, 2014, https://news.agu.org/press-release/scientists-reconstruct-ancient-impact-that-dwarfs-dinosaur-extinction-blast/.

24. Tonje Nygaard Sørensen, "Progressive Deformation in Monocline, San Rafael Swell, Utah" (master's thesis, University of Oslo, 2017).

To the west, the basin-range system began to take form as the Wasatch Plateau was uplifted and the Great Basin depressed. As the layers that make up Emery County and the Colorado Plateau rose, younger rock was stripped away, exposing older strata, which, over time, were carved into dramatic canyons by wind and waters flowing swiftly downhill from the Colorado Plateau south and west toward Arizona.

With the mass extinction of nonavian dinosaurs at the end of the Cretaceous, smaller mammals were able to diversify and exploit a climate that turned warm and humid following the asteroid impact and the resulting long period of global cooling. The first to appear were bulky, primitive mammals that soon went extinct during a period of elevated global temperatures that began around fifty-six million years ago. They would later be replaced by ungulates, along with bats, rodents, turtles, proboscideans (elephants and their extinct relatives), rhinos, and camels, among many other species of animals.[25]

By thirty-four million years ago, the climate had once again cooled, and deciduous trees overtook much of North America. Toward the end of the Tertiary period, plains, deserts, and grasslands covered Emery County and much of Utah.

The Pleistocene Epoch (2.6 Million to 11,700 Years Ago)

Beginning about two million years ago during the Pleistocene epoch, Earth experienced numerous ice ages. During this period, towering Columbian mammoths, bulky ancient bison, short-faced bears, and saber-toothed cats roamed Utah. Remains of two of these mammals, a Columbian mammoth (*Mammuthus columbi*) and short-faced bear (*Arctodus* sp.), were discovered by construction crews from Emery County working along the dam of Huntington Reservoir (now also known as Mammoth Reservoir) in the Wasatch Range.[26] The mammoth, identified as a fifteen-foot-tall, sixty-year-old male, is one of the most recent specimens to have been discovered. About two miles away, the remains of a mastodon, horse, and bison were also uncovered.[27]

---

25. *New World Encyclopedia*, s.v. "Eocene," updated August 29, 2008, https://www.newworldencyclopedia.org/p/index.php?title=Eocene&oldid=794527.

26. David D. Gillette and David B. Madsen, "The Columbian Mammoth, *Mammuthus columbi*, from the Wasatch Mountains of Central Utah," *Journal of Paleontology* 67, no. 4 (1993): 669–80.

27. Wade E. Miller, "*Mammut americanum*, Utah's First Record of the American Mastodon," *Journal of Paleontology* 61, no. 1 (1987): 168–83. Although they became extinct around ten thousand years ago, horses are actually native to the United States.

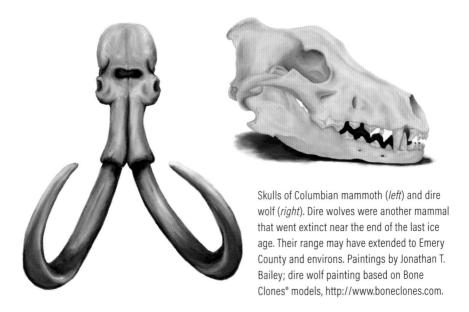

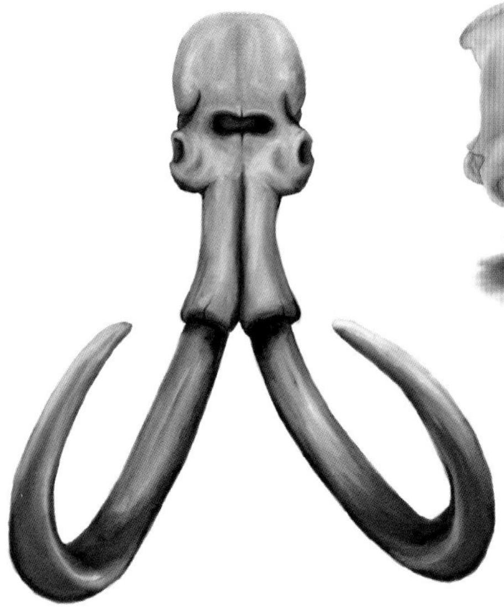

Skulls of Columbian mammoth (*left*) and dire wolf (*right*). Dire wolves were another mammal that went extinct near the end of the last ice age. Their range may have extended to Emery County and environs. Paintings by Jonathan T. Bailey; dire wolf painting based on Bone Clones® models, http://www.boneclones.com.

Just south of Emery County in Horseshoe Canyon, dung from mammoths and bison was identified in Cowboy Cave.[28] Radiocarbon dating indicates that mammoths and bison roamed the San Rafael Desert about twelve thousand years ago.

About ten thousand years ago, an event known as the late Pleistocene or Quaternary extinction event resulted in the demise of many animal species, particularly mammals weighing more than one hundred pounds (megafauna). The cause(s) of this mass extinction remain a mystery. Some researchers propose that humans arriving in North America around this time hunted megafauna to extinction, disrupting the ecological balance, and leading to the decline of other species.[29] Others suggest that climate change, as temperatures warmed and glaciers melted, might have forced animals to occupy environments in which they were unable to adapt and survive.[30] Still

28. Jesse D. Jennings, *Cowboy Cave*, University of Utah Anthropological Paper 104 (Salt Lake City: University of Utah Press, 1980).

29. Christopher Sandom, "Global Late Quaternary Megafauna Extinctions Linked to Humans, not Climate Change," *Proceedings: Biological Sciences*, 281, no. 1787 (2014), https://doi.org/10.1098/rspb.2013.3254.

30. Paul L. Koch and Anthony D. Barnosky, "Late Quaternary Extinctions: State of the Debate," *Annual Review of Ecology, Evolution, and Systematics* 37 (2006): 215–50.

other, less well-regarded hypotheses suggest an asteroid impact or infectious diseases as potential causes.[31]

Reflecting on the decrease in biodiversity in modern times, Alfred Russel Wallace, known for developing the underlying concepts of evolution in parallel with Charles Darwin, wrote that "we live in a zoologically impoverished world, from which all the hugest, and fiercest, and strangest forms have recently disappeared."[32] While Wallace's lament is certainly understandable, we should pause and reflect on those losses in another context: our good fortune in now having tools to explore and understand not only the biological abundance of earlier eras, but the mutuality of life and ever-changing environments. There are few places on Earth where the richness of life and its adaptability over three hundred million years is better documented than in the strata revealed within the boundaries of Emery County. In that, we are truly privileged.

31. Mario Pino et al., "Sedimentary Record from Patagonia, Southern Chile Supports Cosmic-Impact Triggering of Biomass Burning, Climate Change, and Megafaunal Extinctions at 12.8 ka," *Scientific Reports* 9 (2019), article 4,413, https://doi.org/10.1038/s41598-018-38089-y.

32. Alfred Russel Wallace, *The Geographical Distribution of Animals*, vol. 1 (New York: Harper and Brothers, 1876), 150.

Snake petroglyph under the Milky Way. Photo by Jonathan T. Bailey.

History of Emery County's Indigenous Peoples

I lifted the candle, and in a warm orange light appeared round phantom eyes, deep red, filling a featureless, stone face. Our eyes adjusted, picking up the detail of vertical stripes running the length of a painted torso. It stood in a line, accompanied by more figures, narrow and tall, tapering like waterfalls, some into stubby legs, others into levitation. There were rows of them, life-sized. They were intricate and deeply colored, like residual stains of a vision. Smaller, precise figures were inter-spaced as if they had been thrown at the wall from a distance and the paint had congealed into shapes.

— CRAIG CHILDS, *STONE DESERT: A NATURALIST'S EXPLORATION OF CANYONLANDS NATIONAL PARK*

Memory and Place: A Reflection

What is the function of memory? Perhaps, like trees that distribute messages and nutrients through their underground fungal networks, memories are designed to connect and sustain us.[a] These memories extend their roots, twisting and turning, seeking support in nourishing soils, affixing themselves to a place and our communities, whether natural or cultural.

One of my earliest memories traces back to a time shortly after I was born. My mother had gathered my siblings and me as we traveled to the edge of a canyon lined with ridges of colorless shale. Wrapped in a blanket, I was carried down a crevice to the drainage below. Once on the ground, we soon arrived at a masked figure painted below a stone carapace. He was tinged with blood-red pigment and marked with haunting eyes. A curved horn extended on either side of his head, and his lower jaw was crammed with teeth. His face was stained with dripped paint and his shoulders had faded into furls of taupe sandstone. Shortly after our arrival, raindrops fell. Obsidian-black clouds circled overhead. Thunder shook the ground as the cold air moved us from the canyon floor.

Of course, this memory could not have been my own. It is said that many of these stories, our earliest recollections, are connected to childhood photographs, videos, and stories.[b] But whether "real" or borrowed, these are the threads of memory that anchor us to the past and shape who we are.

Memory is persistence; to exist is to remember why one exists. We all become stewards of this memory by capturing these moments through stories, whether visual, spoken, or written. Like birds that dream their melodies, rehearsing their call in deep sleep until an ancestral song emerges, we, as a species, retain memory to recall our own reasons for being.[c] Memories emerge in the language we speak, or in stories, or in song, or in the creation of symbolic imagery—and sometimes we remember through the photographs from our childhood. Like the cascading song of the canyon wren (*Catherpes mexicanus*) from the onset of spring, we sense that it is the remembrance of our "songs," our histories, that revitalizes us as a species.

Viewed in this way, sacred topography is defined by memory. Like the fungal networks that enable trees to speak to the forest, or the song that allows a bird to call to the flock, these landscapes assemble communities of living things, giving each member a voice and opportunity to speak. Indigenous people have shared these spaces since time immemorial, casting memories over millennia through rock art, architecture, and stories that, passed down over generations, connect time and place. A landscape comes alive through these narratives, which highlight its enduring history.

Here, in the greater San Rafael Swell, stories were told and retold in the flickering of a flame. Homes were warmed with the same charcoals tended by their ancestors. One more layer of soot was burned into the ceiling like a fresh coat of paint. Symbols and images were carved. Pigment was applied to the wall. Plants were gathered and prepared just as they had been for millennia. Houses were depopulated and reconstructed, and life began again.

The greater San Rafael Swell embraces those stories, the spinning of life's spiral. They manifest as ocher-stained cliff walls in the creation of rock art, and in the organic residues that blacken alcoves. They appear in the winds and water that give shape to this sacred landscape. As climate change, over-visitation, and mineral extraction scar the skin of our Earth, in these stories—in these memories—lies the opportunity to remember, to heal, and to return.

JONATHAN T. BAILEY

[a] Richard Grant, "Do Trees Talk to Each Other?," *Smithsonian Magazine*, March 2018. Trees can send signals, nutrients, and water through these underground networks. These are particularly beneficial in communicating drought and disease.

[b] Erika Hayasaki, "Traces of Lost Time," *Atlantic*, November 29, 2016, https://www.theatlantic.com/health/archive/2016/11/childhood-memory-amensia/508886/.

[c] Daniel Margoliash, "Do Sleeping Birds Sing? Population Coding and Learning in the Bird Song System," in *Advances in Neural Population Coding*, ed. Miguel A. L. Nicolelis (Amsterdam: Elsevier, 2001), 319–31.

Culture and Place

In the beginning, humans were bug-like creatures, or beings shaped of varicolored clays, or a thought in the empty voids of space. Many present-day tribes draw on these and other origin stories to affix their place in a landscape that is ancestral, sacred, and central to their genesis and identity.

Over time, we have moved a few steps closer to comprehending an Indigenous understanding of origin, place, and history. Still, archaeology often focuses on the "working parts," seeking to understand the past through the study of objects. Similarities in the physical traces of the past are often used to define archaeological cultures—such as Fremont, Hohokam, or Ancestral Pueblo. But these labels do not give us a fully realized description of who people were as individuals, what social labels they identified with, or what beliefs they may have held. To the Hopi, some of these cultural concepts are broadened as *Moti'sinom* and *Hisat'sinom*, encompassing over two thousand years of history that bleed into the present-day representations of Hopi.[1]

In what follows, we use archaeological designations as a rough guide to the Indigenous history of the region, but with the caveat that these are

1. Lyle Balenquah, "Acknowledging the Ancestors: Hopi History in the Archaeological Record," in *Rock Art: A Vision of a Vanishing Cultural Landscape*, ed. Jonathan Bailey, illustrated ed. (Denver, Colo.: Johnson Books, 2019), 21–22.

imperfect labels encompassing diverse peoples, defined by predominately non-Indigenous archaeologists.

Memories in Rock Art

When compared to the people occupying nearby areas in the Four Corners—such as Bears Ears, Chaco Canyon, or Mesa Verde—people in the greater San Rafael Swell were, on average, less sedentary. It is often the case that greater mobility diminishes what is available in the material record. Impermanent, often exposed camps were subject to greater weathering. Material goods would often have to be transported over large distances, rather than situated in permanent settlements. Hence, study of a typical area in this region would likely reveal objects that are fewer in number, and physically smaller (or easier to carry) when compared to, say, Bears Ears in southeast Utah, or Chaco Canyon in northwest New Mexico.

Given those limitations, it is likely that greater mobility fostered the area's abundant and dispersed rock art. While it is typically challenging to provide absolute dates for individual rock art images, we can deduce that certain stylistically similar images (or "rock art styles") may be older than others.[2] For example, if an image from one rock art style is found carved *over* an image from another, the former was clearly made more recently.

When enough of these stylistic similarities are defined, compared with other styles, and are shown to have a limited geographic distribution, we can begin to view rock art in greater context with its natural and cultural surroundings. Given the mobility of Indigenous peoples in these regions, rock art provides perhaps the best window into the past.

The First Inhabitants

For decades, researchers have suspected that the first people to arrive in North America migrated from Siberia and East Asia across a land bridge

2. Radiocarbon dating of rock art imagery presents a few challenges. Many images are not created with the carbon-rich materials necessary for dating. Even when rock art contains organic goods, such as animal or plant products used in the creation of pigment or binding agents, it is difficult to acquire a sample large enough without significantly damaging the original image. And even when samples are able to be taken, they may be contaminated by carbon dioxide present in rainfall or ancient hydrocarbons.

that was exposed when sea levels were lowered by the buildup of enormous glaciers during the Pleistocene (or Ice Age). About twenty-three thousand to thirteen thousand years ago, this land bridge was blocked by the Cordilleran and Laurentide ice sheets, which served as a barrier to entering mainland North America, until a gap between the ice sheets was formed in response to warming temperatures. Islanded in coastal Alaska by an impenetrable wall of ice for perhaps ten thousand years, humans are thought to have forged their way through a newly ice-free corridor around thirteen thousand years ago. However, several archaeological sites in the United States have recently turned up artifacts dating back about fifteen thousand years, a result that suggests that Indigenous peoples may have arrived not only through the Alaskan corridor, but via one or more alternative routes.[3]

The recent and controversial Solutrean hypothesis posits that humans arrived along the East Coast of North America from Europe during the Pleistocene—support for which rests on the similarities observed between stone tools found in North America and in Europe.[4] The equally controversial Cerutti mastodon theory proposes that humans (or perhaps other hominids) were already present in North America about 130,000 years ago, a theory that is based on the humanlike manner in which the mastodon's bones were broken at a site near San Diego, California.[5] Neither of these theories seems likely. The data are more readily explained by assuming that stone tools developed independently, and that the pattern of broken mastodon bones resulted from factors other than human activity.

An increasingly popular hypothesis posits that the first peoples to populate the North American continent skirted the West Coast on boats, possibly arriving near the northwest corner of the present-day United States (Alaska) from Beringia, which is now partially submerged under the Bering Strait.[6] Recent research indicates that the coastlines of Alaska might have been

3. Jessi J. Halligan et al., "Pre-Clovis Occupation 14,550 Years Ago at the Page-Ladson Site, Florida, and the Peopling of the Americas," *Science Advances* 2, no. 5 (2016), https://doi.org/10.1126/sciadv.1600375.

4. Dennis J. Stanford and Bruce A. Bradley, *Across Atlantic Ice: The Origins of America's Clovis Culture* (Berkeley: University of California Press, 2013).

5. Steven R. Holen et al., "A 130,000-Year-Old Archaeological Site in Southern California, USA," *Nature* 544 (2017): 479–83, https://doi.org/10.1038/nature22065.

6. Lizzie Wade, "Most Archaeologists Think the First Americans Arrived by Boat. Now, They're Beginning to Prove It," *Science Magazine*, August 10, 2017.

ice-free beginning about seventeen thousand years ago, perhaps allowing Native peoples to survive and thrive on a diversified diet of plants, larger game animals, and readily accessible marine life.[7] It is possible that early settlers of the continent entered North America both by sea and land.

The Pleistocene Peoples

Beginning about thirteen thousand years ago, people entered what is now the San Rafael Swell and surrounding areas. In high-elevation environments like the Wasatch Plateau, they may have encountered a habitat similar to the present, with towering pines, turquoise lakes, and fields of grasses that lie beneath open forests.

A few things have changed since that time. Active glaciers in the Wasatch Plateau and farther to the south deglaciated at the end of the Pleistocene.[8] Megafauna (large mammals over one hundred pounds) also vanished during this period of climate change. These events are dramatically recorded in the region's archaeological and paleontological deposits.

West of the present-day town of Huntington lies Huntington Canyon, where the Wasatch Plateau has been chiseled by a tree-lined river flowing over polished gray stones. Farther up, at about nine thousand feet, rolling hills surround the present-day Mammoth Reservoir. In summer 1988, a mammoth was discovered on the banks of the reservoir. Estimated to about sixty years of age—near the end of a typical life span for many proboscideans (elephants and their extinct relatives)—this large male had become trapped in a clay-rich bog. Unable to escape, the mammoth was targeted by scavengers, possibly including a short-faced bear (*Arctodus simus*) and early humans.[9] At least one projectile point and numerous stone tools were discovered near the remains, and cut marks were reported within the mammoth's ribs and feet.[10]

7. Lizzie Wade, "New Map of Alaska's Ancient Coast Supports Theory That America's First People Arrived by Boat," *Science Magazine*, May 30, 2018.

8. Richard F. Flint and Charles S. Denny, *Quaternary Geology of Boulder Mountain Aquarius Plateau, Utah*, Geological Survey Bulletin 1061-D (Washington, D.C.: Government Printing Office, 1958).

9. The cranium of a short-faced bear was also discovered in Mammoth Reservoir, also known as Huntington Reservoir.

10. David D. Gillette and David B. Madsen, "The Columbian Mammoth, *Mammuthus columbi*, from the Wasatch Mountains of Central Utah," *Journal of Paleontology* 67, no. 4 (1993): 669–80.

Mammoth skeleton, Utah Museum of Natural History. Courtesy of Daderot, Wikimedia commons.

Additional, now extinct, mammals were found about two miles away within a series of sinkholes: a mastodon (*Mammut americanum*), horse (*Equus* sp.), and bison (*Bison* sp.). During excavation of the site, researchers discovered a single stone tool located a few feet from the remains. The tool may have been deposited with the animals, although the remains exhibit no further signs of human interference.[11]

Elsewhere in Emery County, evidence of Paleo-Indian occupation is sparse. This largely owes to the lifeways of these hunter-gatherers, who moved from camp to camp and left little behind that would have been preserved over millennia. The best evidence of their habitation comes from surviving stone tools, the Clovis point being prominent among them. These projectile points, stone tools used as a projectile for hunting, were first found near today's Clovis, New

11. Wade E. Miller, "*Mammut americanum*, Utah's First Record of the American Mastodon," *Journal of Paleontology* 61, no. 1 (1987): 168–83.

Comparison of Clovis (*left*) and Folsom points. Reproduction by John Olsen. Photos by Jonathan T. Bailey.

Mexico. They are characteristically large, and distinguished by a prominent groove known as a *flute* that is removed from both sides of the point, a feature that would have made it easier to attach them to a wooden shaft. A similar projectile known as a Folsom point is named after the stone tools found at the Folsom site in New Mexico. Folsom flutes are much longer and extend through the length of the point.

In some cases, both Folsom and Clovis points were created using visually arresting stones. The materials for such points were often carried over long distances, even when local materials for point-making were available. This, along with the care that went into crafting them, suggests that they were more than tools, they were perhaps a form of art and expression. However, most of the Paleo-Indian tools found in Emery County are cruder in design and execution.

Researchers have debated whether rock art was created in North America during this period. At Winnemucca Lake in Nevada, for example, abstract petroglyphs appear to have been carved fifteen thousand to ten thousand years ago. Farther south, carved images in the Bears Ears National Monument have been reported to depict mammoths and ancient bison. Although they appear to portray fauna that became extinct during the late Pleistocene, such depictions are not always a reliable indicator of age. There are innumerable reports of "mammoth" images that, when inspected, are found to depict currently living animals, or are determined to be forgeries.

It is also possible that descriptions of extinct animals passed down in oral histories inspired post-Pleistocene rock art, although whether such a description is sufficient to accurately portray an extinct species is uncertain. The limited research available suggests that people in the Pleistocene period *did* create rock art, but we don't know with certainty how often it

Western Abstract Tradition petroglyph. Photo by Jonathan T. Bailey.

was created, how much of it survives, or how often we fail to recognize its antiquity.

Western Abstract Tradition

The Western Abstract Tradition was perhaps one of the earliest and most widespread examples of rock art in North America, encompassing abstract imagery of curvilinear lines, parallel lines, vulvas, grids, and abundant animal tracks. Dating of Western Abstract Tradition rock art is often technically challenging, but in some cases it is possible. In the case of the Lake Winnemucca site, the rock art is estimated to be between ten thousand and fifteen thousand years old. In southern Oregon, Western Abstract Tradition petroglyphs were discovered beneath the ash of Mount Mazama, which erupted 7,700 years ago. More recent examples of Western Abstract Tradition rock art have also been reported. Further research is necessary in order to better define the range of ages over which Western Abstract Tradition rock art was created.

In the Greater San Rafael Swell, Western Abstract Tradition rock art is often found to be heavily repatinated (covered by a dark sheen consisting mainly of iron and manganese that develops on rocks) and often overlain by later Archaic period or Fremont rock art, suggesting that many sites in this region are probably at least several thousand years old, dating back to the Archaic period.

The Archaic Period Peoples

The Archaic period began about 8,000 years ago and ended 2,500 years ago. People who lived in the Greater San Rafael Swell during this time were hunter-gatherers who collected plants for food, ceremony, weaving, and medicine. They hunted game animals—such as deer, bighorn sheep, and rabbits—using a spear-throwing instrument known as an atlatl. They also constructed other hunting tools, like nets, which were used as traps for smaller game animals. Examples of these artifacts are found throughout the region.

During the Archaic period, greater varieties of plant foods were gathered, processed on metates (a surface on which grains, seeds, and nuts were ground), and temporarily stored in cists dug into alcove floors. These peoples often lived in caves and alcoves without any evidence of physical architecture. Many of these sites are still caked with soot from generations of open fires.

Some of the earliest—and perhaps most iconic—material artifacts from the Archaic period discovered in Emery County are unfired clay figurines, and textiles including a beautifully preserved blanket discovered in Clyde's Cavern in the Molen Reef.[12]

In later times, split-twig figurines of large game animals (most likely bighorn sheep or other hooved animals) were constructed by twisting and folding a single stick. Similar artifacts have been found in the Grand Canyon, occasionally with fecal pellets from deer and sheep within their body cavities. In one case, a spear was found in the side of the animal, suggesting that these figurines may have been associated with hunting or ritual activity.[13] Although Grand Canyon split-twig figurines are stylistically distinct from those found in Emery County, they may well be functionally similar.

12. Nancy J. Coulam and Alan R. Schroedl, "Early Archaic Clay Figurines from Cowboy and Walters Caves in Southeastern Utah," *KIVA* 61, no. 4 (1996): 401–12; Henry G. Wylie, *Report of Excavations at Clyde's Cavern (42Em177), Emery County, Utah* (Salt Lake City: University of Utah Department of Anthropology, 1971).

13. Alan R. Schroedl, "The Power and the Glory: Shamanistic Arts of the Archaic Period," *Canyon Legacy*, Spring 1989.

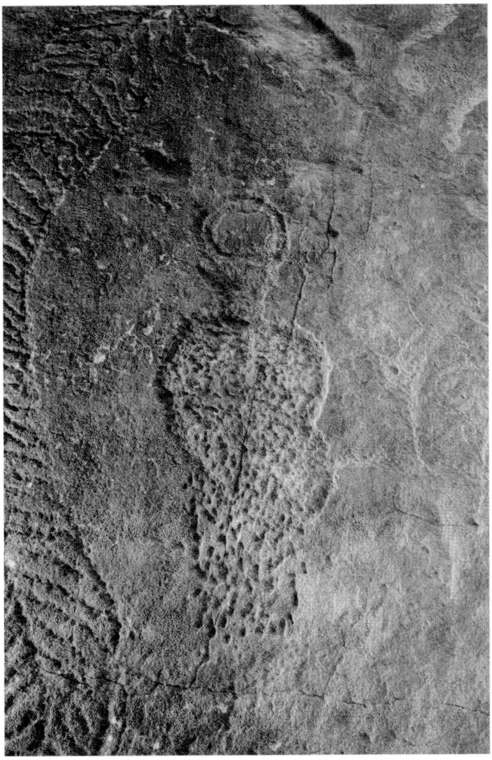

Unusual Archaic period petroglyphs with snakelike features extending from the mouths of bighorn sheep (*top*); and limbless anthropomorphic (humanlike figure) petroglyph from the Archaic period. Photos by Jonathan T. Bailey.

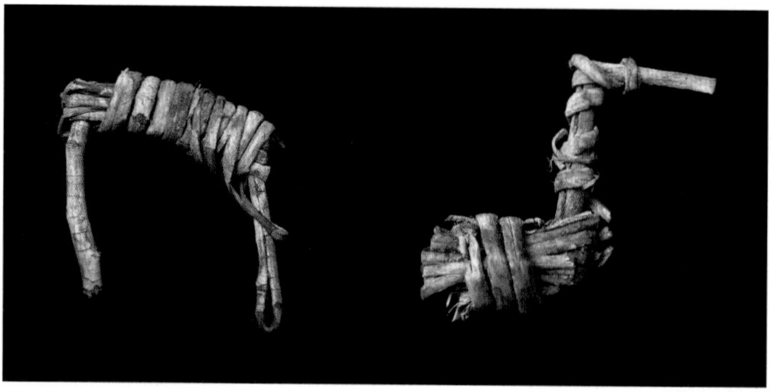

Green River Style split-twig figurines found in the San Rafael Swell. Photos by Jonathan Bailey. The Utah State University Eastern Prehistoric Museum kindly provided access to these artifacts, numbered CEUM 81256 and 77938 in its collection.

Geoglyphs in the San Rafael Swell: A Reflection

In the back of a small aircraft, I am crouched in a cab just large enough for a few people inside, fidgeting with camera equipment in the only space with a view through both windows. In the front, Clark Tenakhongva and Troy Honanie Jr. from the Hopi Cultural Preservation Office discuss the San Rafael Swell exposed below.

In a few moments, we encounter what I have brought them to see—a geoglyph (a large image or design created on the ground) positioned on the earth, slate-black, shaped of stones that are arranged into a curled, distorted image. Twisted and undefined, its features are strikingly abstract, bordering on entoptic, like a vision projected from the mind's eye into physical space. It stretches for perhaps 150 feet before descending toward a field of skunkbush sumac (*Rhus trilobata*), exposed on pale bedrock like blotches drifting through our field of vision.

We drop lower, curving back to the north, the plane rocking in sympathy with buffeting winds. As the image fades in the distance, more glyphs appear—giant circles, contoured arches, and parallel lines that buck the pattern with camel-brown stones propped on small pedestals. To date, we have located over a dozen of these features throughout the greater San Rafael Swell. Some of these are small, only a few feet in diameter, while a few can exceed a hundred feet in length. There is no telling who made these, when they were constructed, or why they were built.[a]

JONATHAN BAILEY

[a] At present, there is no way of directly dating these geoglyphs. They are tentatively placed in this section because of their proximity to specific rock art styles and the lack of ceramics.

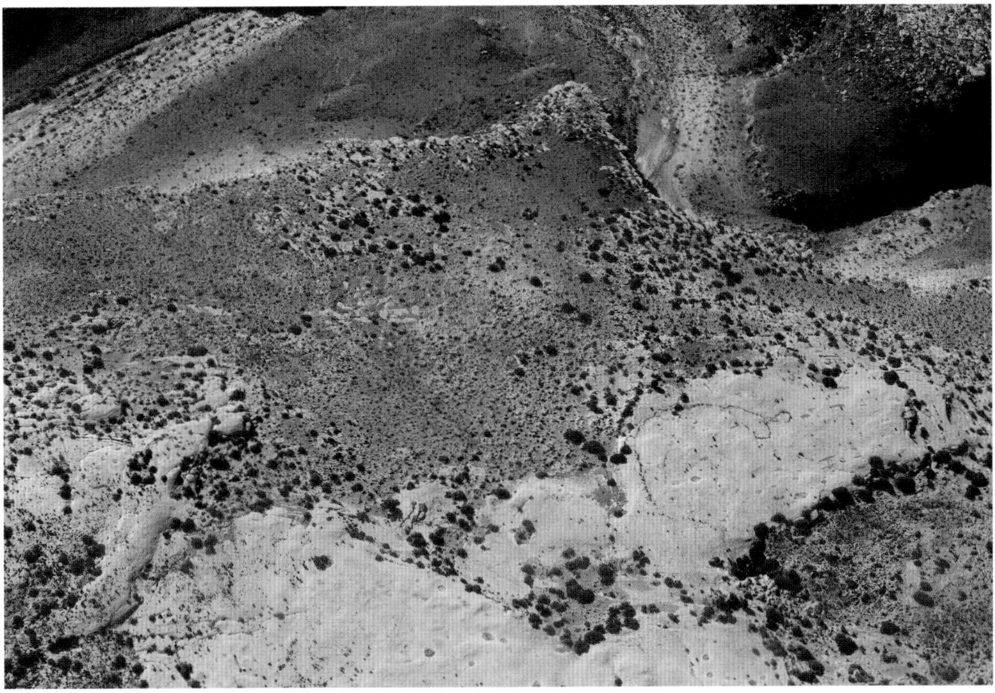

Geoglyph on sandstone exposure measuring approximately 150 feet. Photo by Jonathan T. Bailey.

Barrier Canyon Style

Imagine characters painted with haunting, empty eyes, arms outstretched, and long, curved claws reaching downward to the earth. They are marked in blood-red pigment, overcoated by nearly invisible traces of chalk-white paint. Some are tall and limbless, others short and humanlike. A horned serpent slithers above, bleeding from its face, mirrored by a bird with long, spindling legs. Beyond, a ghostly form with hollow eyes clutches an object, possibly a flute, accompanied by a figure with roots that erupt from his feet.

These painted panoramas typify the Barrier Canyon Style: chilling characters, frequently portrayed with elongated torsos, limbless bodies, and vacant, circular sockets to mark the eyes. In some panels, these figures are accompanied by evocations of rain clouds, canines with curled tails, birds, serpents, and companion figures, sometimes described as "spirit helpers," on or near the shoulder blade of larger characters. These figures evoke a nearly paralyzing

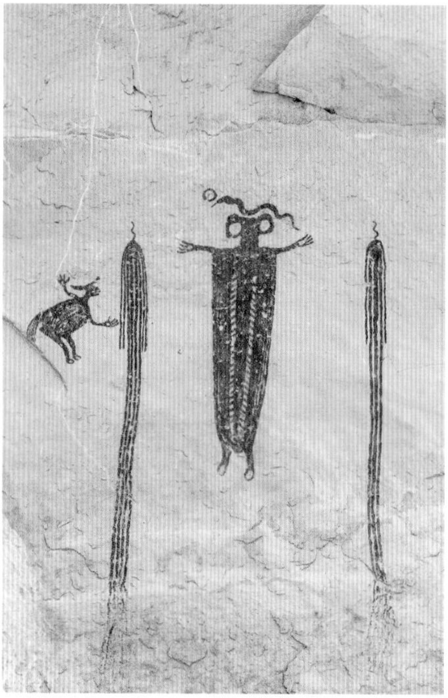

Barrier Canyon Style pictographs with human and animal characteristics. Photos by Jonathan T. Bailey.

feeling of power, as if apparitions had manifested from the shadows to walk the shallow interior of canyon alcoves.

The name Barrier Canyon Style was first proposed by Polly Schaafsma in 1971 in recognition of the style's dramatic manifestation in the two-hundred-foot-long, fifteen-foot-high "Great Gallery" in Barrier Canyon (later renamed Horseshoe Canyon), located a mile south of the Emery-Wayne county border in a unit of Canyonlands National Park. Some of the humanlike figures, or anthropomorphs, along the gallery wall tower over seven feet in height, stained in pigments ranging from maroon and umber to white.

Unusual Barrier Canyon Style panel with a birthing scene on the right. Photo by Jonathan T. Bailey.

Some researchers believe that these powerfully enigmatic Barrier Canyon Style images were painted in the Pueblo IV period, about seven hundred to four hundred years ago, citing similarities between Barrier Canyon Style depictions and present-day Pueblo rites and beliefs.[14] For example, many human figures are reminiscent of kachinas, known as life-bringers in present-day Hopi ceremonies. Although these images could be portraying comparable events, characters, or objects, these similarities are insufficient to compel either a date or a direct connection to the Pueblo IV period.

Based on analysis of nearby artifacts, some archaeologists believe that Barrier Canyon Style panels could be far older.[15] About ten miles from Barrier Canyon, on the southern border of Emery County, ten unfired clay figurines were found in Cowboy and Walters Caves.[16] Each of these figurines is modeled from a single piece of clay into haunting, largely featureless forms. They are arresting, some incised with marks that flow like lines of virga,

14. Steven J. Manning, "A Hypothesis for a Pueblo IV Date for the Barrier Canyon Style," in *Utah Rock Art*, vol. 1 (Salt Lake City: Utah Rock Art Association, 1981), 28–37.

15. Coulam and Schroedl, "Early Archaic Clay Figurines from Cowboy and Walters Caves in Southeastern Utah."

16. Jesse D. Jennings, *Cowboy Cave*, University of Utah Anthropological Paper 104 (Salt Lake City: University of Utah Press, 1980).

Footprints of the Hopi in the Greater San Rafael Swell

Footprints of the Hopi are global, at the directive and advice of the supreme creator, "Massau." The Hopi traveled the entire globe, the four directions. We have roots and ties to most major lands that exist today: South America, Easter Island, Middle East, Egypt, China, and both the North and South Poles, to name a few. The San Rafael Swell is no different. The evidence of our connections and place names is still in our oral history and ceremonies. Who in this world has a more complex life, religion, culture, and continuous study? I say proudly that the Hopi have been there in southern Utah. Four to seven clans occupied the region for many years, until the time was told for us to continue the journey to the center of the universe at a place now called "Final Resting Place Home." We have a purpose in the cycle of life, for the benefit of all life-forms. Hopi still have the destiny to carry out the message as care takers of his land, stewards of the land, people of the short ear of corn, for the supreme ruler "Massau."

Kwak'kwy. Thank you.

CLARK TENAKHONGVA, VICE CHAIRMAN OF THE HOPI TRIBE

others with stippled dots arranged in horizontal bands. The figurines share these spectral attributes with the painted apparitions of Barrier Canyon Style, some even marked with similar patterns streaked over their faces and torsos. Associated material was radiocarbon dated to 5600 to 5000 BCE. However, the current consensus among archaeologists is that the morphological similarities of these clay figures and the pictographs found in Barrier Canyon Style do not appear to indicate that they are contemporary.

Regardless of the range of time over which Barrier Canyon Style panels may have been painted, it appears most likely that the people who created these images were hunter-gatherers, whose lives differed dramatically from the Indigenous peoples who lived in multistoried pueblos and mass produced the high-quality ceramics typically associated with the Pueblo IV period. There are, for example, almost never physical structures or ceramics found near Barrier Canyon Style pictograph panels. Moreover, these sites are generally located along rivers, drainages, or other migratory routes, suggesting a mobile rather than stationary way of life. Finally, anatomical figures (rock art characters with genitalia), which tend to be created by people having developed agricultural practices, are largely (albeit with some notable exceptions) absent in Barrier Canyon Style paintings. The conflicts and contradictions surrounding Barrier Canyon Style artwork are summed up best

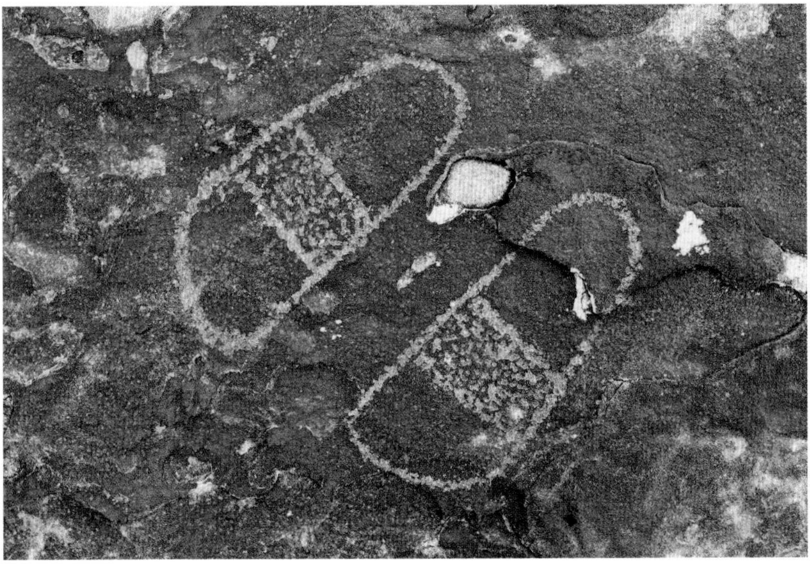

Fremont sandal designs on horizontal bedrock. Photo by Jonathan T. Bailey.

by archaeologist Sally Cole, who mused that "[perhaps Barrier Canyon Style rock art] is not frozen in time."[17]

The Arrival of the Fremont

The shift from Archaic period foragers to Fremont farmers, estimated to span the period between about AD 300 and 1300, was not seamless. The bow and arrow, agricultural practices, and the production of ceramics were not adopted at once as a wholesale package.[18]

The timing of this transition is a matter of disagreement among archaeologists, who hold conflicting views regarding the origins of the Fremont. Similarities between the Fremont and the Basketmaker farther to the south—particularly the Eastern or White Dog Basketmaker II tradition—have led some researchers to suggest that the Fremont and Basketmaker people descended from common or similar ancestor groups. Still, other researchers contend that the Fremont were in situ descendants of Archaic period populations,

17. Sally J. Cole, *Legacy on Stone: Rock Art of the Colorado Plateau and Four Corners Region* (Boulder, Colo.: Johnson Books, 2009).

18. Archaeologist Jody Patterson, pers. comm.

Fremont panel on horizontal bedrock (*top*); and Fremont pictographs with intricately incised interior designs. Photos by Jonathan T. Bailey.

Fremont moccasin panel on a vertical surface, with feet and other images. Photo by Jonathan T. Bailey.

and that the similarities are the result of interaction between the Fremont and Basketmaker peoples, with both groups diversifying over time.

In any event, the Fremont appear to have been present in the greater San Rafael Swell from around 1,700 to 700 years ago. During this time, the Fremont adorned cliff walls with images of bighorn sheep, snakes, geometric patterns, and triangular- or trapezoidal-bodied human figures. Moccasins and sandals are also commonly seen carved on horizontal bedrock surfaces within juniper-pinyon mesas.[19]

The Fremont take their name from the nearby Fremont River—which honors the nineteenth-century explorer John C. Fremont—along which many distinct rock art images, granaries, and artifacts were noted by archaeologist Noel Morss in 1931. The Fremont moniker now encompasses numerous and diverse groups that cannot be accurately described as a homogenized "culture"; hence archaeologists often use the term Fremont Complex. The Fremont were most

19. These track sites present management and preservation issues. Placement on exposed ground puts them at increased risk of fracturing as livestock wander over Bureau of Land Management (BLM) grazing allotments, and as off-highway vehicles (OHVs) traverse areas farther away from existing roads and trails.

Eroded slab-lined Fremont granary. Photo by Jonathan T. Bailey.

prevalent within the borders of present-day Utah, especially around the Greater San Rafael Swell, although they also occupied areas in Nevada, Colorado, and Wyoming.

When compared to their Ancestral Pueblo contemporaries to the south and east, the Fremont likely remained peripatetic and generally less sedentary after the introduction of agriculture—hunting, gathering, and/or growing crops. Marks of their movement are scattered across the landscape. Examples include crude, dry-laid structures that take shape beneath shallow overhangs, or the occasional jumble of ceramics—some blackened from years of cooking over open fires, others marked in black pigment. There are rarely vast ensembles of ceramics in the greater San Rafael Swell, just a few sherds exposed on pale sandstone, blistering under the desert sun.

At times the Fremont were apparently less mobile, building small "rancherias," including partially subterranean structures, pit houses, stone-lined buildings, and small storage structures along rivers, mesas, and valleys. Several of these complexes are found near modern-day towns and farms, testimony to the Fremont's judicious selection of places favorable for settlements.[20]

Between 1200 and 1300 CE, the Fremont were likely affected by the same drought that disrupted the Ancestral Pueblo way of life to the south and east. No archaeological evidence has been found that indicates continued occupation by the Fremont after 1300 CE. They may have moved, or chosen to scatter, perhaps riven by social upheaval following the drought. Some researchers have suggested that the Fremont might be distant ancestors of the present-day Ute, Paiute, and Shoshone tribes. Others have claimed that the Fremont moved south and assimilated into Ancestral Pueblo populations.[21] Many archaeologists now suggest that a combination of these hypotheses is plausible, if not probable.

20. James Gunnerson, *An Archaeological Survey of the Fremont Area*, University of Utah Anthropological Paper 28 (Salt Lake City: University of Utah, 1957).

21. Tamara Stewart, "Who Were the Fremont?," *American Archaeology* 10, no. 4 (2006–7): 26–33.

Bighorn and Olivella: A Refection

We have arrived at a panel at least a hundred feet long with spirals, sheep, and canines migrating through the porous stone canvas. Some are much older: dotted, limbless characters and large, featureless apparitions that appear like bands of desert varnish. Above, more recent human figures are situated to face one another, shields in hand, with long spears in tow—perhaps a signal that interpersonal violence preceded the demise of the Fremont. Farther up, a carved hunter crouches behind a ram, his bow poised, his head crowned with headgear fashioned from the skull of a bighorn.

Many years after reaching this panel, I spoke with archaeologists Timothy Riley, adjunct professor and curator of archaeology at the Prehistoric Museum in Price, Utah; and Alan Gold, the director and founder of the California Rock Art Foundation. They were examining headgear constructed from the cranium of a ram.[a] It was joined with cordage fashioned from milkweed (*Asclepias* spp.) and decorated with six Olivella shell beads.[b] These marine mollusks would have arrived from the eastern Pacific Ocean, traded from the present-day California coast or farther south from Mexico. They were clutched tightly in ancient hands, these small bundles of lavender-tinged calcium carbonate, and traveled perhaps seven hundred miles before reaching areas around the San Rafael Swell.

The headdress was removed without provenance in the 1960s, but Timothy and Alan had pinpointed several locations where it may have been discovered. All of them were adjacent to the hunter, the character shown crouched, bow poised, and capped with the horns of a ram.

It is possible that this co-occurrence is coincidental, two separate relics found at a confluence of time and place. Regardless, the relics render the past palpable. One can imagine the hands that once trailed along its weathered surface, bleached white under the midday sun. Look away, and time comes flooding back.

JONATHAN T. BAILEY

[a] This object is in the collection of Utah State University Eastern Prehistoric Museum in Price, Utah.

[b] Alan P. Garfinkel et al., "Age and Character of the Bighorn Sheep Headdress, San Rafael Swell, Utah" (AGG Associates, interim report, last modified May 19, 2015), ResearchGate, https://www.researchgate.net/publication/287207447.

The Ute, Paiute, and Shoshone

Around 1000 CE, Numic-speaking groups of hunter-gatherers migrated eastward from the Sierra Nevada into the Great Basin. By 1400 CE, their descendants—bands of Utes and Paiutes—inhabited most of Utah, western and central Colorado, and the watershed of the San Juan River.

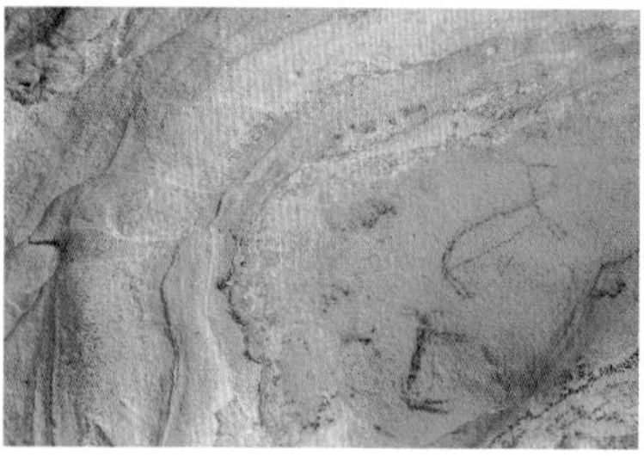

Solidly pecked Numic petroglyphs with bison and horned horseback rider (*above*); and Numic pictographs using a crayon-like mineral block. Photos by Jonathan T. Bailey.

The Ute primarily lived in teepees and wickiups, although nonhabitation structures such as shades, windbreaks, and sweat lodges were also constructed. Few remnants of these structures have survived.

After the acquisition of the horse in trade with Spanish settlements in the mid-1600s, the Ute began traveling great distances—hunting bison, and ranging as far as Wyoming, Oklahoma, Texas, and New Mexico. Elements of these hunts are preserved in their unique rock art, where horses and bison are often scratched or incised in petroglyphs, or appear in pictographs painted with crayon-like mineral blocks. Solidly pecked and painted images also exist.

Like other Numic tribes, the Southern Paiute were primarily hunter-gatherers, although they occasionally grew corn, squash, gourds, melons, and eventually wheat. They lived in caves, wickiups, and, during the summertime, brush shades. While Paiute rock art and habitation sites are found in Emery

Unusual Plains-like bison etched on a canyon wall. Photo by Jonathan T. Bailey.

County, their identification as distinctly Paiute is rarely decisive, as Numic art and artifacts share numerous similarities with many postcontact sites.

Other present-day tribes claim ancestral affiliation to the area in and around Emery County. They include the Numic-speaking Shoshone, as well as Pueblo groups, who may well share ancestry with the Fremont, Archaic period, and Paleo-Indian groups. The Navajo Nation has also asserted ties to the area, although no archaeological sites have yet been identified as Navajo.

One unusual and unidentified rock art panel in Emery County depicts several incised bison with heartlines (interior features that extend from the mouth and expand near the heart) and flared arrows pierced into their sides. This imagery is consistent with styles present within the Great Plains region. Its cultural affiliation is uncertain.

Concluding Observations

It is no doubt an oversimplification to speak in absolutes, and to assume unambiguous lineages when examining the histories, cultures, and artistic styles of the diverse peoples and cultures who once occupied Emery County.

Caverns and Carved Horses: A Reflection

Diane Orr and I are in the back of a pickup in the backcountry of the greater San Rafael Swell. We often shared these afternoons with locals: ranchers, coal miners, maybe a public servant or two, many of whom insist on traveling in their well-traveled trucks, doors rattling, the cab penetrated by the scent of aged leather.

Our vehicle sputters to a stop on a two-track road, a canyon carved below, while our traveling companion—a man in his forties with a thin build, ash-blond hair, and an unkempt "Mark Twain" mustache—gestures toward a cliff in the distance. We pack lunch and descend the talus to the canyon floor, heading eastward over sage-covered tablelands buzzing with cicadas, the ground occasionally revealing the sinuous path followed by a passing rattlesnake.

Before long, we move up into the cliffs, navigating on hands and knees to a small cavity located behind pockets of sagebrush. The cave—if you can call it that—is barely noticeable, a small den or burrow, now abandoned by rodents that have filled its cracks with needlelike juniper leaves. Our hirsute companion dives into the small opening on his elbows, his feet vanishing from view.

From inside, the passage opens into a small room, just large enough to fit two crouched people. We huddle against the back wall, peering up to discover charcoal images—many marked in pigment, once black, that has oxidized into a shimmering dark blue. Among the charcoal figures is a canine, painted with ears erect, staring down at the cavernous floor.

Many years ago, not far from here, I stumbled across a cache: a basket and cooking vessel, packed together and padded with shredded juniper bark. Both were downturned, placed in the back of an alcove, and concealed by flagstones.[a] Like the painted canine, this cache had once belonged to a Numic-speaking person, who must have walked this canyon less than two hundred years ago.

These places date to the period when Indigenous peoples first encountered newly arriving European settlers. In the aftermath, perhaps as many as fifty-six million Indigenous people in North, Central, and South America perished—many of smallpox, cholera, and other diseases to which they had little immunity.[b] And here in the Southwest, the people whose rock art adorns canyon walls, and whose art and culture once flourished in these deserts, were enslaved, brutally tortured, raped, murdered, and torn from their families and the ways of life that had sustained them for millennia.

Let these places serve as a somber reminder of the people who once—and still—call these places home. We walk, recreate, and live on stolen land.

JONATHAN T. BAILEY

[a] Arie W. Leeflang et al., "The Bailey Basket (42Em4090): An Unusual Late Prehistoric Artifact Cache in Emery County, Utah," *Utah Archaeology* 22, no. 1 (2009): 51–62.

[b] Lauren Kent, "European Colonizers Killed So Many Native Americans That It Changed the Global Climate, Researchers Say," CNN, February 2, 2019, https://www.cnn.com/2019/02/01/world/european-colonization-climate-change-trnd/index.html.

Nevertheless, many writers and researchers have chosen to place varied Indigenous groups into narrow cultural "boxes" by assuming that "culture" and "style" are synonymous with the people themselves. For present-day tribes, culture is a meaningful expression of tradition, and style is presented in traditional forms of artistry. By contrast, archaeologists speak of "culture" to define inferred similarities in lifeways and the expressions of those lifeways. Similarly, archaeologists use "style" to denote like features in artwork or in the construction of objects. Different "styles" or "cultures" do not necessarily equate to different people, nor is the opposite necessarily true. People are not pots. People are people. And people are diverse.

From the distant past to the present, the land that would become Emery County was alive with stories and traditions of multiple peoples. Hundreds of generations were born, raised, and laid to rest in the serpentine canyons that give shape to sacred spaces. As we encounter traces of the past, we should be reminded of the individuals who participated in these cultural landscapes. Behind our monolithic labels used to define "groups" and "styles" are people—individuals—who have stories and lives of their own.

The traces they left as mothers, fathers, and children are not just "objects" of the past, but memories of their love, aspirations, and beliefs, and sometimes even the fears that may arise in the beautiful—but harsh and unforgiving—landscapes that make up present-day Emery County.

We, part of a nation of immigrants, are newcomers to a cultural landscape that has endured for millennia. It is our collective responsibility to work with our Indigenous neighbors to care for these sacred places; to treat them wisely and respectfully, so that these places and the stories they hold can continue to serve not only as testaments to imagination and endurance, but as inspiration to future generations. Absent a thorough inventory of these places—which are currently poorly understood and barely documented in Emery County and environs—we stand to lose a profound connection to the past.[22]

---

22. Less than 10 percent of Utah's public land is comprehensively inventoried for cultural resources; see Arie Leeflang, "Quantifying Utah's Past: An Archaeological Data Synthesis of Utah Through 2015," *Utah Archaeology* 29, no. 1 (2016): 59–90.

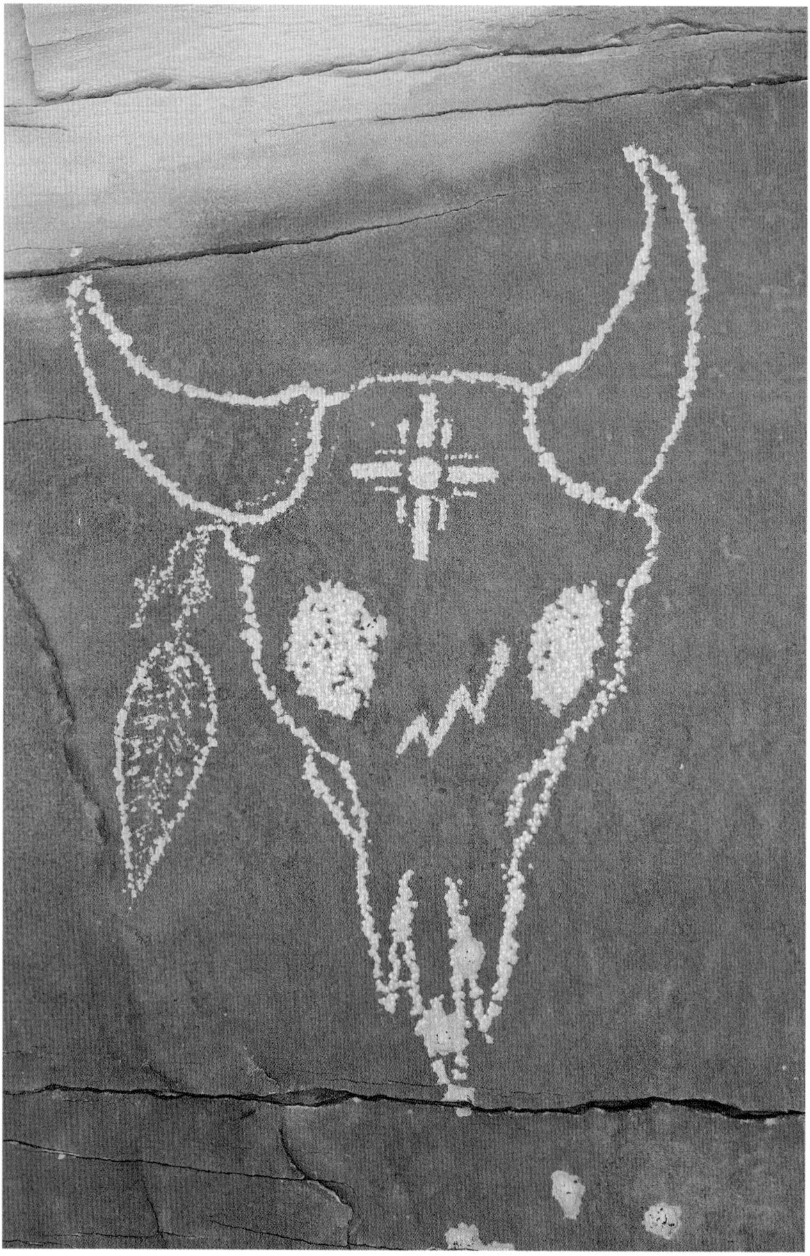

Historic cowboy art pecked on canyon walls. Photo by Jonathan T. Bailey.

Modern History of Emery County

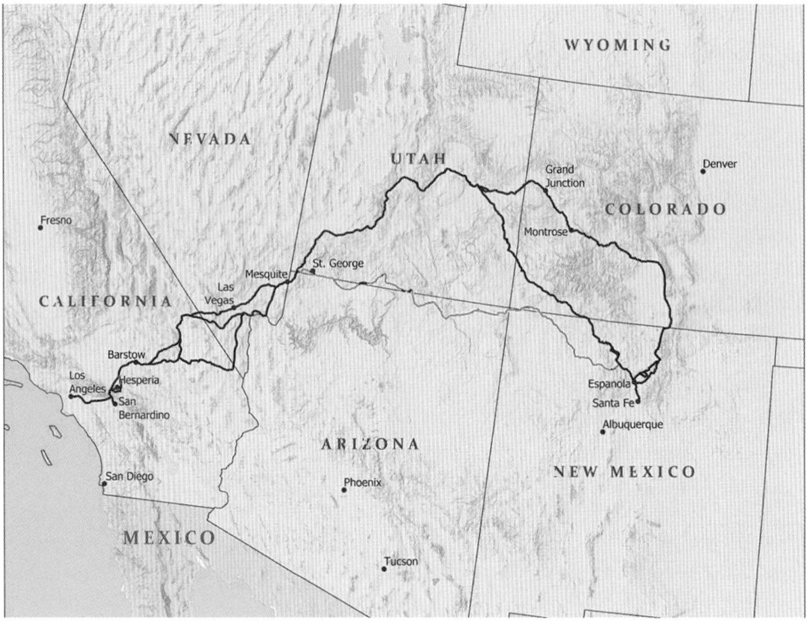

Old Spanish Trail routes. The two northern (*dark brown*) routes passed through Green River and Emery County. Map by the National Park Service.

Early European Arrivals

Exactly when Europeans first arrived in the Emery County region is uncertain, though it seems likely that Spanish traders from New Mexico interacted with members of the Ute Indian Tribe in Emery County during the latter half of the eighteenth century.[1]

The first reliable account of U.S. arrival in the county is provided by the writings of frontiersman, fur trapper, cartographer, and explorer Jedediah Smith, who passed through the area in 1826.[2] His logs suggest that he explored valleys of the Wasatch Plateau, and possibly passed through Castle Valley. Fur trappers likely entered the region in the 1830s, though records of their forays into the county are superficial. From the 1830s to the mid-1850s, mule trains, driven by traders, traveled through Emery County along

1. Edward A. Geary, *A History of Emery County* (Salt Lake City: Utah State Historical Society, 1996), 24, http://utahhistory.sdlhost.com/#/item/000000011019471/.

2. Geary, 25.

Boats assembling in Green River, Wyoming, for the Second Powell Expedition (1871), photo by E. O. Beaman (*top*); and John Wesley Powell speaking with Paiute chief. Both photos are from the U.S. Geological Survey.

the northern path of the Old Spanish Trail, on their way between Santa Fe and Los Angeles.[3]

Era of Exploration

During the 1840s and 1850s, government explorers and engineers, among them John C. Fremont, John Gunnison, and Kit Carson, journeyed through the Emery County area, seeking to map optimal routes for rail and wagon

3. Geary, 27; Elizabeth von Till Warren, "The Old Spanish National Historic Trail," 2004, Old Spanish Trail Association, accessed June 1, 2021, https://oldspanishtrail.org/our-history.

travel from the Midwest to the West.[4] In 1869, geologist and explorer John Wesley Powell led the first of his pioneering, and now legendary, scientific and mapping expeditions, starting in Green River, Wyoming.[5] He followed the Green River southward through Desolation, Gray, and Labyrinth Canyons in Emery County, to its confluence with the Colorado River, and along the Colorado through the Grand Canyon, into Nevada, where the Colorado joins the Virgin River. Powell's descriptions of the region's geology, flora, and fauna are beautifully, ofttimes poetically captured in a classic volume titled *Exploration of the Colorado River of the West and Its Tributaries*, published in 1875.[6]

Arrival of Mormon Settlers

Following the arrival of the first party of Mormons in Salt Lake Valley in 1847, Brigham Young, president of the Church of Jesus Christ of Latter-day Saints (LDS Church), embarked on an ambitious program to extend settlements throughout the West. He envisioned creating a state of Deseret, whose boundaries would encompass lands between the Rocky Mountains on the east and the Sierra Nevada on the west, from the Oregon Territory on the north to the Mexican border on the south, as well as the California coast south of Santa Monica.[7]

During his thirty years as leader of the LDS Church, Young called Mormon pioneers to settle almost four hundred towns, among them areas encompassing today's Sanpete and Sevier Counties, just to the west of Emery. Mormon families brought with them thousands of cattle, which foraged on the rich grasslands in the area. The burgeoning settlements drove the Northern Ute from their ancestral lands—which once spanned much of Utah and

---

4. Geary, *A History of Emery County*, 28–36.

5. Carolyn J. Hursch, "John Wesley Powell: Mapping the Colorado River," *American History Magazine*, June 2000, https://www.historynet.com/john-wesley-powell-mapping-the-colorado-river.htm.

6. John Wesley Powell, *Exploration of the Colorado River of the West and Its Tributaries* (Washington, D.C.: Government Printing Office, 1875), https://pubs.usgs.gov/unnumbered/70039238/report.pdf.

7. Richard D. Poll, "Deseret," in *Utah History Encyclopedia*, ed. Allan Kent Powell (Salt Lake City: University of Utah Press, 1994), https://www.uen.org/utah_history_encyclopedia/d/DESERET.shtml.

Colorado—depriving them of access to game and traditional food resources, including grain from the very grasslands on which Mormon livestock grazed.

Clashes with Indigenous Peoples

With the ecosystems on which they depended destroyed, much of the Northern Ute population starved. As happened throughout the period of U.S. expansion across, and colonization of, North America, disease imported by white men and women also took a grave toll on the Indigenous population.[8] Tensions between the settlers and the Utes intensified, as Native Americans raided Mormon stock in response to diminished resources, and Mormons retaliated in a series of tit-for-tat skirmishes.

One of the more significant flare-ups in the ongoing hostilities took place in summer 1853, when a series of incidents led to what became known as the Walker War. White settlers killed a relative of Ute chief Walkara in the Sanpete River Valley, west of Emery County; Utes retaliated by killing and sometimes mutilating Mormon settlers and soldiers; and in turn, Mormons sought revenge.[9]

During the height of these conflicts, members of the Ute Indian Tribe encountered a party led by Captain John Gunnison of the Corps of Topographic Engineers. Gunnison, charged with assessing the suitability of land between the thirty-eighth and thirty-ninth parallel for a transcontinental railroad route, had just crossed through Emery County from east to west before camping on the lower Sevier River. On the early morning of October 26, 1853, Gunnison's party was attacked and killed by a band of Pahvant Utes.[10]

The back-and-forth skirmishes came to a temporary end in spring 1854, following a meeting between Walkara and Brigham Young. Young, who had

8. Kenneth L. Alford, "Indian Relations in Utah during the Civil War," in *Civil War Saints*, ed. Kenneth L. Alford (Provo, Utah: Religious Studies Center, 2012), 203–25, https://rsc.byu.edu/civil-war-saints/indian-relations-utah-during-civil-war.

9. "Walkara—Walker War Leader in Utah," Legends of America, accessed June 1, 2021, https://www.legendsofamerica.com/na-walkara/; Tina Kelley and Kathryn L. MacKay, "Wakara," *Utah History Encyclopedia*, https://www.uen.org/utah_history_encyclopedia/w/WAKARA.shtml.

10. Sue Schrems, "The Gunnison Massacre by Colonel Dick Kindsfater (Retired)," *Western Americana: History of the American West* (blog), May 17, 2010, http://westernamericana2.blogspot.com/2010/05/gunnison-massacre-by-dick-kindsfater.html.

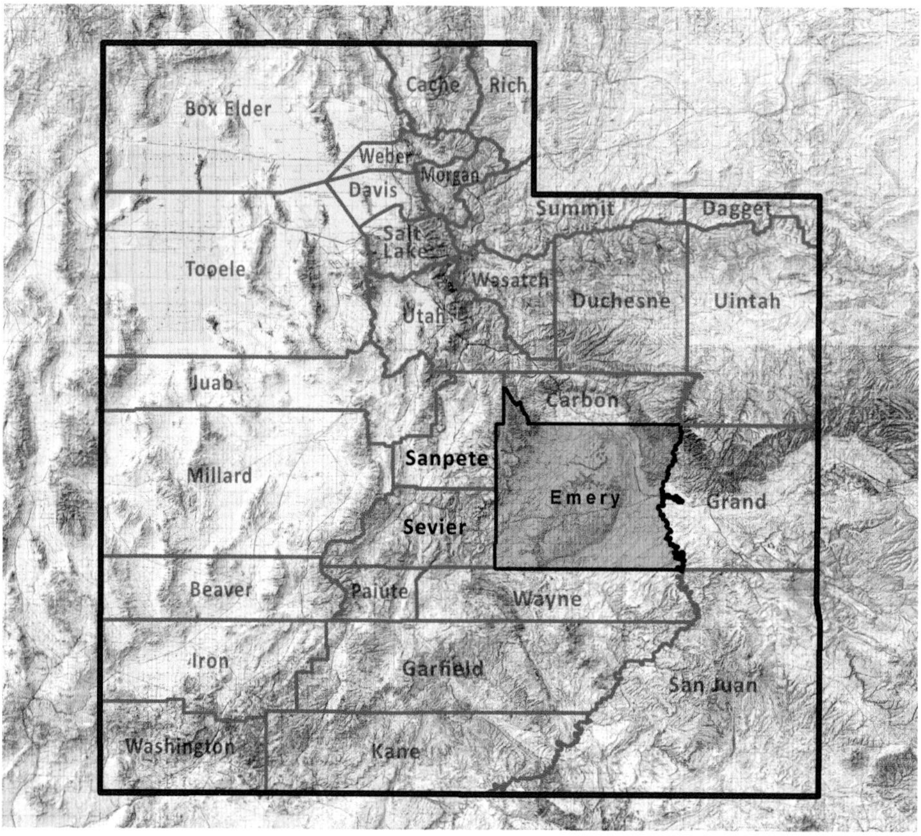

Map of Utah counties, with Sanpete, Sevier, and Emery Counties highlighted.

initially tried without success to quell the violence, traveled to Walkara's camp on Chicken Creek in what is now Juab County to negotiate a settlement. Unfortunately, bloody quarrels between settlers and Utes resumed and escalated until an all-out war was triggered in April 1865.[11] The precipitating event ironically took place in the course of one of the many efforts to negotiate peace between tribal members and Mormon settlers. An inebriated Mormon apparently jerked a Ute chief from his horse, thereby insulting the Ute negotiators, who left the gathering determined to retaliate. Thus began the Black Hawk War, named after the Ute chief Antonga (or Black Hawk). Mormons built forts and recruited a militia. The Utes engaged Paiutes and

11. John A. Peterson, "Black Hawk War," *Utah History Encyclopedia*, https://www.uen.org/utah_history_encyclopedia/b/BLACK_HAWK_WAR.shtml.

Early ranch house in Emery County, circa 1885. Emery County Archives.

Navajos on their behalf. And a war of mutual vengeance replete with unspeakable atrocities raged for seven years.

The war was ended in 1872 as federal troops entered the fray and quelled Black Hawk's insurgence. The Northern Utes were forced onto the Uintah Valley Reservation in northeast Utah, an area far smaller than the vast ancestral lands that once sustained them.[12] Their population plummeted as they were forced to eke out a meager existence in one of the more inhospitable areas in Utah, and to relinquish their traditional way of life.

In the course of the hostilities, the Utes frequently transported cattle stolen from Mormon settlers to Castle Valley, on the west side of Emery County. In summer 1865, a Mormon militia was sent from Sanpete to Castle Valley to recover the cattle. In the course of their forays, Mormon militiamen began to sense the potential of Castle Valley and the Wasatch Plateau for agriculture and grazing as a place favorable for future settlement.[13]

Calling Mormon Families to Emery County

Five years after the Black Hawk War ended, Brigham Young issued what historian Edward Geary calls the founding document for Emery County. In it, Young asks the stake bishop of Sanpete County, Canute Peterson, "to select good, energetic, God fearing young men, whether single or with families, and others who can be spared without interfering with the interests of the settlements in which they now reside, such ones as will be a strength to the new settlement and an aid to its growth in all that we as Latter-day Saints desire to see increase upon the earth." Their destination was Castle Valley.[14]

12. "History: The Northern Utes," Utah American Indian Digital Archive, accessed June 1, 2021, https://utahindians.org/archives/ute/history.html.

13. Geary, *A History of Emery County*, 60.

14. Geary, 58–59.

The first Mormon families to arrive occupied areas adjacent to three of the major creeks flowing eastward from the Wasatch Plateau: Huntington, Cottonwood, and Ferron. They cleared and plowed the arid land and began to farm.

In 1880, just three years after the arrival of the first settlers in Castle Valley, the Utah Territorial Legislature formally recognized Emery as a county, naming it after the then governor of the territory, George W. Emery.[15]

Emery County Begins to Flourish

Over the next decade, the population of Emery County grew fivefold from approximately 550 to 2,000.[16] During that period the towns of Castle Dale, Ferron, Molen, Huntington, Orangeville, and Green River were founded. Residents of the county were sustained by farming along Huntington, Cottonwood, and Ferron Creeks, and by raising cattle and sheep both in Castle Valley and on the slopes of the Wasatch Plateau.

Governor of Utah Territory, George Emery, 1875. Emery County Archives.

In 1883, completion of the Denver and Rio Grande Western Railroad turned Green River, on the eastern side of the county, into an important shipping center for livestock and mining equipment.[17] Railroad workers, along with ranchers, sheepherders, and mining prospectors, flocked to Green River, and the town's population fluctuated between 350 and 800 during the 1880s and 1890s. The railroad linked Emery County with Salt Lake City and Denver, providing access to markets for sheep, cattle, wool, and grain.

Outlaws in Emery County

No history of Emery County during the last two decades of the nineteenth century would be complete without a brief recounting of its outlaw history. Among Utah's early Mormon settlers, Robert LeRoy Parker, known widely

15. Geary, 75; Utah Division of State History, "George W. Emery," History to Go, June 1, 2021, https://historytogo.utah.gov/george-w-emery/.

16. Geary, *A History of Emery County*, 94.

17. Geary, 108.

by his nom de guerre, Butch Cassidy, became one of the most infamous desperados in the history of the Southwest. Butch and his gang, the Wild Bunch, regularly took advantage of hiding places in remote canyons east of the San Rafael Swell, often evading law enforcement in the Robbers Roost region of the San Rafael Desert.[18]

Not far north of Emery County, in the town of Castle Gate, Butch Cassidy and Elzy Lay robbed the Pleasant Valley Coal Company's payroll, plundering about $7,000 in gold (about $180,000 today).[19] Brazenly, they pulled off this stunt in broad daylight in front of nearly a hundred onlookers, many awaiting their pay. The gang then rode off, escaping through Gordon Creek near Price—where they were supplied with fresh horses—across Washboard Flat, and through the San Rafael Swell to the Book Cliffs. A third man, Joe Walker, is said to have assisted them by cutting the telephone lines between Castle Gate and communities farther to the south, but word had already reached Emery County. Posses from Huntington and Castle Dale were sent after the men, but they soon lost track and called off the chase.

While it is often difficult—if not impossible—to separate fact from fiction in the life of Butch Cassidy, he almost certainly left his mark throughout Emery County. A plank structure, still visible today on Cedar Mountain, was allegedly constructed by Butch. Blackened alcoves in Buckhorn Wash are believed by many to be locations of Cassidy camps. Elsewhere, in the western part of the San Rafael Swell, a small wall-lined shelter is marked with the outlaw's faintly visible signature, painted in what appears to be axle grease. Some Ferron residents also insist he occupied a cabin on Ferron Creek. Some of these theories (for example, the signature) certainly seem more probable than others. Recently, Price resident Layne Miller rediscovered a hand-stitched holster made from a weathered boot and incised with Butch's name. It was originally found not far from the Robbers Roost in the San Rafael Desert by a late friend of the family who worked with wild horses and burros in the area. Of note is at least one punch or "loop" used to firmly attach the holster to the leg—a feature that allowed its user to draw a gun quickly.

From 1885 to 1889, Butch Cassidy was joined by fellow outlaw Willard Erastus Christianson (a.k.a. Matt Warner). When he was thirteen years old,

18. "Robbers' Roost—Outlaw Trail," Utah.com, accessed June 1, 2021, https://utah.com/old-west/robbers-roost.

19. Timothy Draper, "Butch Cassidy and the Castle Gate Robbery," Treasures in America, accessed June 1, 2021, https://treasuresinamerica.com/outlaw-loot/butch-cassidy-and-the-castle-gate-robbery/.

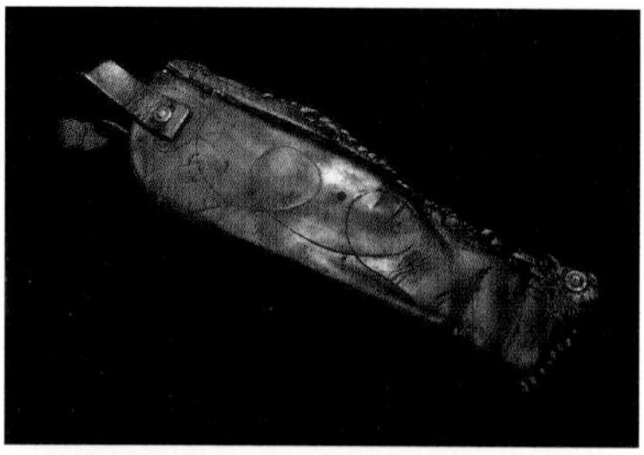

A makeshift holster made from a discarded boot, possibly by the celebrated outlaw Butch Cassidy (*left*); his carved signature appears near the top of the holster. Photos by Jonathan T. Bailey.

Willard (Matt) ran away from his parents, thinking he had murdered a boy during a fight. As he roamed through the West, he became a livestock thief and then a bank robber. As a member of Cassidy's Wild Bunch, Matt was said to have "robbed the Telluride Bank, held up numerous railroad lines, and plundered from New Mexico to Washington."[20]

Matt Warner would later reform, settling down in Price, Utah, where he was elected justice of the peace and later served as deputy sheriff, emblematic of the uniquely American possibility of reinventing oneself in the "Wild West."[21] Butch Cassidy was apparently less fortunate. Most believe he was killed in Bolivia during a shoot-out with police, although some speculate that

20. Eileen Hallet Stone, "Living History: A Utah Boy Who Ran with Butch Cassidy's Wild Bunch," *Salt Lake Tribune*, September 26, 2016.

21. David E. Jensen, "Matt Warner: Utah's Outlaw," Utah Stories, August 11, 2015, https://utahstories.com/2015/08/matt-warner-utahs-outlaw/.

Butch "Casady" left his mark on a sandstone wall in Emery County. Photo by Jonathan T. Bailey.

he faked his death, traveled back to the United States, and lived out the rest of his years under a different pseudonym in an undisclosed location.

Toward the end of his life, Matt Warner left his mark in Emery County along a canyon wall in Buckhorn Wash: Matt and a sheepherder by the name of William Hambrick painted their names and an image of a bull dated 1920. Hambrick's "signature" adorns many other sites throughout the Molen Reef and the Manti-La Sal National Forest.

Farming, Coal Mining, and a Peach Boom

During the first two decades of the twentieth century, Emery County's population grew, increasing to 7,400 in 1920. Growth was spurred both by a peach boom in Green River, in the eastern part of the county, and by an increase in farming following newly constructed irrigation networks on the west side.[22] Wealth from livestock increased as well as ranchers brought in large herds of cattle and sheep. At one point, more than eight hundred thousand head

22. "Green River: A History of Booms and Busts," Destination Green River, December 17, 2012, http://destinationgreenriver.com/green-river-a-history-of-booms-busts/.

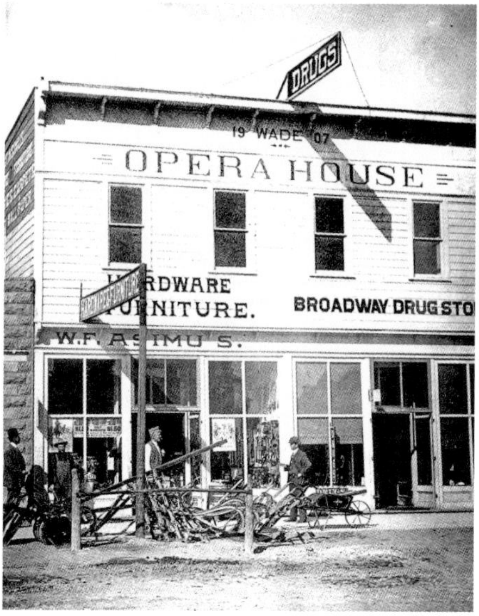

Main Street, Green River, circa 1900 (*left*); and the Green River Opera House. Emery County Archives.

of sheep grazed on the slopes of the Wasatch Plateau.[23]

Mining of coal from rich deposits on the Wasatch Plateau served local markets.[24] Over time, multiple large companies were drawn to the county's ample coal deposits and invested heavily in Emery's coal mines. Coal camps proliferated, and the demand for miners increased. Throughout much of the twentieth century, coal mining has served through booms and busts as a foundation of Emery's economy.[25]

Challenges to Emery County Between the World Wars

Between the end of World War I and the beginning of World War II, Emery County's residents experienced a number of challenges. Directly after World War I, livestock and grain prices plummeted, and save for a modest uptick toward the end of the 1920s, they remained low.[26] Droughts plagued Emery

23. Geary, *A History of Emery County*, 197.

24. Edmund M. Spieker, *The Wasatch Plateau Coal Field, Utah*, USGS Bulletin 819 (Washington, D.C.: Government Printing Office, 1931), https://pubs.er.usgs.gov/publication/b819.

25. Allan Kent Powell, "Coal Industry," in *From the Ground Up: A History of Mining in Utah*, ed. Colleen Whitley (Logan: Utah State University Press, 2006), 126–41.

26. Geary, *A History of Emery County*, 260–65.

The Price-Emery stagecoach, 1912 (*left*); and a home in Castle Dale, 1898. Emery County Archives.

Coal mine in Emery County, 1900. Emery County Archives.

County during the 1930s, ushering in an era of poverty and grief for farmers and stockmen.

Prices for coal dropped as demand for the mineral plummeted at the end of World War I, leading to substantial, years-long layoffs, and lower returns to county coffers during most of the period between 1920 and 1940. At the peak of the Depression, Emery was one of the hardest hit counties in Utah.

In a county of proud and fiercely independent citizens, nearly four in ten residents were receiving public assistance in the mid-1930s.[27]

Perhaps the only bright spot in Emery County's economy during the 1930s was the growth of the melon industry in Green River.[28] The combination of hot summer temperatures and ample irrigation from the river consistently produced (and continues to produce) high-quality melons known nationwide for their sweetness. During the depths of the Depression, Green River melons commanded exorbitant prices from Americans who could afford them.

Agricultural reforms and subsidies instituted during the early days of the New Deal offered some help to the county's farm economy. Ranching was aided following passage of the Taylor Grazing Act in 1935, as reductions in herd size resulting from the introduction of grazing regulations on public lands led to increased prices and a slow return to sustainable incomes.[29]

During the 1930s, when Emery County faced its most dire challenges, the Civilian Conservation Corps (CCC), another innovative program initiated during the early days of the New Deal, hired jobless men to work on public land projects, including "the prevention of forest fires . . . plant pest and disease control, the construction, maintenance and repair of paths, trails and fire-lanes in the national parks and national forests and such other work . . . as the President may determine to be desirable."[30]

One notable achievement of the CCC was the construction of a road linking Castle Dale to Buckhorn Draw. From there, the corps built a bridge over the San Rafael River, allowing the road to continue eastward across the county. The completion of the bridge in 1937 was celebrated by a crowd estimated to be more than two thousand in size. Although traffic no longer uses the CCC "Swinging Bridge," it still stands, a monument to the country's willingness to invest in its people and infrastructure during desperate economic times.[31] Other CCC projects included construction of a road linking

27. Geary, 274–81.

28. Geary, 279.

29. "Taylor Grazing Act (1935)," The Living New Deal, accessed June 1, 2021, https://livingnewdeal.org/glossary/taylor-grazing-act-1935/.

30. "Civilian Conservation Corps (CCC) (1933)," The Living New Deal, accessed June 1, 2021, https://livingnewdeal.org/glossary/civilian-conservation-corps-ccc-1933/.

31. "San Rafael Bridge—Emery County UT," The Living New Deal, accessed June 1, 2021, https://livingnewdeal.org/projects/san-rafael-bridge-emery-county-ut/.

Civilian Conservation Corps camp in Joe's Valley, Utah. Emery County Archives.

The Swinging Bridge, constructed by the CCC, spans the Green River. At the time that the bridge was built, it provided an important link between the western and eastern portions of Emery County. Emery County Archives.

Castle Dale and Green River, as well as construction of a large number of facilities for watering sheep and cattle. Many members of the CCC fell in love with the land and decided to settle in Emery County following completion of their tours in the corps.

During the 1930s and extending into the war years, paleontologists from the University of Utah, the Smithsonian Institution, and the California Institute of Technology discovered rich fossil beds in Emery County that contained the remains of a large number of dinosaurs and other denizens of the Jurassic period (201–145 million years ago).[32] The Cleveland-Lloyd Dinosaur Quarry has long served as an important research site, and is now included

32. Martha Hayden, "Dinosaurs of Utah," *Utah History Encyclopedia*, https://www.uen.org/utah_history_encyclopedia/d/DINOSAURS_OF_UTAH.shtml.

A car crossing the Swinging Bridge soon after its 1937 completion. Emery County Archives.

The reconstructed head of an allosaur, discovered in Cleveland-Lloyd Dinosaur Quarry. Emery County Archives.

as part of the Jurassic National Monument, declared in the 2019 Dingell Conservation, Management, and Recreation Act.[33]

With the beginning of World War II, demand for coal and agricultural products once again increased.[34] While many men in Emery County left for the service between 1940 and 1945, Emery County's citizens still managed to modernize their housing stock, build new schools and other public facilities, and enhance the quality and number of roads in the county during that period.[35]

33. "Jurassic National Monument," Utah.com, June 1, 2021, https://utah.com/cleveland-lloyd-dinosaur-quarry; Matcha, "Hidden Secrets of the Jurassic National Monument's Cleveland Dinosaur Quarry," Utah Office of Tourism, accessed June 1, 2021, https://www.visitutah.com/articles/cleveland-lloyd-dinosaur-quarry.

34. Geary, *A History of Emery County*, 304–7.

35. Geary, 297–301.

Challenges After World War II and a Boom During the Early Cold War Years

At the end of the war, the economy of the area once again deteriorated as the demand for coal decreased. At first the decrease was modest, but from the 1950s to the early 1970s mined tonnage decreased by nearly a factor of three. Agricultural prices dropped as well and, coupled with another long drought, wrought havoc on farmers. In response to economic stress, the county population dropped, and by 1960, the unemployment rate reached 14 percent.[36]

One bright spot in the otherwise dismal economic environment was the resurgence of uranium mining. The demand for uranium soared as the Cold War began to accelerate in the 1950s, producing a temporary mining boom. Spurred by incentives from the Atomic Energy Commission, corporate mining enterprises and hundreds of mom-and-pop explorers alike ranged over Emery County searching for the suddenly valuable mineral.[37] Old radium mines around Temple Mountain and Tidwell Bottom were reopened and expanded.[38]

Uranium mining camp near Temple Mountain (*upper left*). During the peak of the Cold War, Emery County experienced a uranium boom. The boom petered out toward the end of the 1960s. Emery County Archives.

Some weekend prospectors found their fortunes in valuable uranium deposits in Lucky Strike Mine in Reds Canyon, and in rich deposits near Tomsich Butte and Green Vein Mesa. Perhaps the best-known uranium mine that sprung up during the 1950s is Hidden Splendor, near one of the most beautiful parts of the San Rafael Swell, where Muddy

36. Geary, 316–17.

37. Michael T. Searcy, *A History of the Copper Globe, Lucky Strike, Tomsich Butte, Hidden Splendor, and Little Susan Mines within the San Rafael Swell Mining District* (Provo, Utah: Brigham Young University Office of Public Archaeology, 2012), https://fs.ogm.utah.gov/PUB/MINES/AMR/A015/917/SanRafaelOralHistoryReport4-16-2012.pdf.

38. Geary, *A History of Emery County*, 330–34.

Creek pierces the San Rafael Reef. The boom was short lived, as the demand for uranium dropped precipitously as the 1960s came to an end. Rusting remnants of the atomic era are still visible: once thriving, now-abandoned mines and hundreds of abandoned digs abound throughout Emery County.

During the 1950s and 1960s, Green River once again became an important shipping center as the town served as a locus for staging and supplying miners working the Temple Mountain, Hidden Splendor, and Tidwell Draw Mines. Town residents also found short-lived but lucrative employment in the mines or at the newly constructed Union Carbide ore-sampling plant.

Green River's economy was also boosted by an influx of tourists, and a miniboom in construction of motels and other amenities. In the early 1960s, the U.S. Army established a branch of the White Sands Missile Range near the town. Site engineers and technicians were involved in testing a variety of military missiles including the iconic Atlas and Athena rockets.[39] The development of the Green River missile facility brought with it a number of individuals who grew to love the area, stayed, and joined longtime residents to improve schools and raise the level of other civic amenities.[40]

Despite relative prosperity in Green River, the overall economy and population in Emery County both declined. And yet, even in the face of high overall unemployment, mitigated only partially by the uranium boom and Green River's flourishing, many residents still chose to stay in Emery County. Their reasons for staying were many, but perhaps most significant were the family ties and deep cultural and spiritual attachments to a land that is startling in its beauty and that has sustained families for multiple generations.

Investment in Emery County's Future During the 1960s and 1970s

Later in the Cold War era, public-spirited leaders persuaded county residents to invest in major infrastructure developments, including a telephone network that spanned towns spread across 2.7 million acres. With support from the federal government, three major infrastructure projects key to Emery County's future were initiated in the 1960s: the Emery County Project,

39. "Green River: A History of Booms and Busts," Destination Green River.

40. Geary, 353; "Green River History," Destination Green River, September 25, 2010, http://destinationgreenriver.com/green-river-history/.

Senator Frank Moss (D-Utah) at the dedication of the Joe's Valley Dam, 1963. Emery County Archives.

the Ferron Watershed Project, and the construction of Interstate 70 through the heart of the county.[41]

The Emery County Project provided for storage of water in Joe's Valley Reservoir, which was created by a dam capturing water from a tributary of Cottonwood Creek in the Wasatch Plateau, and channeled when needed to fields in Castle Valley below.[42] The reservoir is located in a serene mountain valley, and it attracts recreationists from Emery County and beyond.[43]

41. William Joe Simonds, "A History of the Emery County Project," Water History, accessed June 1, 2021, http://www.waterhistory.org/histories/emery/emery.pdf; Edward A. Geary, "Ferron," *Utah History Encyclopedia*, https://www.uen.org/utah_history_encyclopedia/f/FERRON.shtml; Edward A. Geary, "Interstate 70," History to Go, accessed June 1, 2021, https://historytogo.utah.gov/interstate-70/.

42. Julie Johansen, "Joe's Valley Reservoir: The Jewel of Emery County," ETV News, January 10, 2019, https://etvnews.com/joes-valley-reservoir-the-jewel-of-emery-county/.

43. "Joe's Valley Reservoir," Utah Fishing Information, accessed June 1, 2021, http://www.utahfishinginfo.com/utahlakes/joesvalley.php.

The primary feature of the Ferron Watershed Project is the Millsite Dam, which stores water from Ferron Creek in a reservoir behind the dam, located high on the Wasatch Plateau. The reservoir-dam system controls the flow of water through Ferron Creek, feeding farms below. The reservoir serves as another locus for boating and fishing.[44]

Initial plans for completing Interstate 70 from its origin outside Baltimore to its terminus at Interstate 15 near Fort Cove, Utah, imagined a route through Utah that would roughly follow the path of the Old Spanish Trail: leaving Utah Highway 6 north of Green River, crossing Buckhorn Flat, and joining Utah Highway 10 in Castle Dale. Following a tour across the San Rafael Swell with Emery County officials, highway planners decided on a far more challenging and expensive route: a path from Green River to Salina, Utah, a 108-mile stretch directly through the middle of the geologically breathtaking and extraordinarily rugged swell. The road was opened to traffic in 1970, but the highway was not fully completed as a continuous, four-lane divided road joining the two towns until 1990.[45] It is without doubt one of the most arresting sections of highway in the United States. The beauty and the rhythms of the swell, though far better appreciated on foot or on four-wheel-drive roads, can still be sensed even driving along Interstate 70 at the posted speed of eighty miles per hour.[46]

While travel through the swell on Interstate 70 whets the appetite for "more Swell," the only consistent benefit to the county accrues to businesses and recreation activities in Green River. The western towns of Huntington, Cleveland, Castle Dale, Orangeville, Moore, and Emery lie well to the north of the interstate and are thus rarely visited by those who drive by. As a result, the development of amenities in the western part of the county has been slowed, although the 2019 declaration of the San Rafael Swell Recreation Area and the wilderness areas to the south and east may soon begin to attract recreationists, investors, and perhaps new residents.

---

44. "Millstone State Park," Utah Office of Tourism, accessed June 1, 2021, https://www.visitutah.com/places-to-go/parks-outdoors/millsite-state-park.

45. Matthew Brown, "I-70 Project Reaches End of Road at Last," *Deseret News*, September 28, 1990, https://www.deseret.com/1990/9/28/18883456/i-70-project-reaches-end-of-road-at-last-br.

46. "A Guide to I-70 Through Southeastern Utah," Moab Area Travel Council, June 22, 2007, https://www.moabtourismcenter.com/i70.pdf.

Resurgence in Coal Mining and the Coming of Coal-Fired Power Plants

The economy of Emery County began an upward turn in the 1970s. The fear that worldwide energy reserves would be depleted within a few decades led to a resurgence in coal mining in the county. The availability of vast quantities of coal along the Wasatch Plateau, as well as access to water stored in Joe's Valley and behind the Millsite Dam, led Utah Power and Light Company to construct two large coal-fired power plants: one, the Huntington Power Plant, located in the eponymous town; and the other, the Hunter Power Plant, located two miles south of Castle Dale. The Huntington and Hunter plants (now operated by PacifiCorp) have the capacity to generate 1,073 and 1,577 megawatts of electricity, respectively.[47] Together, they exceed the generating capacity of the Hoover Dam.

Construction of the power plants transformed the county's economy dramatically. Emery's population grew by 150 percent from the early 1970s to the early 1980s (from 5,100 to more than 12,000 residents) as the number of jobs in construction and coal mining surged. By the late 1970s, Emery County, which once suffered with 14 percent unemployment, was transformed into the second wealthiest of Utah's twenty-nine counties.[48] The unemployment rate dipped to 4.2 percent in 1982.[49]

Former Emery County commissioner Randy Johnson recalls the evolution of the county's economy from the late 1960s to the early 1980s.

> When I was a boy, many, many years ago, the school board and the county were the largest employers, and the largest industry was the cattle industry. You either went into the coal mines, or you left for elsewhere when you grew up if you wanted work. Then, in the late seventies, early eighties, because of the water that we had in our reservoirs, and their proximity to the huge amounts of coal resources, the power company came down here and proposed five power plant units. Those five units were built over a period of a

47. "Huntington Power Plant," Global Energy Monitor Wiki, last updated April 30, 2021, https://www.gem.wiki/Huntington_Power_Plant; "Hunter Power Plant," Global Energy Monitor Wiki, last updated April 30, 2021, https://www.gem.wiki/Hunter_Power_Plant.

48. Geary, *A History of Emery County*, 374.

49. Geary, 395.

The Hunter Power Plant, south of Castle Dale. The plant makes use of the abundant local supply of coal and water that flows down from the Wasatch Plateau. Courtesy of ETV News.

> decade or so, and when they were in full swing they represented 83 percent of Emery County's tax dollars. It provided a huge number of jobs building them, and then a fairly substantial number of jobs continuing to operate the power plants.[50]

By 1983, the Emery County economy was once again in trouble, as the demand for Emery County coal dropped. The boom of the 1970s became the bust of the 1980s, as the county's population once again began to decline, doing so at a rate of four hundred people per year over the decade.[51] While demand dropped, coal mining itself became more automated, with a consequent dramatic effect on the number of mining-related jobs.[52]

Imagining a Dynamic Future for Emery County

Randy Johnson reflects on the challenges of the declining number of coal jobs and the prospective closing of the Hunter and Huntington plants sometime before the year 2040:

---

50. Randy Johnson, pers. comm. Except where otherwise noted, subsequent quotations in this book from Johnson and others come from direct conversation with the speakers.

51. Geary, 395–97.

52. Devashree Saha and Sifan Liu, "Increased Automation Guarantees a Bleak Outlook for Trump's Promises to Coal Miners," *Brookings*, January 25, 2017, https://www.brookings.edu/blog/the-avenue/2017/01/25/automation-guarantees-a-bleak-outlook-for-trumps-promises-to-coal-miners/.

> When I was a commissioner between '95 and 2002 we made about $4 million plus dollars in mineral lease money every year from the production of coal and a few other things. We were one of the three counties in the state that provided the most money to the [State] Mineral Lease Board. Now they're lucky to get a million dollars in mineral lease money. And the power plants are projected to run their course in about 2034 or 2035. So we need to be doing something to broaden our economic horizons and to have more variety in our economic possibilities. [That's] been on the minds of commissioners for twenty-five years, and it continues to be in the forefront.[53]

With the certainty in public land use gained by passage of the Emery County Public Land Management Act in 2019, Emery County leaders hope to develop plans with a clear understanding of how their public lands can be used.

Emery County commissioner Kent Wilson underlines the importance of certainty:

> Certainty in public land use was one of the motivations for my supporting this [the Emery County Public Land Management] bill. If you look at the economies of Garfield County, Kane County, Piute County, San Juan County, who are all heavily relying on the tourism industry, they are poor counties. So for Emery, where we've been an extraction county with coal, our economy had a good middle class for the last thirty years. Where else can you go [other than coal mining or the power plants] and graduate high school and get a $60,000-a-year job? You gain experience and you get into management and you go up from there.
>
> The challenge for us is how do you replace that? Tourism doesn't do that. The business owners, they do well, but then you have the lower spectrum, the ten- to fifteen-dollar-an-hour jobs, that can't survive in the economy that you've created. We want to focus on the $60,000 jobs for the most part, and then also see what we can do to take advantage of the good will from the public lands bill.

Wilson's and other leaders' discussions have focused on enhancing the recreation economy, taking advantage of the extensive electric grid infrastructure already in place to serve the power plants, supporting renewable energy

---

53. See also Brian Maffly, "Poll Says Utahns Support Closing Coal-Fired Plants Early," *Salt Lake Tribune*, March 3, 2020, https://www.sltrib.com/news/environment/2020/03/02/poll-says-utahns-support/.

projects, researching alternative uses of coal, and leveraging their investment in high-speed internet to attract entrepreneurs and small businesses to an area with unusually compelling natural amenities.

In May 2019, the county authorized the Hunter Solar Project.[54] The plan envisions installing a field of solar panels covering 1,300 acres south of the Hunter Power Plant. The eventual goal is to develop utility-scale solar power generation that can serve up to thirty-five thousand people.

Emery County's leaders have also reached out to the three major universities in the state—Utah State University and its nearby USU Eastern campus in Price, Brigham Young University in Provo, and the University of Utah in Salt Lake City—to explore initiatives to diversify the county's economy.

In another step to build a robust economic future, the county has purchased an abandoned building in Orangeville and is refurbishing it to house the San Rafael Energy Research Center.[55] The research center will be operated as a business incubator by Emery and six nearby counties: Duchesne, Daggett, Carbon, Uintah, Sevier, and San Juan. Initial facilities include a thorium-based nuclear power generation plant, which will enable production of medical isotopes, and a coal combustion research plant.

"We are not giving up on coal," says Kent Wilson:

> One of the things that we've been working on the last six months is [developing a research center] in a twenty-five-thousand-square-foot building that housed mining parts for several coal mines. [After the building had sat] vacant for the last five or seven years, Emery County went and bought the building. [The first project at the facility] started out as thorium [reactor] research through the seven-county coalition. . . . [The project involved] professors from BYU, Utah State, and University of Utah who felt like they [could develop a new approach to building] thorium nuclear reactors. To this point, we've secured a $1 million grant from the State of Utah. We secured a $2.6-million grant from [the Utah Permanent Community Impact Fund Board] to bring that facility up to speed.

54. Traci Bishop, "Emery County Makes Progress on Hunter Solar Project," ETV News, October 25, 2019, https://etvnews.com/emery-county-makes-progress-on-hunter-solar-project/.

55. Scottie Draper, "Emery County Commissioners Develop San Rafael Research Center," ETV News, June 26, 2019, https://etvnews.com/emery-county-commissioners-developing-san-rafael-research-center/; Scottie Draper, "Emery County Receives $7 Million Grant for San Rafael Energy Research Center," ETV News, October 9, 2020, https://etvnews.com/emery-county-receives-7-million-grant-for-san-rafael-energy-research-center/.

Solar panels for the proposed Hunter Solar Project. Pixabay.

> [We also have] a combustion machine [used to] analyze coal emissions and burning coal with different ingredients like wood or mulch. [The machine analyzes] the data on CO_2 emissions and such.
>
> There have been people coming to us wanting to rent space for doing research on batteries for solar. So that's an exciting concept that's just in its infancy. We've got consultants chasing Department of Energy grants. So it feels like it's going to take off.
>
> We feel like with these power plants here, we have billions of dollars of infrastructure [in our] transmission lines, so we want to be a part of the next generation of electricity, whatever that might be. Because if the power plants go away, the infrastructure is still here to transport electricity out of here to the rest of the western United States. It has value. It gives us an advantage. Right now there's a lot of interest in solar. And also there's some interest in taking coal and turning it into low-cost carbon fiber.
>
> We're also trying to put a package together for tourism. We recognize with the [new] public lands bill that tourism could be an important part of our future. It seems like there's willingness among our taxpayers to go and create a trail plan for motorized and nonmotorized, equestrian, bouldering, all sorts of recreation. Our goal is to make ourselves appealing to motels, KOA types, and other businesses in the tourism realm.

Wilson sees good days ahead for Emery County. "I have a lot of optimism for our economy going forward. It has never been easier to make a living in rural Utah than it is now."

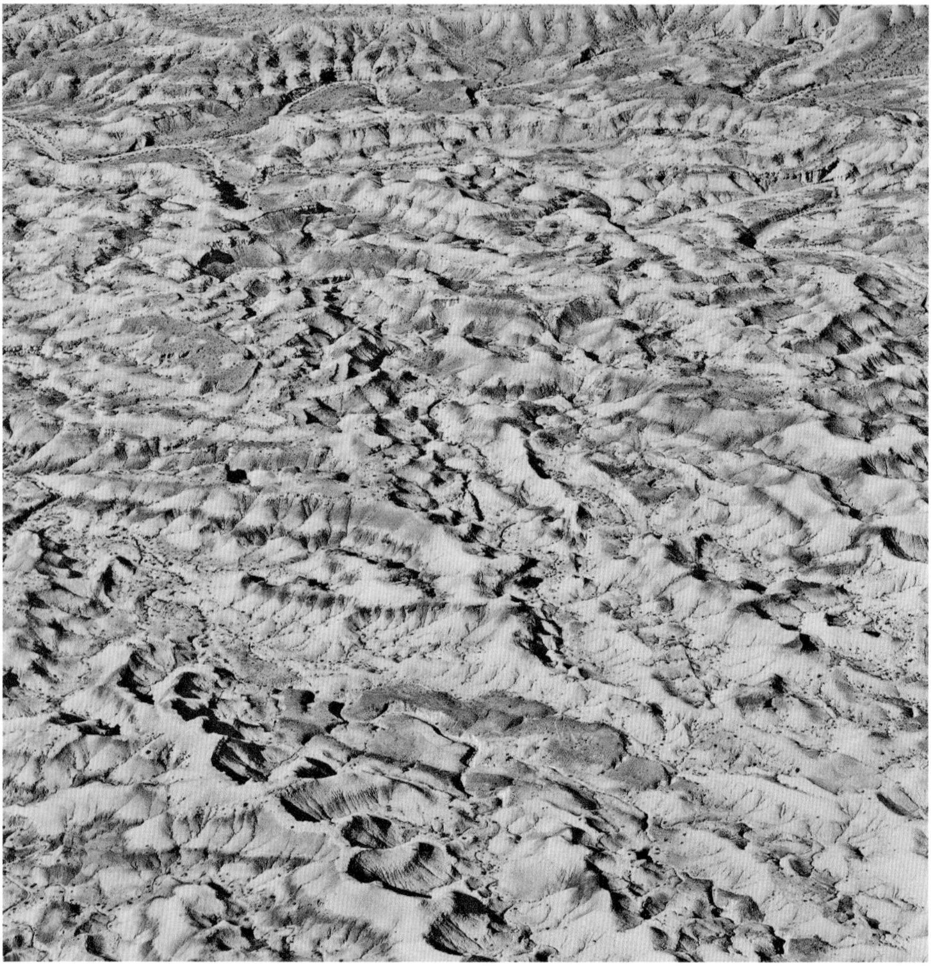

Mussentuchit Badlands. Aerial photo by Stephen E. Strom.

Collaboration and Compromise

Forging the Emery County Public Land Bill

[Emery County] is to me . . . a combination of one of the most remarkable natural places in the world, and one of the most incredible human histories in the world. The outlaw heritage, and the Indian heritage, and the natural history . . . all kind of meshed into this incredible, beautiful place. But more than anything else, [what makes Emery County remarkable are] its people and what they went through to settle a land that was so hostile.

—FORMER COUNTY COMMISSIONER RANDY JOHNSON

We are deeply involved with this land. We had ancestors that came in here in the 1870s with their livestock. I have a grandfather who died while he was prospecting in the Lost Spring Canyon. And we have our Easter season. The population of every county practically doubles during Easter weekend because everybody comes home [to be in the land]. It's those feelings about the land [that make it special to us].

—EDWARD GEARY, EMERITUS PROFESSOR OF HISTORY,
BRIGHAM YOUNG UNIVERSITY

Families "Eastering" in the San Rafael Swell, 1928. Emery County Archives.

Coal mining during World War II. Emery County Archives.

Public Lands and the Citizens of Emery County

Emery County's eleven thousand residents today—80 percent of them Mormons, many of them descendants of families that first settled the region in the late 1870s—share deep attachment to public land that provides economic sustenance through ranching, farming, and mining, as well as spiritual nourishment.

Crucially, nearly all the land in Emery County is public land, held by the federal government and managed for the benefit of all Americans. As has been the case for all states admitted to the union since its inception, the federal government retained title to these lands when Utah was granted statehood in 1896.[1]

Currently, the federal government oversees 83 percent of the county's 2.7 million acres (75 percent is managed by the Bureau of Land Management, BLM; 8 percent by the U.S. Forest Service, USFS), while the state of Utah manages 12 percent of the land as school trust land, or land that was carved out from federally owned land and granted to Utah at the time of statehood to use as a resource for funding schools and hospitals or to use as state parks.[2]

Both the economy and culture of Emery County's citizens are intimately linked with how these public lands are managed. Ranchers depend on per-

1. John D. Leshy, *Debunking the Creation Myths of America's Public Lands,* 2018 Wallace Stegner Center Lecture (Salt Lake City: University of Utah Press, 2018).

2. "Emery County, UT," Economic Profile System, Headwaters Economics, accessed June 1, 2021, https://headwaterseconomics.org/apps/economic-profile-system/49015.

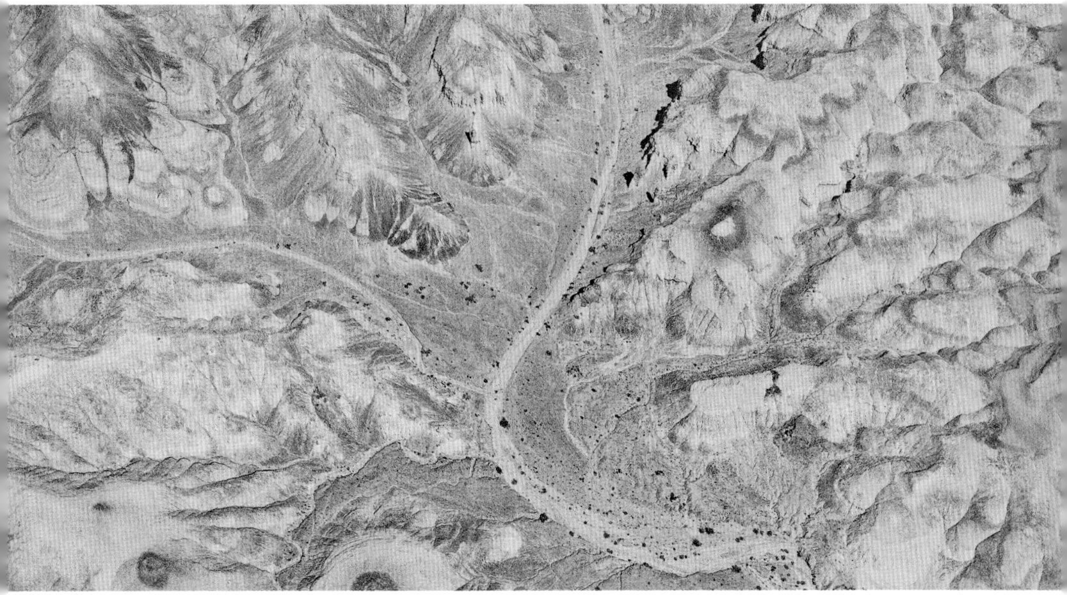

Badlands near the Moroni Slopes. Aerial photo by Stephen E. Strom.

mits issued by the BLM and USFS to graze livestock. Mines past and present depend on these federal agencies to issue leases and grant water rights. How residents are permitted to recreate on nearby lands depends on how the BLM and USFS manage roads and campsites, motorized and nonmotorized recreation, hunting, and fishing.

A Movement to Conserve Public Lands

Starting in the 1960s, prosperity in the United States reached new heights. Travel by air, train, and auto increased dramatically, and the development of the interstate highway system and improvement of secondary roads provided far more convenient access to remote regions of the West.

At the same time, the conservation movement, which had been relatively dormant during the war years, began to grow into a significant political force. Building on the efforts of late nineteenth- and early twentieth-century pioneers like John Muir, Gifford Pinchot, and Theodore Roosevelt, and on the visionary work of Interior Secretary Harold L. Ickes during the 1930s to expand protections for public land in Utah, the new generation of

Muddy Creek winding through the area near Tomsich Butte. Aerial photo by Jonathan T. Bailey.

conservationists forged politically powerful coalitions to support protection of America's wild lands, forests, and waterways.

Publication of Rachel Carson's *Silent Spring* raised awareness of some of the more egregious effects of human activity on ecosystems, and further inspired efforts to demand legislative and executive action to protect sensitive environments.[3]

These efforts culminated in the passage of the Wilderness Act—signed into law by President Lyndon B. Johnson in 1964—which created the Wilderness Preservation System to protect "areas where earth and its community of life are untrammeled by man, and where man does not remain."[4] The act empowers Congress to declare tracts of public lands "wilderness areas," which are then managed to ensure that they retain their wilderness character.

Continued advocacy by conservation groups and like-minded citizens resulted in passage of the National Environmental Policy Act (NEPA) and the Clean Air Act in 1970.[5] The NEPA brought into being two government bodies that together provide a broad national framework for developing policies aimed at protecting our environment: the Council on Environmental Quality and the Environmental Protection Agency.[6]

As citizen interest in conservation grew during the 1960s and 1970s, and the natural beauty, paleontological richness, and cultural significance of remote western lands became more widely known, major efforts to protect the public lands managed by the BLM and USFS were launched. Those urging protecting Utah's red rock country in its natural state found a literary champion in Edward Abbey, whose love for the land and fury at its perceived violation were fiercely manifest in *Desert Solitaire* and *The Monkey Wrench Gang*.[7]

3. Rachel Carson, *Silent Spring* (Boston: Houghton Mifflin, 1962).

4. "The Wilderness Act of 1964," U.S. Department of Justice, updated May 12, 2015, https://www.justice.gov/enrd/wilderness-act-1964.

5. "What Is the National Environmental Policy Act?," U.S. Environmental Protection Agency, last updated September 17, 2020, https://www.epa.gov/nepa/what-national-environmental-policy-act; "Clean Air Act Requirements and History," U.S. Environmental Protection Agency, last updated January 10, 2017, https://www.epa.gov/clean-air-act-overview/clean-air-act-requirements-and-history.

6. "Welcome: The Council on Environmental Quality," National Environmental Policy Act, accessed June 1, 2021, https://ceq.doe.gov/; "EPA History," U.S. Environmental Protection Agency, last updated May 17, 2021, https://www.epa.gov/history.

7. Edward Abbey, *Desert Solitaire* (New York: McGraw-Hill, 1968); Edward Abbey, *The Monkey Wrench Gang* (Philadelphia: Lippincott, Williams and Wilkins, 1975).

While raising public awareness of the scarring of Utah's public lands by loosely regulated miners and ranchers and the careless mutilation of its fragile landscape by motorized vehicle operators, Abbey's depictions of locals, along with those of zealous conservation groups, angered some citizens living adjacent to public lands who felt misunderstood, belittled, and disrespected. By contrast, they believe profoundly that, with few exceptions, they have been good stewards of the land, using it prudently and preserving their heritage.

The Challenges of Balancing Multiple Uses of Public Lands

The daily lives of a significant number of Emery County's residents are tied directly to decisions made about public lands. Finding a balance between their economic needs—which historically have been met by using public lands for resource extraction and grazing—and the protection of lands that conservation groups, as well as many local citizens, believe to be national treasures represents a significant challenge.

The magnitude of the challenge increased significantly during the 1980s following a survey of all BLM lands in Emery County that was aimed at assessing whether they possessed wilderness characteristics: "[areas of] sufficient size, naturalness, and outstanding opportunities for either solitude or primitive and unconfined recreation."[8] The survey—a legal requirement of the Federal Land Policy and Management Act (FLPMA) of 1976—designated several wilderness study areas (WSAs) in the county and raised the possibility that some of them would become prime candidates for congressional designation as wilderness, the highest form of protection for federal lands.[9]

The designation of WSAs was attacked by many county residents, who feared the potential of "locking up" public lands and precluding access for ranching, mining, and recreation. At the same time, many conservation groups believed that the BLM failed to include lands that should qualify as wilderness.

---

8. Bureau of Land Management, *Utah Wilderness Inventory: 1999* (n.p.: U.S. Department of the Interior, 1999), https://www.blm.gov/sites/blm.gov/files/Utah%20Wilderness%20Inventory%201999.pdf.

9. Roger Flynn, "Daybreak on the Land: The Coming of Age of the Federal Land Policy and Management Act of 1976," *University of Vermont Law Review* 29 (2004): 814–45.

Efforts to declare large tracts of public lands in Emery County as wilderness were led by the Utah Wilderness Coalition, a consortium of environmental groups spearheaded by the Southern Utah Wilderness Alliance (SUWA). Their cause was championed in 1989 by Representative Wayne Owens (D-Utah), who introduced a bill, America's Red Rock Wilderness Act, to protect 5.7 million acres of wilderness in Utah, including much of the BLM land in Emery County since 1989.[10] As of 2021, the bill has been introduced in every session of Congress since.

Not surprisingly, many citizens and political leaders in Emery County became concerned that their economic future and cultural connections to the land would be compromised. Indeed, it has been reported that to survive politically in the 1980s and early 1990s required that an Emery County commissioner respond "Hell no, we don't want any" to any wilderness proposal.[11]

Early Efforts to Forge Compromise

In the mid-1990s, political leaders in Emery County initiated discussions to develop proposals aimed at finding a balance among competing visions for the future of the 2.1 million acres of public lands in their county. They believed that a proactive approach would offer the best way of ensuring that the citizens of Emery County would have a voice in defining how those lands would be used. Absent a locally based plan, Emery's residents were fearful that decisions regarding the future of nearby public lands could be decided in Washington by legislative action creating wilderness areas, or executive declaration of a national monument. "There [was] a sense here in Emery County for quite some time that we needed to have some influence over what was going to happen to our public lands," former county commissioner Randy Johnson recalls. "That to just sit and wait and watch was a very dangerous game to play."

In 1995, in what would be a critical development that would play out over the next several decades, the County Commission formed a twelve-person Public Lands Council that comprised a diverse body of stakeholders

10. "The Story of America's Red Rock Wilderness Act," Southern Utah Wilderness Alliance, accessed June 1, 2021, https://suwa.org/issues/arrwa/the-story-of-americas-red-rock-wilderness-act/.

11. Jeffrey O. Durrant, *Struggle Over Utah's San Rafael Swell* (Tucson: University of Arizona Press, 2007), 165.

Former county commissioners and members of the Emery County Public Lands Council Randy Johnson (*above*) and Ray Peterson. Photos courtesy of ETV News and Ray Peterson, respectively.

(e.g., ranchers, recreationists, representatives of the mining community, off-highway vehicle [OHV] enthusiasts) spanning a wide range of local views regarding how Emery's public lands should be used or protected. The council then signed formal agreements with all the agencies and entities that manage or have interest in the use of public lands, including the BLM; USFS; Utah State Parks; Utah Division of Oil, Gas and Mining; and the Utah School and Institutional Trust Lands Administration (SITLA). The agencies and Public Lands Council met monthly (and continue to do so), and over time the various stakeholders developed mutual trust and understanding despite their often-conflicting views.

In 1998, following three years of discussion and debate, the Public Lands Council proposed legislation that would have protected public land in Emery County, designating some as a national heritage and conservation area, and other land as wilderness. The council envisioned having significant influence on the BLM's management of the heritage and conservation area through participation in an advisory council that was partially composed of Emery County residents representing a broad range of local expertise and opinion.

"We had all the different stakeholders at the table," Johnson says:

> We held monthly meetings and took a large number of field trips and came up with a proposal for Congress that [the late] congressman Jim Hanson (R-Utah)

Meeting of the Emery County Public Lands Council. The council has met monthly since 1995. Courtesy of ETV News.

> carried for us: the San Rafael Swell National Conservation/National Heritage Area that included half a million acres of Wilderness, a conservation area that was six hundred thousand acres, and a heritage area laid down over the top of it [which included] most of the county.
>
> The reasoning behind [our thinking was] that unlike many of the red rock areas around the state, the San Rafael is an extremely unique mix and blend of history and pretty rocks. It's got extensive outlaw history and mining history and Civilian Conservation Corps history and Native American history. The thinking of Emery County folks is that many of those historic elements are just as important to preserve and recognize as the beauty of the rocks surrounding them. So we've always sought a solution that would include recognizing and working to preserve that element of the San Rafael along with the pristine areas.

After failing to receive sufficient support in Congress for its 1998 initiative, Emery County tried again two years later. It put forward the framework for a bill that would have declared the area west of the San Rafael Swell a western legacy district, and a region including the swell as a national conservation area. The legislation initially enjoyed significant support, but in the end, opposition from OHV enthusiasts and other groups killed the bill.

The county leaders persisted in their efforts to seek certainty regarding the future of public lands, and next proposed that Emery County advocate for creation of a national monument centered on the San Rafael Swell. Their proposal was rejected by county citizens in a referendum held in 2002.

Bringing Stakeholders Together

Further efforts were put on hold until 2009, when the County Commission and Public Lands Council decided to try again. This time, they sought the participation of a large cross section of county residents before proposing a new plan for public lands use. "We had earlier versions or earlier attempts in 1998 and 2000 to do something legislatively but lessons were learned when they weren't successful," former county commissioner Ray Peterson says:

> So when we started in 2009 we cast this broad net. Who are all the stakeholders? Let's talk to them. Let's invite them to come and talk to us and be part of this. We knew by then it had to be a process, it had to involve everyone that had a stake in this.
>
> I think we held eight or nine [scoping meetings] right off the bat. What are the clear range of issues according to resource use? We created subcommittees [under the auspices of] the Public Lands Council, and they held public meetings for the people that they represented: water users, livestock grazers, recreation folks, etc. For most meetings, the first question was, does Emery County want to pursue something legislatively? Do we have support to do that? And if we do, what are your thoughts? What do you want to tell us as we proceed?
>
> [People agreed that] we better try and do something. We can be proactive and try to get some certainty through legislation before [something] takes place where we don't have any control. So the citizens of Emery County and other stakeholders said yeah, let's try and do something. That gave us buy-in. That gave us a base to grow on.

A New Opportunity

In 2013, after four years of work, the county had a nearly completed draft bill in hand when Representative Rob Bishop (R-Utah), then chair of the House Committee on Natural Resources, urged the county to participate in a broader effort to resolve outstanding public lands issues in eight counties in eastern Utah. Efforts to shape and pass Bishop's comprehensive Public Lands Initiative ultimately failed in 2016, and with them, Emery County's latest effort.

However, in return for Emery County's willingness to put its own initiative aside and to participate in the Public Lands Initiative, Bishop promised to support the county's bill at the next politically favorable opportunity. That occasion presented itself in 2018, when Utah's senior senator, Orrin Hatch, at the time the longest-serving Republican senator in U.S. history (having served forty-two years in office), announced his retirement. Hatch gathered his staff together to identify the best opportunities to develop and pass legislation important to his legacy before he retired.

"We knew before [the senator] announced it publicly, we knew internally that he was going to retire," former Hatch staffer Romel Nicholas shares. "And he called in his senior staff and sat around a big table. He said, in all of your portfolios—I handled environmental issues and lands issues—I want you to make a graph of impact versus likelihood [of passing legislation] and wherever the graph intersects, that is where I want you to focus your efforts. . . . So when you put together the graph and look at likelihood versus potential impact, one arrives at Emery County."

Representative John Curtis (R-Utah) in Arches National Park. Photo courtesy of Jake Bornstein.

Senator Hatch's support rekindled interest in crafting a version of an Emery County bill that could conceivably muster the backing needed to pass. However, crafting a version of the bill that enjoyed the support of a range of conservation and recreation groups, local mining and ranching interests, rock climbers, mountain bikers, OHV enthusiasts, Emery County's citizens, tribes who trace their ancestry to the region, and a bipartisan majority in the House and Senate still presented major challenges. Meeting those challenges required a combination of leadership and persistence by the Emery County Commission, the Public Lands Council, Senator Hatch and his staff, and Republican congressman John Curtis and his staff, who represented Emery County.

Seeking Support, Building Trust

The first major challenge was winning the support of conservation groups, which were deeply mistrustful of the Utah congressional delegation following the bitter battle over the fate of the Bears Ears National Monument. Bears Ears, declared in 2016 near the end of President Barack Obama's second term, protected 1.35 million acres in Utah's San Juan County, and provided the five tribes that advocated for the monument a significant role in managing it. The Utah congressional delegation opposed Bears Ears prior to Obama's declaration, and lobbied President Donald Trump to reverse the monument declaration. Of note, Senator Hatch played a central role in the Trump administration's decision to alter the boundaries of Bears Ears and Grand Staircase-Escalante National Monuments. Hatch had been asking the president to rescind or shrink the two Utah monuments since the earliest days of Trump's presidency. Trump responded to the delegation in 2017 by reducing the area protected within Obama's Bears Ears boundaries by 85 percent. The tribes, along with a wide spectrum of conservation groups and outdoor industry representatives, sued to restore the original Bears Ears boundaries. As of this writing (2021), the newly elected Biden administration has announced its intention to review the status of Bears Ears and Grand Staircase-Escalante. In parallel, the constitutionality of Trump's executive order to reduce the size of the two monuments has been challenged in the U.S. District Court for Washington, D.C. As yet, no decision has been rendered.

Ron Dean, staff member for former senator Orrin Hatch, in Huntington Canyon, Utah (*left*); and Romel Nicholas, speaking in February 2019 at a public meeting hosted by the Emery County Commission and the Emery County Public Lands Council. A few weeks after this meeting, the Emery County Public Land Management Act passed both houses of Congress. Photos courtesy of Ron Dean and ETV News, respectively.

When Senator Hatch and Representative Curtis and their staffs sought support for an Emery County bill, they were not surprisingly met at first with deep skepticism if not outright hostility. Ron Dean and Romel Nicholas from Hatch's office, and Jake Bornstein from Representative Curtis's staff, continued to reach out as no bill could pass without support from the conservation community.

Romel Nicholas describes the breakthrough moment:

> In this fateful conversation, Jason Keith [of the Access Fund, a group dedicated to protecting public lands and the rock climbing areas within them] goes, "You know Jake, we're all sick of this winner-take-all approach to Utah politics." That was all Jake [Bornstein] and I needed to say, alright, we got it. We now know that they're willing to compromise. Then the environmental groups start dancing. They're not in the middle of the dance floor at the wedding having a good time, but they're tapping their feet underneath the table. And we knew that we were moving.

Hatch, Curtis, and their staffs quickly learned that three key concerns of environmental groups involved: designating as wilderness land they believed possessed wilderness characteristics; finding a designation that would protect other areas of high natural and cultural value from new road construction, excessive OHV use, and mineral extraction; and ensuring that tribal interests in protecting cultural resources were respected.

Steps Toward a Compromise Land Use Bill

With a broad range of conservation groups indicating a willingness to negotiate, Curtis, Hatch, and their staffs began discussions with other stakeholders whose support was key to creating viable legislation. Representative Curtis put it this way:

> We needed stakeholders in the [negotiating] box. And if by pulling a stakeholder into the box it pushed somebody else out, we were very careful about letting them in. [In contrast to the Bears Ears negotiations,] in Emery, the box was teeming with people. I will tell you, there were a couple of groups on both sides who wouldn't climb into the box. In my opinion, as a result, [those groups] lost huge influence over the bill, by staying outside the box and insisting on what Jake [Bornstein] and I call the winner-take-all philosophy.

As Utah's legislators and their staffs reached out, the concerns of other groups came into focus. While the interests of recreation groups largely overlapped with those of conservation groups, their organizations wanted to ensure adequate access for nonmotorized recreation (and, in some areas, motorized recreation) and options for rock climbing in protected areas not designated as wilderness.

The OHV community lobbied strongly to keep as many roads as possible open to motorized use, and to seek an expansive definition of what constitutes a road. An open letter from the organization Ride with Respect to Utah political leaders in January 2019 specified the concerns of many in the OHV community. In summarizing their objections, the authors of the letter claimed, "For over a decade, Emery County's stated purpose for pursuing legislation has been to provide assurance to each stakeholder and actually resolve controversy. The current bill doesn't do so for OHV riders, other than putting the word 'recreation' in the Swell Recreation Area, with both the word and the designation lacking clarification."[12]

Other OHV groups were vociferous in advocating for little-constrained access to public lands. The more zealous among them regard any regulation as a threat to individual liberty.

Finally, Emery County was adamant in its desire to maintain access to mineral resources thought to be critical to the county's economic future. It also wanted to ensure that the designations of protected lands reflected their potential for supporting recreation, as well as for honoring and vivifying Native and Anglo historical and cultural legacies. As was the case in earlier efforts, the county advocated for the creation of an advisory council through which participants from Emery could help determine management of protected public lands.

Finding a Path Forward

Outlines of proposed wilderness areas were drawn fairly early in the process, as the boundaries of wilderness study areas designated by the BLM provided a starting point for discussion. The Southern Utah Wilderness Alliance took the position that a large fraction of the public lands in Emery County should

12. Clif Koontz, "An Open Letter from Ride with Respect on the Emery County Public Lands Bill," Castle Country Radio, January 31, 2019, https://www.castlecountryradio.com/2019/01/31/an-open-letter-from-ride-with-respect-on-the-emery-county-public-lands-bill/.

be designated as wilderness, based on SUWA's evaluation of regions that merited wilderness characteristics.

In criticizing a proposal put forward by Emery County early in the process, SUWA executive director Scott Groene argued that "[Emery County's proposed bill is] worse than the status quo. [It] would designate less wilderness than already has protection as Wilderness Study Areas. Over 900,000 acres of deserving wild lands are left unprotected as wilderness. At the same time, the bill makes off-road vehicle abuse worse by enshrining 800 miles of off-road vehicle routes, effectively perpetuating an old, illegal and overturned travel plan."[13]

Other groups shared SUWA's goals but chose to calibrate their advocacy to balance what was desirable with what could be supported by a broad range of stakeholders and political interests. The Pew Charitable Trusts, the Wilderness Society, Access Fund, and the Conservation Alliance, as well as recreation groups such as the Outdoor Industry Association and the Outdoor Recreation Roundtable, strove to find a workable compromise so as to avoid missing out on the unique opportunity for passing a major conservation bill.

Hatch's and Curtis's staffs worked with willing conservation and recreation groups, OHV representatives, and representatives from Emery County to reconcile often divergent interests and to find a path forward.

Jake Bornstein, Representative Curtis's deputy chief of staff, remembers:

> Everybody wants to preserve and protect. We spend so much time focusing on what we call it. If we could just change the name and have the same intent, you could accomplish the same thing. We went through every potential name in the book. We tried National Heritage Area, we tried National Conservation Area, a National Conservation and Recreation Area, a National Recreation Area, and we ended on Recreation Area. We tried everything. We eventually just found one that worked for the locals [and the conservation groups]. It's [a] shame that we don't do it more often [for land use bills]. It's basically what we did in Emery County.

---

13. "Utahns Call for Protection of San Rafael Swell at People's Hearing in Salt Lake City," Southern Utah Wilderness Alliance, August 30, 2018, https://suwa.org/utahns-call-protection-san-rafael-swell-peoples-hearing-salt-lake-city/.

Left to right: Lorie Fowlke, district director for Representative Curtis; Representative John Curtis; Jake Bornstein, Representative Curtis's deputy chief of staff; and Emery County commissioner Kent Wilson. Photo courtesy of Jake Bornstein.

In the end, the groups were able to agree to protect 217,000 acres as the San Rafael Swell Recreation Area.[14] The legislative language creating the recreation area precluded development of new roads and mineral withdrawal, satisfying the conservation community; kept existing roads open for OHV use, an issue of importance to the OHV community; emphasized recreation possibilities so that Emery County could begin to grow its tourist economy; and created an advisory committee to guide the BLM's management of the recreation area, an important ask from the county.[15] The willingness by all

14. "An Overview of the Emery County Public Land Management Act," Southern Utah Wilderness Alliance, accessed June 1, 2021, https://www.arcgis.com/apps/MapJournal/index.html?appid=fe945411e7684dddab3dc53dac3596b0.

15. "San Rafael Swell Recreation Area Advisory Council," Bureau of Land Management, accessed June 1, 2021, https://www.blm.gov/get-involved/resource-advisory-council/near-you/utah/San-Rafael-Swell-RAC.

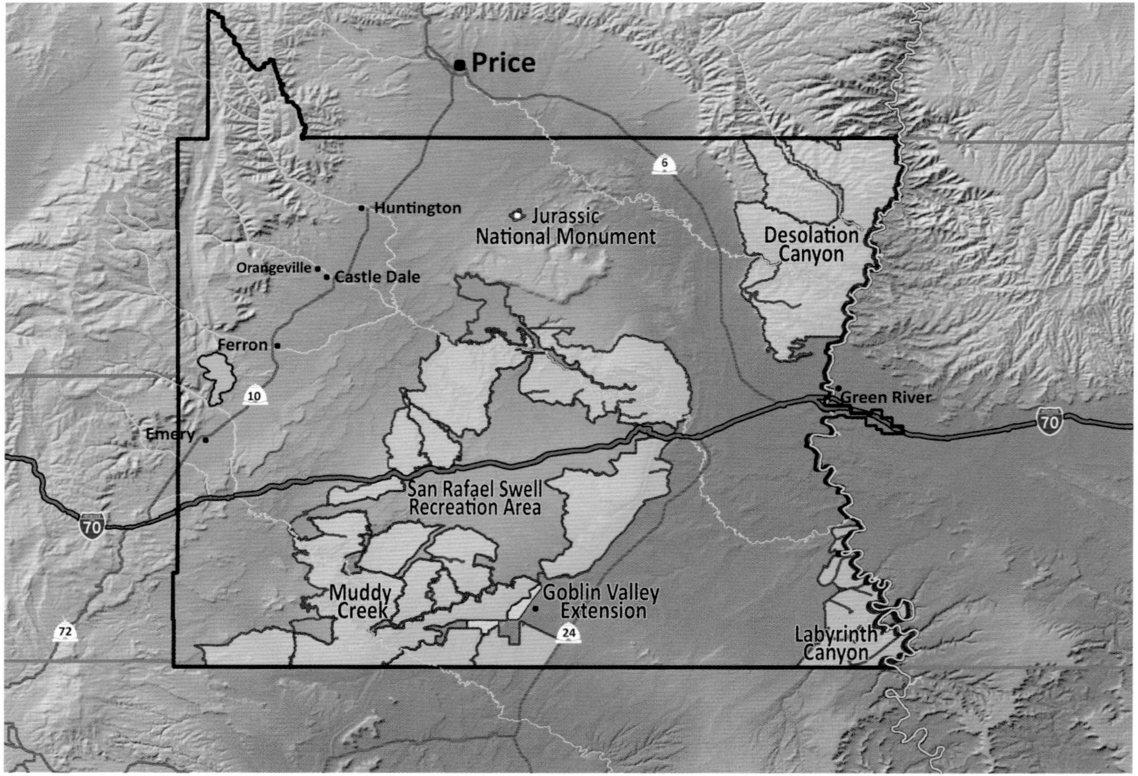

Public land designations in the Emery County Public Land Management Act: Desolation Canyon, Labyrinth Canyon, and Muddy Creek Wilderness Areas (*butterscotch*); the San Rafael Swell Recreation Area (*blue*); and an extension of Goblin Valley State Park (*light green*).

sides to be flexible in accepting unconventional nomenclature represented an important breakthrough.

Although the acreage and final boundaries of these areas remained unsettled until the very end of the legislative process, the bill ultimately designated 660,000 acres as the Muddy Creek, Desolation Canyon, and Labyrinth Canyon Wilderness Areas.

A Solution for School Trust Lands

Another major challenge to drafting a bill that could win sufficient support in Utah involved the fate of school trust lands located within the boundaries of the recreation and wilderness areas. As each state entered the union, the U.S. Congress granted square-mile (640-acre) blocks of federal land in order that revenue derived from those lands—called trust lands—could be used to support public schools and other public institutions. When Utah achieved statehood in 1896, 7.5 million acres of trust lands were granted with the provision that revenue earned from sale or lease of trust lands be used to support twelve entities: public education, Utah School for the Deaf, Utah School for the Blind, Utah State Hospital, Juvenile Justice Services, Miners Hospital, University of Utah, Utah State University, colleges of education, University of Utah's College of Mines and Earth Sciences, reservoirs, and public buildings.[16]

Trust lands in Utah are administered by the State Institutional Trust Lands Administration, which is charged with generating maximum revenue from these lands, typically from mineral royalties, grazing leases, and timber sales. More than one hundred thousand acres of school trust parcels were located within the boundaries of the proposed recreation and wilderness areas in Emery County.

If the Emery County legislation proceeded, the isolated school trust parcels would be subject to use restrictions for the proposed protected areas and would thus no longer be able to generate revenue. As a result, supporters of the legislation needed to develop language that would enable exchange of parcels within the protected area for other public lands in Utah deemed to have more significant revenue potential. An early candidate for exchange was

16. "SITLA and Trust Lands Explained," Trust Lands Administration, accessed June 1, 2021, https://trustlands.utah.gov/our-agency/sitla-and-trust-lands-explained/.

mineral-rich public land located in the Uinta Basin. However, the Ute Indian Tribe (whose current homeland is centered in western Uintah and eastern Duchesne Counties, to the northeast of Emery County) has for years claimed legal rights to these lands, and any attempt to exchange state trust lands from newly protected land in Emery County into the basin would likely trigger a long and contentious court battle.[17]

Conservation groups were firm in opposing such a trade, while SITLA regarded unlocking the potential economic return from Uinta Basin lands as aligned with its charter obligations.

Accommodating Tribal Concerns

In 2018, as the Emery County bill was taking form, the Ute Indian Tribe was deeply concerned that initial drafts had been prepared without adequate participation by tribal members. They believed that without changes in those drafts, the resulting legislation would threaten tribal homelands and, in their view, override treaties and agreements between the United States and the Ute Indian Tribe. In a scathing press release, the tribe argued that "despite claims of decades of outreach and negotiation, Curtis failed to include the Tribe in the drafting of his bill. Now his bill threatens the homelands of Utah's oldest residents."[18]

Allen Freemyer, former chief of staff on the House Committee on Natural Resources and an advisor to SITLA, notes:

> SITLA always looks to take a piece of scenery like in the San Rafael Swell and exchange that for a place more appropriate in the state for raising revenue off of that land. Of course, the top targets are always oil and gas or other leasable minerals. It just so happened that the vast lion's share of oil and gas in the state is in the Uinta Basin. So that was SITLA's original target, oil and gas properties, in the Uinta Basin.

---

17. "Ute Indian Tribe of the Uintah and Ouray Reservation," Utah Division of Indian Affairs, accessed June 1, 2021, https://indian.utah.gov/ute-indian-tribe-of-the-uintah-ouray-reservation/.

18. "Defeat H.R. 5727 Another Indian Land Grab!," Ute Indian Tribe Political Action Committee, September 27, 2018, https://utepac.com/media-1/2018/9/27/defeat-hr-5727-another-indian-land-grab.

Representative Curtis meets with members of the Ute Indian Tribe at a buffalo ranch on the Uintah and Ouray Reservation. Photograph courtesy of Jake Bornstein.

> But the Ute Indian Tribe has sued the federal government and is claiming ownership for about 75 percent of the Uinta Basin. The Emery bill was going to be so difficult to get done [anyway], we finally decided in order to get something done that we would conduct an exchange that did not involve [lands claimed by the Ute Indian Tribe]. We selected targets that were not oil and gas, that were other leasable minerals, other development opportunities. That was a major concession on the part of SITLA to do that, because that was not [its] first preference.

Congressional leadership was crucial as well in coming to an agreement that avoided conflict with the Ute Indian Tribe. John Sterling of the Conservation Alliance recollects, "Jake [Bornstein] and Romel [Nicholas] both told us regularly 'SITLA will come to the table when this bill is real. . . . We're not going to [undermine the interests of the Ute Tribe].'"

At the end of February 2019, the tribe announced its satisfaction with the framework for SITLA land exchanges included in the final version of the bill. In a press release following passage of the bill, the Ute Indian Tribe Business Committee offered the following praise to supporters: "The Ute Indian

Tribe has forged lasting partnerships with many Utahns who understand the importance of responsible energy development as well as the value of a thriving recreational and tourism industry. The Business Committee appreciates the strong statements that the Pew Charitable Trusts, the Wilderness Society and others made to Congress in support of the Tribe's Reservation lands and resources." The release, however, reiterated the tribe's displeasure with the earlier versions of the bill introduced by Representative Curtis and Senator Hatch.[19]

Athan Manuel, director of the Sierra Club's Lands Protection Program, gives great credit to Representative Curtis. "Mr. Curtis gets so much of the credit for this thing," Manuel says. "He had to negotiate with us and the environmental community and Indigenous peoples, especially the Utes in southern Utah, to make sure liberals and enviros were happy."

"Curtis is a person of extraordinary conscience because Curtis says, 'I'm going to go out to the Ute Reservation and sit down and [talk about the SITLA land exchange],'" Romel Nicholas recalled. "No one saw that coming, including Hatch's office and SITLA."

Ron Dean echoes Nicholas: "Curtis says 'we're going to take care of the Tribes. Period. I don't care. If the whole thing fails, then the whole thing fails. I've met these guys. They're good people.' That is what resulted in [including in the Emery County bill] a rather robust advisory council that included a seat for the Tribes." Underscoring the importance to the Indigenous community of having a role in crafting the management plan for the San Rafael Swell, Hopi vice chairman Clark Tenakhongva reflected on the historical and cultural importance of the swell from the perspective of Hopi people:

> The Hopi people have placed their footprints on the land, at the approval of the creator, and made the covenant to be stewards of the land. To this day the Hopi Sineom are still stewards of the land. We have a long living and recorded history of our scared sites—rock art, petroglyphs, and artifacts—left upon lands we traveled. The swell [contains the history of] several clans—the Snake, Sand, Flute, and Katchina people. Hopi was there yesterday. They remain and thrive in their ancient ways, humble, humility, farming, and knowledge acquired still lives amongst the people, land, water, and air.

19. "Ute Tribe Victory in Congress," Ute Indian Tribe Political Action Committee, March 1, 2019, https://utepac.com/media-1/2019/3/1/ute-tribe-victory-in-congress.

To assuage concerns that a solution would be imposed on Emery County and its citizens by negotiations carried out two thousand miles away in Washington, D.C., both Senator Hatch and Representative Curtis made it clear that they would withdraw the bill if it failed to achieve broad support from the county. This proved an essential element of building trust with the county and earning its support for the final version of the bill.

Toward the Finish Line

As the bill neared completion, the possibility that Emery County might in the end reject the bill seemed quite real. Bringing the county on board with the final drafts of the bill first required meeting with the Southern Utah Wilderness Alliance and making its representatives aware that the county was opposed to wilderness designation or any other form of protection for two areas that SUWA believed to be of great significance: the badlands extending

Representative Curtis meets with Hopi vice chairman Clark Tenakhongva. A tribal member will serve on the seven-person advisory council for the San Rafael Swell Recreation Area. Photo courtesy of Jake Bornstein.

from Mussentuchit through the Molen Reef, and the San Rafael Desert. SUWA was concerned that not including these lands in the bill would make their future protection more challenging.

Other conservation groups thought that the bill offered enough wilderness acreage and advised SUWA to take the deal. Despite their differences in approach during the process, representatives of most conservation organizations involved in efforts to protect public lands in Emery County acknowledge that SUWA's forceful, decade-long advocacy ultimately led to protection of significantly more acreage as wilderness than would have been included in the bill without its persistent endeavors.

Another, perhaps crucial element to cementing Emery County's support for the bill was the potential revenue return from a land exchange framework negotiated with SITLA. In the words of the Wilderness Society's director of wilderness policy, Paul Spitler, "The amount of revenue that the county is going to generate through SITLA land exchange is going to be significant to the county [over time]. It's not a one-time thing. I think Emery County will do well."

Creating a seven-person advisory council charged with working collaboratively with the Bureau of Land Management to develop management plans for the San Rafael Swell Recreation Area ensured that the county would have a voice in shaping the future of the region.

Last-Minute Opposition

Nevertheless, the county faced significant last-minute opposition to the bill's final draft. Commissioner Kent Wilson remembers that

> the [OHV folks] were in the process of giving us a hard time. [There] were a couple of things that upset them: some verbiage in the bill [precluding construction of] new roads, which they felt was a major mistake, and their belief that sixty or seventy miles on the south-central part of the county were going to be closed. So they were quite vocal.
>
> I remember being told once that there was an internet poll: is Commissioner Wilson an idiot? But we [the county commissioners] decided we would fight and do all we could to help [the bill] pass. We felt like the public lands bill was the best thing for Emery County but the worst thing possibly for the commissioners that made that decision. There was talk about a statewide boycott of my convenience store. A lot of the local OHV [folks] quit coming. That's how

A meeting of the Emery County Commission. The commission members serving at the time the final version of the Emery County Public Lands Bill was agreed to by the county are (*left to right, foreground*): Kent Wilson, Lynn Sitterud, and Gil Conover. An unidentified individual sits to the far left. Courtesy of ETV News.

> personal it got. For me personally, the easiest thing to have done would be to vote no, for my personal life. It's still quite emotional for me.

In January 2019, two months before the bill passed, the outlook for Emery County support seemed grim. The tide was turned at the decisive community meeting by the intervention of Brock Johansen, CEO of Emery Telcom. Emery Telcom, based in Orangeville in Emery County, provides phone service, DSL Internet, cable TV, and cable Internet to much of eastern and southeastern Utah. As the leader of a successful and highly visible local company, as well as a rancher, Johansen commands considerable respect in the county. According to Commissioner Wilson, Johansen "stood up and supported Emery County commissioners and talked about how a long time ago Emery County decided to pursue legislation instead of a federal designation. If you ask what turned the tide as far as public sentiment, he is well respected in the community. A lot of the locals, when he voiced support for it, it legitimized it. He rose to the occasion and saved the day for us."

Winning the support of Emery County residents for the final version of the bill was validation of the nearly quarter-century-long effort by Emery County commissioners and the Public Lands Council.

"There's no doubt the presence of the people that we were able to get to the table—especially in the final two years in getting this passed—was the

Brock Johansen, CEO of Emery Telcom. Courtesy of ETV News.

result of the respect that Emery County had built over the years because of the Public Lands Council and the work that they had done," former Emery County commissioner Randy Johnson says. "The hundreds of people involved [by the PLC] and the hundreds of tours on the San Rafael, and the hundreds and hundreds of meetings, was a process that gathered people in. They [also realized that when I took the draft of the bill] to Washington, that there would be things they would have to do to compromise and get the thing actually passed."

With support obtained from conservation and recreation groups, OHV groups, major stakeholders in Emery County, and the County Commission, the bill now awaited action in Washington, D.C.

Finding a Legislative Vehicle for Passing the Lands Bill

Athan Manuel of the Sierra Club notes that the Emery County bill benefited from another conservation effort on Capitol Hill:

> Running in parallel to what was happening with the Emery County bill was an effort to permanently reauthorize the Land and Water Conservation Fund [LWCF]: a bill that uses offshore oil and gas royalties to fund land and water conservation projects, recreational activities, and preservation of historic landmarks. The bill was enacted in 1964 and originally authorized for fifty years. It had been temporarily extended for two more years twice but was expiring. The latest extension was ending in 2018. So advocates for that program were pushing for permanent reauthorization so that it wouldn't have to be reauthorized every fifty years. That bill was also pretty bipartisan and, [like the Emery Bill, had considerable momentum.] These two bills were running on parallel tracks.
>
> So once Mr. Hatch and Senator Richard Durbin (D-Ill.), the second-ranking Democrat in the Senate, [reached] an agreement on how Emery County would look, it was decided that [the Emery County bill] would be the nexus for a larger public lands bill. [After] Emery was worked out, they put the LWCF on it [along with] a bunch of other bills. Senator Maria Cantwell (D-Wash.) had a bill, Senator Lisa Murkowski (R-Alaska) had a bill, Senator Ron Wyden

> (D-Ore.) had a bill, Senator Martin Heinrich (D-N.Mex.) had a bill. So it snowballed from there. That [omnibus] package would not have gotten done without Emery County being the centerpiece of it. It had to be something big, and it had to have bipartisan support.[20]

Rob Bishop (R-Utah) and Raúl Grijalva (D-Ariz.), chairman and ranking members of the House Committee on Natural Resources, and their Senate counterparts, Lisa Murkowski (R-Alaska) and Joe Manchin (D-W.Va.), worked with their staffs and members of the committees to develop a bill that eventually included long-stalled conservation and recreation initiatives brought forth by legislators from both parties. With agreement among committee leadership and members in both chambers, the bill was introduced toward the end of the 115th Congress. However, objections from Utah's junior senator, Mike Lee (R-Utah), prevented the bill from being adopted before Senator Hatch retired on January 3, 2019.

The Final Bill

Final tweaks were made to the bill during the early days of the 116th Congress. Crucial to the effort was the support of Senator Hatch's replacement, Senator Mitt Romney (R-Utah). With his support, along with bipartisan support from the chairs of the House and Senate Committees on Natural Resources and the leadership teams on both sides of the aisle, the bill passed with wide margins in both the House (363–62) and Senate (92–8). The omnibus bill, designated the John D. Dingell Jr. Conservation, Management, and Recreation Act in honor of the late Democratic congressman from Michigan who served in the House for fifty-six years, was signed into law on March 12, 2019.[21]

---

20. See also John D. Dingell Jr. Conservation, Management, and Recreation Act, S. 47, 116th Cong. (2019); Tom Pfister, "Land and Water Conservation Fund Activated by 'Dingell Act,'" *Forbes*, March 13, 2019, https://www.forbes.com/sites/tompfister/2019/03/13/land-and-water-conservation-fund-activated-by-dingell-act/.

21. "John D. Dingell, Jr.," Bureau of Land Management, accessed June 1, 2021, https://www.blm.gov/about/laws-and-regulations/dingell-act; Doug Eiken, "How America's Lands Became Common Ground; The Journey for Passage of the John D. Dingell, Jr. Conservation, Management and Recreation Act of 2019," National Organization of State Outdoor Recreation Liaison Officers, October 17, 2019, https://www.nasorlo.org/how-americas-lands-became-common-ground-passage-of-the-john-d-dingell-conservation-management-and-recreation-act-of-2019/.

Looking to the Future

Passing the Emery County Public Land Management Act required balancing the needs of multiple stakeholders, and asking each to make compromises that were sometimes painful.

Emery County made significant concessions within the San Rafael Swell Recreation Area. The county agreed to cease road development in the area, and to adhere to a more limited interpretation of what constitutes a "road." Moreover, it accepted a stipulation precluding mineral extraction in the recreation area. Perhaps most significantly, it also went considerably beyond its initial comfort level in accepting wilderness designations in the Muddy Creek and Labyrinth Canyon regions. "[Those wilderness areas] were a huge give from the perspective of the county," former commissioner Randy Johnson says. "We stretched [to accept for wilderness designation] well beyond what we felt were lands that qualified for pure wilderness."

"Some of the areas we ultimately agreed to designate as wilderness were in our mind considerably more developed, particularly by historic oil and gas development, than what should meet the definition of wilderness under the Wilderness Act," Curtis staffer Jake Bornstein says. "But in the end, we and the county decided that it was better to include them as wilderness in the [Emery County bill] to increase the chance of passing the bill."

Johnson waxes philosophical about the long-term process that finally led to a resolution of public lands issues in Emery County. "[It's really gratifying] to see how far we've come [over these last twenty-five years]," Johnson says. "I think that as a result [of compromises like the Emery County bill], we're going to get more conservation, we're going to get more done. Nothing was done in those couple of decades when all we [county and conservation community] did was mark our positions, and then stand and lob bombs. Nothing at all. But once we started to sit down and talk, then we started [making progress]." He speculates that the effort made in Emery County might serve as a model for future conservation efforts in Utah and elsewhere: "And so I'm thinking that [in the future] we're going to end up with more conservation and a lot more certainty in these rural areas [if we engage in collaborative conservation]."

The conservation community had hoped to designate more acreage as wilderness than was finally incorporated in the bill. SUWA, which had conducted an extensive survey of public lands in Emery County, had argued for two decades for additional lands to be protected as wilderness or national conservation areas: the Molen Reef, the Mussentuchit Badlands, the San Rafael Desert, and the Price River drainage. None of these areas were included in the final bill. Accepting the exclusion of these areas represented a significant concession for many conservation organizations, but one that they recognized as necessary to ensure wilderness protection for what turned out to be more than a third of the public land in Emery County.

Following the decades-long effort to reach a compromise regarding protection of public lands in Emery County, neither local political leaders nor many in the conservation community appear to have the appetite for additional conservation efforts, at least on the scale of the Emery County bill. Indeed, such major, landscape-scale efforts would undermine one of the key gains sought by Emery County in negotiating the framework for the bill: certainty regarding the uses of public lands.

However, there remain compelling arguments for pursuing approaches to managing the remaining public lands in Emery County in a manner that would enable both preservation of cultural sites and the landscape on the one hand, and the building of an economic future and sustaining of traditional uses of these lands on the other.

Based on Emery County citizens' and stakeholders' shared success in achieving landmark public lands legislation, there is every reason to hope that the trust relationships built over the past two decades can serve as a foundation for identifying mutually acceptable compromises.

Barrier Canyon pictographs. Photo by Jonathan T. Bailey.

Successful Land Use Compromises

Three Case Studies

We shall never achieve harmony with the land, anymore than we shall achieve absolute justice or liberty for people. In these higher aspirations the important thing is not to achieve but to strive.

—ALDO LEOPOLD, *ROUND RIVER: FROM THE JOURNALS OF ALDO LEOPOLD*

Foster's columbine (*Aquilegia fosteri*), Washington County, Utah. Photo by Jonathan T. Bailey.

The Washington County Land Bill

Washington County, Utah—located in the southwest corner of the state and bordering Nevada to the west and Arizona to the south—is a place of contrasts: lush evergreen forests, red rock, lava flows, deep canyons, and arid desert populated by Joshua trees and mesquite. The Virgin River courses through the varied landscapes of the county, starting at 9,200 feet just east of the border with adjacent Kane County, descending through aspen and evergreen forests, passing through the Narrows in Zion National Park at 6,000 feet, flowing toward the city of St. George at 2,500 feet and the eponymous gorge carved by the river, to its final destination: Lake Mead in Nevada, where the Virgin feeds the waters of the Colorado.

The eastern part of the county lies at the very western edge of the Colorado Plateau, containing the plateau's characteristic amalgam of mesas, cliffs, and red rock canyons. The western two-thirds of the county is part of North America's basin-range province, which comprises soaring mountain ranges separated by wide valleys.[1] Washington County's southwestern corner, adjacent to Arizona on the south and Nevada on the west, shares climate, flora, and fauna with the Mojave Desert. Of the county's 2,400 square miles (1.5 million acres), 75 percent is public land, managed by either the U.S. Forest Service (USFS), the Bureau of Land Management (BLM), or the National Park Service.[2]

More than 90 percent of the county's population of 180,000 is concentrated in and around St. George, located in the southwest part of the county along the Interstate 15 corridor, which connects Las Vegas with the Los Angeles metropolitan area.[3] In the early 2000s, St. George was the fastest growing city in the United States, and it continues to experience rapid growth today. The remainder of the county is sparsely populated, with approximately 10,000 people spread among small towns outside the St. George metropolitan region.

1. "Basin and Range Province," National Park Service, last updated April 15, 2020, https://www.nps.gov/articles/basinrange.htm.

2. "Washington County, UT," Economic Profile System, Headwaters Economics, accessed June 1, 2021, https://headwaterseconomics.org/apps/economic-profile-system/49053.

3. "Resident Population in St. George, UT," FRED Economic Data, Federal Reserve Bank of St. Louis, accessed June 1, 2021, https://fred.stlouisfed.org/series/STGPOP.

Canyon in Red Cliffs National Conservation Area (*left, facing page*); and canyon in the Canaan Mountain Wilderness. Bureau of Land Management.

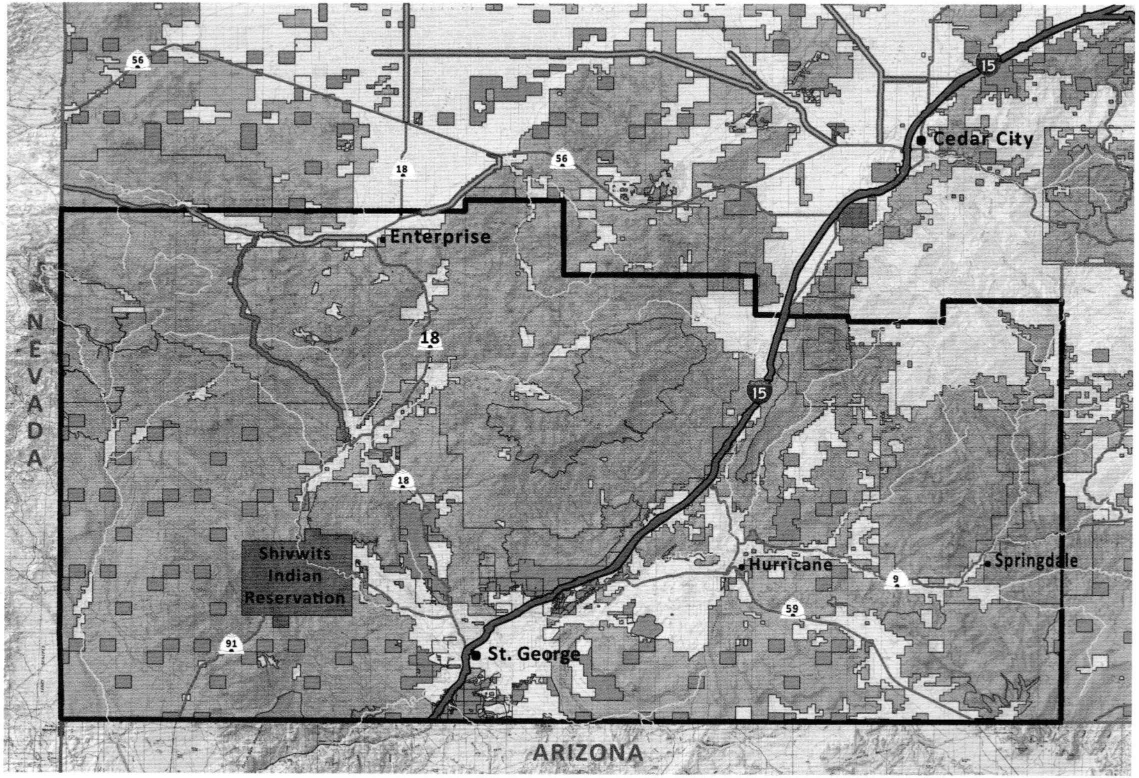

Land designations in Washington County, Utah, including public lands (*green*), school trust lands (*purple*), and private land (*off-white*). Public lands account for 75 percent of the land area in the county. Adapted from Utah Automated Geographic Reference Center, https://gis.utah.gov/.

A development in rapidly growing St. George, Utah. Aerial photo courtesy of Ted Wood, with support from LightHawk.

Despite the county's rapid growth, its demographics still reflect the influence of its earliest settlers: 85 percent white, non-Latino; 10 percent Hispanic or Latino; 0.5 percent Native American; and 4.5 percent mixed race. Of Washington's population, 70 percent are members of the Church of Jesus Christ of Latter-day Saints (Mormon), 4 percent are Catholics, and the rest are nonbelievers (22 percent) or followers of other faiths (4 percent).[4]

Indigenous History

Native occupation of the region dates back over ten thousand years, as is evident in isolated projectile points knapped into distinct typologies including Clovis and Silver Lake (a small lanceolate point with a contracting stem). Most of the region's rock art is attributed to Virgin Pueblo, the westernmost

4. "Washington County, Utah," Best Places, accessed June 1, 2021, https://www.bestplaces.net/religion/county/utah/washington.

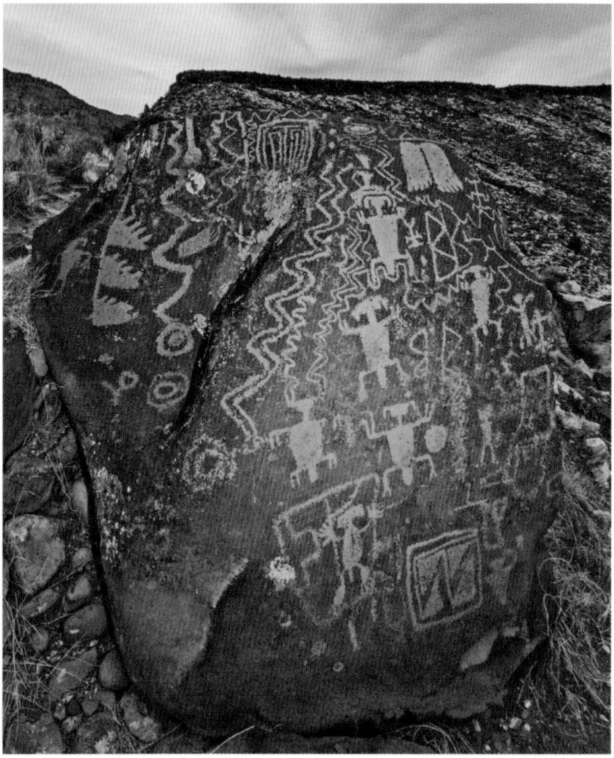

Ancestral Pueblo petroglyphs, Washington County, Utah. Photos by Jonathan T. Bailey.

Ancestral Pueblo rock art, Washington County, Utah. The pictographs (*right*) are attributed to the Cave Valley Style. Photos by Jonathan T. Bailey.

Ancestral Pueblo group, who occupied the area from about 1 to 1200 CE.[5] They left the region at approximately the same time as their contemporaries in southeast Utah, possibly as a consequence of the great drought that parched the American Southwest through a substantial fraction of the twelfth century.

A branch of the Southern Paiute, the Shivwits Band of Paiutes reached the Washington County area around 1100 BCE. Archaeological evidence indicates that they settled primarily along the Santa Clara and Virgin Rivers, cultivating a variety of crops, and hunting deer, mountain sheep, and smaller animals.

5. "Anasazi: The Ancient Ones," Zion Area Info, Paragon Adventures, accessed June 1, 2021, https://www.paragonadventure.com/zionarea/home/southern-utah-info/sw-utah-history/anasazi/.

European Contact and the Arrival of Mormon Settlers

First contact with Europeans by the Shivwits Band of Paiutes was with members of the Dominguez-Escalante Expedition in 1776. Over the ensuing seventy-five years, fur trappers and explorers and, later, government geographers and surveyors passed through Washington County. Among them was one of the most well-known explorer-trappers of the era, Jedediah Smith, who followed the path of the Virgin River on his way to California in 1826. Following Brigham Young's arrival to Utah in 1847 with his party of Latter-day Saints, the Mormon prophet began to send groups of settlers from Salt Lake City to other areas in Utah and beyond. In 1852, small parties began to arrive in Washington County. By the late 1850s, the agricultural potential of the land in and around the St. George region was evident. By the beginning of the next decade, Mormons largely occupied former Paiute lands, and as a result, the Paiutes were forced to abandon their traditional lifestyles.[6] In 1891, displaced members of the tribe were granted a small reservation (twenty-seven thousand acres) on the Santa Clara River west of St. George.[7]

In 1861, church leaders called several hundred families to settle the area, where they quickly established productive cotton and grape fields. A large fraction of the new settlers came originally from the American South, and the land around St. George became known as the center of "Dixie."

Growth of Washington County

Mining in the area boomed briefly in the late 1870s, but agriculture remained the main source of jobs and income until the 1970s. Since the completion of Interstate 70 and the upgrading of Utah State Route 89 and secondary roads in the early 1990s, the population has boomed. From 1970 to 2018, the population of the county increased by nearly 1,100 percent. The economy has diversified as well, with the St. George area becoming a mecca for tourists and retirees. Nearly a fifth of the jobs in the county now depend directly on travel and tourism, two-thirds provide services to tourists and residents,

6. "Paiute Indian Tribe of Utah: History," Paiute Indian Tribe of Utah, accessed June 1, 2021, https://www.utahpaiutes.org/news-2/history/.

7. "History: The Paiutes," Utah American Indian Digital Archive, accessed June 1, 2021, https://utahindians.org/archives/paiutes/history.html.

and government jobs account for most of the remainder. Employment in agriculture, once dominant, now provides merely 0.6 percent of the jobs in the county.

By the early 2000s, St. George was listed as one of the fastest growing small cities in the country. Residents recognized that future growth of the region depended on expanding into public lands managed by the USFS and BLM. However, many of those public lands were treasured by conservationists and their allies across the country, who wanted to protect the red sandstone cliffs above Quail Creek and nearby archaeological and paleontological sites; the wild transition zone between the Mojave Desert and the basin-range province, where Joshua trees and creosote bushes are home to the endangered Mojave Desert tortoise; and the wilderness surrounding Zion National Park.

Balancing Growth and Conservation Goals

The elements of a long battle were in place, one that would potentially pit many county residents and their supporters against environmental groups and their advocates. In 2003, shortly after Republican Olene Walker succeeded Republican Mike Leavitt as Utah governor, Walker approached all the counties in the state to ask what each would like to do to shape the future of public lands in Utah. Her question was presented in the context of ever-escalating contention between conservation groups and counties throughout the state. At a meeting held in St. George, county commissioners from across Utah agreed that rather than simply waiting for events (for example, declaration of national monuments) to overtake them, they would try to resolve disputes regarding public lands use on a county-by-county basis. Given the pressure to find a path for expanding the boundaries of the St. George metropolitan area, Washington County volunteered to be the first county to try.

The decision to proceed county by county reflected a belief that statewide approaches had failed in the past and were likely doomed to fail in the future. Tyler Owens, a staff member working with the now-late senator Robert Bennett (R-UT), commented:

> When you do a statewide bill you have to line up all the county commissioners and all of the counties if that's what you're interested in. And then you've

got to go to the cities, and get the BLM and the Forest Service and the Park Service and so on, on board with all these things. Washington County because it was small enough, you have the ability to talk to the mayors, to talk to the county commissioners, talk to the land managers and get a very good sense of what kinds of things they were interested in. And because we kept it within the geographical boundary of the county, that became the entire chessboard upon which you started to move. So if you were going to trade things—trade some wilderness here for some other things there—it was all within the county.

Steps Toward Resolving the Land Use Controversy

Senator Bennett's leadership proved key to establishing a favorable environment for resolving Washington County's public lands issue. Randy Johnson, who took on the task of facilitating and moderating public lands discussions in the county, recalled: "I was in a meeting with Bennett and his staff when he pointed at Tyler Owens and said 'from this moment forward, in your assignments, there's Washington County and then there's everything else. And everything else will be handled by other staff. You will handle Washington County.' For a number of years, that's all Tyler did. That's the kind of work it took. I probably flew to D.C. once every three to four weeks, and yeah, it was intensive work."

Senator Robert Bennett (R-Utah, 1922–2016). Official portrait, U.S. Senate.

For three years, as Owens explains, he "traveled pretty much every road in that county, because [access to] roads was a really big issue to the county commission. And what we wanted to do is establish fact-based, on-the-ground information at a given point in time. And so I spent a lot of time with the county, with the BLM, and I spent time with the refuge managers, spent time with the city folks, spent time with the wilderness advocates, spent time with the Nature Conservancy, and really got to have a very deep understanding of the issues of each particular area of the county."

In Bennett's and Owens's view, three levels of negotiation needed to take place for a Washington County land bill to be forged and passed. "The first one is you have to deal with the local leaders, the county; and the second one is you have to deal with the environmental community; and the third one is you have to [deal] with the congressional committees," Owens says.

Building Trust with the Conservation Community

In the early 2000s, the relationships between the Utah environmental community, the county commissioners, and Utah's political establishment were fraught. Owens recalls:

> It was always the environmentalists against us. And they were always diametrically opposed. We had our wilderness bill. They had theirs, neither of them was ever going to pass. . . . One of the things that Senator Bennett was good at, and one of the things that I think he brought me on for, was to create a process where we could be an honest broker. And over a period of time, we were able to develop a relationship with the environmental group at the staff level and at the principal level; to really be able to have a dialogue about the areas that really mattered to them. And it was that breakthrough that enabled us to craft a compromise.

Speaking just before his death in 2016, Senator Bennett emphasized that

> the dynamic that really made it possible for us to do what we did is that the cooler heads in the conservation community realized, for the first time, time was not on their side. I remember my first meeting with Bill Meadows (of the Wilderness Society), which (now-retired senator) Harry Reid (D-Nev.) had helped to broker. I said to Meadows, "I am not ideological about this. I know that there are a lot of people who have very strong ideological, emotional, almost religious feelings about wilderness. I do not. I am a politician who wants to solve a problem, and I'm looking for somebody who is willing to make a deal," and he said, "I would much rather meet with a politician who wants to solve a problem, and let's see if we can make this work."

In his Senate testimony supporting an early version of the Washington County land bill, Meadows noted Bennett's efforts to forge consensus among a broad group of stakeholders. "Senator Bennett and his staff have spent countless hours listening to the concerns and recommendations from all interested parties, including significant time spent on the ground in Washington County examining a great many of the proposed wilderness areas."

Meadows also noted that Bennett, "has demonstrated real leadership keeping these diverse interests focused on what is possible."[8]

According to Randy Johnson, the willingness of national conservation organizations such as the Pew Charitable Trusts and the Wilderness Society to engage in dialogue with local and congressional leadership in Utah was critical. Until that point, he and other political leaders had been at loggerheads with the Utah Wilderness Coalition and its effective leader, the Southern Utah Wilderness Alliance (SUWA).

Johnson noted: "For the first time in the state of Utah, we had relationships with Pew, with the Wilderness Society, with people outside of just SUWA in Utah. That carried over into all the efforts [to reach a compromise regarding public lands issues] that we made after Washington County."

Another factor in advancing discussion with both conservation groups and the county was an openness to considering protections of public lands other than the most restrictive designation, wilderness.

Exploring Alternative Public Land Protection Options

Owens and Bennett needed to educate both conservationists and their opponents about the possible advantages of alternative mechanisms for managing public lands. "When you say 'wilderness,' you immediately raise the hackles of some people, because that's a 'bad word,'" Owens says:

> Some people think when you mention wilderness that "you kill the cattle grazing, and kill extractive industries, and you do this and that and so on." It may not necessarily be true [for wilderness], and in addition to wilderness there are other land designations and other ways that the BLM or the Park Service or so on could manage these lands. And [that really isn't clear to] people who are participating in the process. There's a learning curve and there has to be a lot of trust in the process.
>
> Many believed that if there were a wilderness designation then that will kill the OHV [off-highway vehicle] rides. And there were other people who were worried about grazing, or people who are worried about the tourists, or

8. *Miscellaneous Public Lands Bills: Hearing on S. 934, S. 2833, S. 2834, Before the Senate Subcommittee on Public Lands and Forests*, 110th Cong. 30–31 (2008) (statement of William H. Meadows, president of the Wilderness Society).

> people who are worried about fires. The wilderness folks wanted it all to be wilderness. The fun part about [drafting] these bills is the beauty of being able to understand all of the views and to be able to craft a solution that fits. We were able to create a National Conservation Area [NCA, as a designation for protection and use], and [for example] part of the NCA had no roads in it, and part of the NCA did have roads in it. And so we kept it that way. And we said in this portion here, the roads that are going to be open, and here [are] the roads that are going to be closed.

Senator Bennett added, "there are other ways of protecting the land besides creating wilderness that the [BLM] managers said we can handle. That we can do. The more we got that input into the conversations the more encouraged the Bill Meadows types were that we could protect some of the crown jewels as wilderness, but maybe we should stop trying to protect some of these other things as wilderness and settle for a form of protection that would probably in practical terms be just as good."

Flexibility to consider alternative designations can be essential to reaching solutions that can be embraced by a large range of stakeholders. "You figure out where the special areas are and what things are special," Owens said. "You figure out what the existing uses on the ground are. You figure out the roles, and the situation, and the maps, and then you sit down with all this knowledge and you come up with a plan, and a management regime that might work. And then your job is to go back and sell that to the stakeholders. But in order to do that, you've got to make sure that your stakeholders have a real say in what goes on and that your solution isn't the only solution. There are a lot of smart people out there. It really became an iterative process."

A Public Process for Envisioning Washington County's Future

As an outgrowth of Randy Johnson's dialogue with the county commissioners and the citizens of Washington County, the county's residents initiated an ambitious process: Vision Dixie.[9] "We made the decision in our collaborative meetings that we needed to go well beyond what we were doing just

9. Washington County, Utah, *Vision Dixie: Making a Better Washington County, 2007* (n.p.: n.p., 2007), http://www.visiondixie.org/pdf/VisionDixie-Book-SM.pdf; "Welcome to Vision Dixie," Vision Dixie: Making a Better Washington County, accessed June 1, 2021, http://www.visiondixie.org.

on public lands, and create a process where people could have major input across the county on what Washington County should look like in the future [in terms of] areas of growth and land use," Johnson recalls. "As a result, we took the steps necessary to get more people involved and to create the Vision Dixie process. It evolved into a process of its own, separate from the public lands, although part of the Vision Dixie effort was to discuss the elements of proposed legislation and how it would fit into their planning."

"They held open houses, the public had a lot of comments and they crafted a plan. It dealt with transportation infrastructure, which was critical to the bill," Owens says. "We needed to know where the roads were going to be; we needed to know where the rights of way were going to be; we needed to know whether we would impact any power lines or any gas pipelines that would go through the county."

Owens believes that Vision Dixie could serve as a model for other communities trying to chart their future and offer lessons for resolving the conflicts between use and protection of public lands. "I think it's [important to begin] these kinds of efforts where you have the opportunity to sit down and examine the place that you live in, and what you want this place to look like, and then figure out how to arrange your destiny. Then meet with whoever you have to deal with—state or federal or private or Congress—but to have those conversations as a community and plot your own course."

Shaping Compromise Land Use Legislation

The Vision Dixie effort provided the impetus for bringing Washington County commissioners and the citizens of the county together on a compromise bill. "You are the fastest growing county in the country," Bennett told the commissioners. "What you need more than anything else is certainty. You've got zoning problems. You've got water problems, extra challenges as the fastest growing county. Everybody wants to move to your county. You can't have this [dispute over the future of public lands] hanging over your head with uncertainty while you address those problems. You need resolution even if it's not the resolution you want. It's worth it if you get certainty out of the process."

Owens and Bennett invested a good deal of time with the county, trying to understand what might be needed to gain its support. "One of the things we were able to do for Washington County as we were doing negotiations, we said, 'what do you guys need? Is there land you need? Do you need a shooting range? You know, what is it?'" Owens says. "And they named off four or five things that we were able to convey to the county through the bill that helped."

To further gain the locals' trust, Owens and Bennett promised that they would not advance a bill that was opposed by the county. "We weren't willing to move forward without buy-in from the environmental community, and we weren't willing to move forward without the buy-in of the county commission," Owens recalls. "In fact, Senator Bennett told the county, if you tell me [you don't like the bill], I'll pull the plug."

In order to include the interests of Native peoples in shaping the bill, Owens and Bennett also held discussions with the Paiute Indians to ensure that land adjustments in the final draft of the bill would have a positive impact on the Shivwits Paiute Reservation in Washington County.

The Key Components of the Compromise Legislation

In the end, the bill that was sent to Congress—the Washington County Growth and Conservation Act of 2008—reflected a compromise between protecting wild areas and addressing the needs of a rapidly growing community.[10] The highest priority preferences of the conservation community were met by designating 256,000 acres as wilderness, including a large area surrounding Zion National Park. Rather than insisting that Red Cliff and Beaver Dam be protected as wilderness, however, the community accepted the designation of national conservation areas.

Conservationists also agreed to the federal government's selling BLM lands considered to be environmentally nonsensitive and using the resulting funds to purchase lands judged to be biologically significant. And they accepted a management plan for OHV use, including designation of a High Desert OHV Trail.

Washington County's needs were addressed by allowing the federal government to sell environmentally nonsensitive lands to developers, and by releasing public land for development. The county also agreed to work with federal agencies to establish a framework for permanent protection of the endangered desert tortoise.

---

10. Washington County Growth and Conservation Act of 2008, S. 2834, 110th Cong. (2007–8).

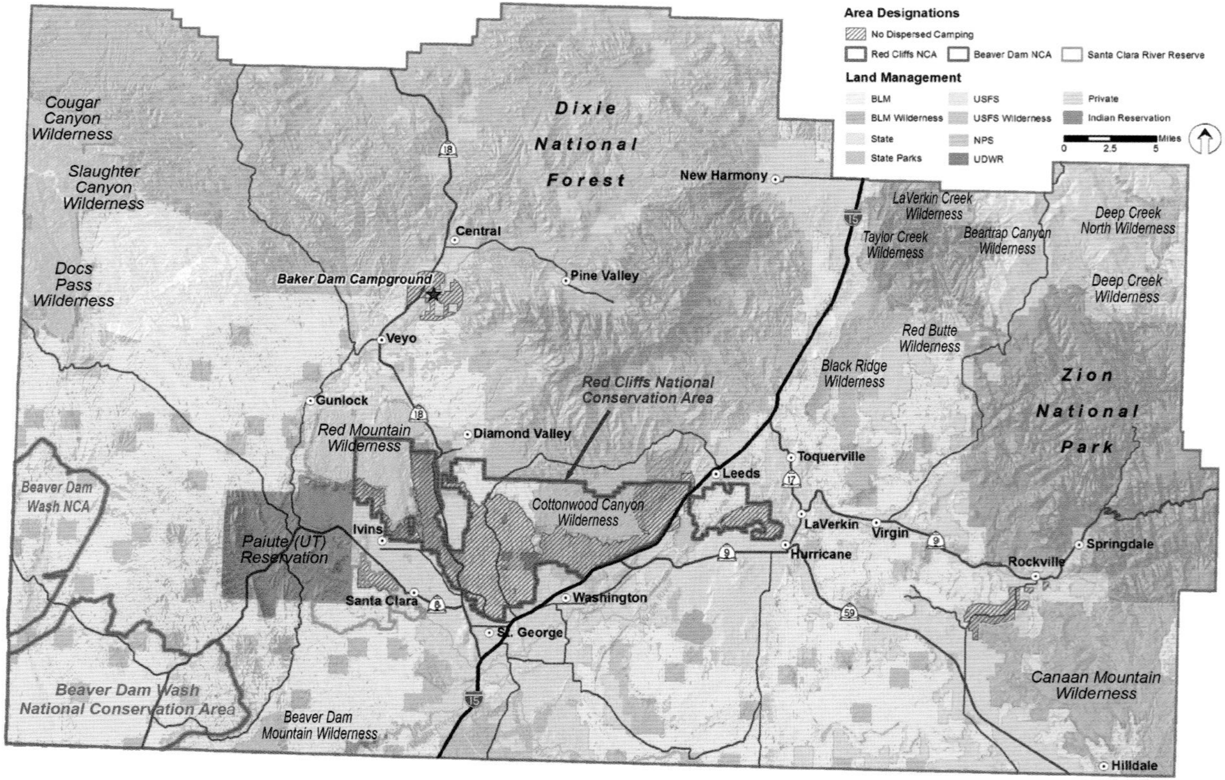

Areas protected in Washington County in the Omnibus Public Land Management Act of 2009, which included the Washington County Growth and Conservation Act of 2008. The boundaries indicated on the map were drawn by the Bureau of Land Management St. George Field Office and lie slightly within the boundaries of Washington County. Base map from the Bureau of Land Management; modifications for clarity by Stephen E. Strom.

Red cliffs at sunset, Red Cliffs National Conservation Area. Bureau of Land Management.

Joshua trees in Beaver Dam Wash National Conservation Area. Bureau of Land Management.

Mobilizing Congressional Support for the Washington County Land Bill

The final hurdle faced by supporters of the Washington County bill was mobilizing support in Congress to enable passage. When the bill was introduced for consideration in early 2009, both houses of the 111th Congress were in Democratic hands. Gaining support would thus require buy-in from Democratic leadership. Senator Bennett, a Republican, and Representative Jim Matheson, the only Democrat serving in Utah's delegation, joined forces to lobby for the bill. Bennett, Matheson, and their allies maneuvered to have the Washington County bill included in an omnibus public lands bill, the same legislation that would include the Owyhee Public Land Management Act (discussed later in this chapter).

Senator Bennett recalled with some satisfaction, "Matheson was talking to the Democrats on the House side. I remember I called Senate majority leader [Harry] Reid, whom I know well. I called him, and he said 'well, Jim Matheson says it's a good deal.' And I said, 'It is. I'm just calling to see if we can break it loose and bring it along,' and he said 'well sure, Senator.'"

As the effort started to gain momentum, its bipartisan prospects became clear. Owens told Bennett, "Senator, we're going to do something that nobody ever, ever thought was possible. We're going to pass this as a Democratic bill in regular order [relying on committees rather than on a partisan task force]."[11] "Tyler told me 'we've got all the opposition taken care of. It's going to move across the floor in regular order,'" Bennett remembered. "'Harry Reid will shuffle it along, and the president will sign it. We're going to do it in a Democratic Senate and [have it] signed by a Democratic president in regular order.'"

Passing the Bill

The Omnibus Public Land Management Act was signed into law on March 30, 2009.[12] Embedded within the ambitious legislative package (which comprised

11. "Regular order" refers to "a systematic, step-by-step lawmaking process that emphasizes the role of committees: bill introduction and referral to committee; the conduct of committee hearings, markups, and reports on legislation; House and Senate floor consideration of committee-reported measures; and the creation of conference committees to resolve bicameral differences." See U.S. Library of Congress, Congressional Research Service, *The "Regular Order": A Perspective*, by Walter J. Oleszek, R46597 (2020), summary.

12. Omnibus Public Land Management Act of 2009, H.R. 146, 111th Cong., sec. 1972 (2009–10).

President Barack Obama signs the Omnibus Public Land Management Act of 2009. Courtesy of Mike Matz, Pew Charitable Trusts.

170 separate bills) was the Washington County Growth and Conservation Act (commonly referred to as the Washington County Land Bill).

"I went down to the White House and stood behind Barack Obama while he signed the bill," Senator Bennett shared. "It was very satisfying to say 'okay, the ideologues have lost and the guys dedicated to a practical solution have won.' Ken Salazar [then secretary of the interior] said, formally and informally, to anybody who would talk to him, 'From now on the position of the Obama administration is that we're going to deal with wilderness the way we dealt with wilderness in the Washington County Land Bill.'"

Representative Matheson celebrated the moment: "For the first time, people who live and work in Washington County have come together on a plan that envisions preserving the remarkable quality of life here." Bill Meadows of the Wilderness Society was similarly pleased with the outcome: "The passage of this bill will mean permanent protection for some of the nation's most remarkable wild lands as well as the promise of a new future for wilderness protection in the state of Utah." He added what no doubt was an understatement, "Getting to this day was no easy task."[13]

Washington County commissioner Jim Eardly commented with considerable pride, "This has been a very thorough process that has led not only to this legislation, but also the Vision Dixie planning process. We believe this bill sets a historic precedent."[14] Randy Johnson, too, looked ahead with some optimism. "Agreement [on future lands bills] is much more likely after the Washington County bill," he noted. "That's how Washington County has changed the environment."[15]

13. Lee Davidson, "Senate Approves Sweeping Public Lands Bill," *Deseret News*, January 15, 2009, https://www.deseret.com/2009/1/15/20296535/senate-approves-sweeping-public-lands-bill.

14. Davidson, "Senate Approves Sweeping Public Lands Bill."

15. Matt Canham, "Washington County Lands Bill May Be the Wilderness Model," *Salt Lake Tribune*, March 30, 2009, https://archive.sltrib.com/story.php?ref=/ci_12032209.

Alpine Lake, Boulder Mountains. Photo courtesy of Ed Cannady, https://www.edcannadyphotograph.com.

"I did everything I wanted to ever do with Washington County," says Tyler Owens. "I could leave [my job here in Washington] a happy man, and think I accomplished some things."

Forging Compromise in Custer County, Idaho

The lands of Custer County, located near the center of Idaho, are remote and expansive. The county ranges over 4,900 square miles (3.1 million acres, or about four-fifths the size of Connecticut), 92 percent of which is managed as public land by the Bureau of Land Management and the U.S. Forest Service.[16] Custer's broad valleys are interlaced by scenic rivers and pastoral ranch country. Above the valleys, the Lost River Range soars in the east, and in the west rise the Sawtooth Range and the White Cloud Mountains.[17]

The Lost River Range is Idaho's highest, extending for seventy-five miles between Challis on the Salmon River to Arco on the Snake. Seven peaks in the range rise more than twelve thousand feet above sea level, among them Mount Borah, the highest peak in Idaho. The Lost Rivers' steep terrain, deep canyons, and alpine lakes offer a wild and still only partially explored landscape.

The area around the jagged peaks of the Sawtooth Mountains and pale gray-white pinnacles of the White Cloud Mountains is equally striking: dense forests, subalpine lakes, flower-filled meadows, creeks, and deep canyons, all hosting a diverse mix of wildlife and rare flora. Four river systems have their headwaters in this region: the Big Wood, Boise, Payette, and Salmon.

Indigenous History

The earliest known occupants of this land arrived at least ten thousand years ago. Numerous examples of handheld spear points and other implements for hunting big game have been found throughout Custer County. Paleo-Indian presence abounds in the Salmon River Mountains, with the Redfish

16. "Custer County, ID," Economic Profile System, Headwaters Economics, accessed June 1, 2021, https://headwaterseconomics.org/apps/economic-profile-system/16037.

17. "Lost River Range," Summit Post, accessed June 1, 2021, https://www.summitpost.org/lost-river-range/171539; "Sawtooth Mountains," Visit Idaho, Idaho Department of Commerce, accessed June 1, 2021, https://visitidaho.org/things-to-do/natural-attractions/sawtooth-mountains/; "White Clouds," Summit Post, accessed June 1, 2021, https://www.summitpost.org/white-clouds/171219.

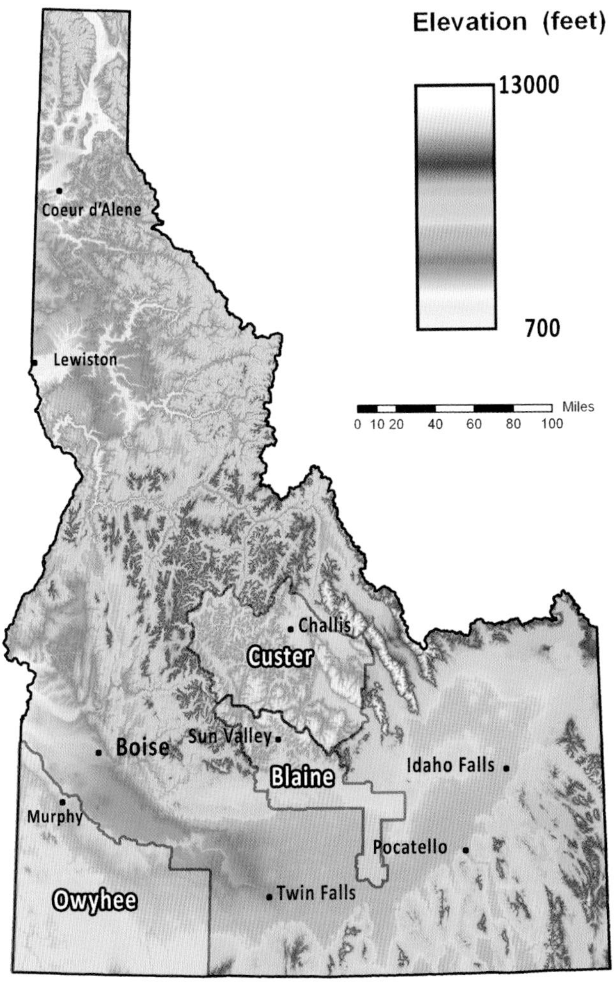

Elevation map of Idaho with Custer, Blaine, and Owyhee Counties indicated. Selected cities and towns in Idaho are shown for reference. U.S. Department of Agriculture, Natural Resources Conservation Service.

Overhang site being among the most prominent archaeological sites in the county. The tribes that occupy Custer County today—Shoshone, Bannock, and Paiute—trace their ancestors to these early inhabitants.[18]

18. Kathryn Estel Sargeant, *Final Report on the Archaeology of the Redfish Overhang Site* (Pocatello: Idaho State University Museum, 1973), https://archive.org/details/CAT31363420/page/n1/mode/2up.

Boulder Mountains in fall. Photo courtesy of Ed Cannady, https://www.edcannadyphotograph.com.

Alice Lake in the Sawtooth Wilderness. Photo courtesy of Ed Cannady, https://www.edcannadyphotograph.com.

Carbon dating of stone tools found at the Redfish site indicate that they were created around ten thousand years ago. Tens of thousands of cultural resources are estimated to be located within Custer County. Their true number may be considerably larger as only a small fraction of the county has been adequately studied.

Arrival of European and American Settlers

The first documented contact with Euro-Americans took place in the early part of the nineteenth century when the Lewis and Clark Expedition passed through central Idaho.[19] Reports from the expedition of abundant wildlife led to an influx of independent fur trappers and companies formed to harvest pelts for clients in the East and in Europe.[20]

Toward the middle of the century, prospectors began to travel east- and northward from gold country in California to seek deposits of precious metals in what is now northeastern Washington and Idaho. Small groups of miners began searching in and around the tributaries of the Salmon River in Custer County in 1863. Early mining efforts were unsuccessful largely because hauling supplies and minerals to and from the rugged landscape was challenging and expensive. But for a few, persistence paid off, and a decade later, mining began to boom in Custer County as the Montana, Charles Dickens, and Custer Mines began to extract profitable quantities of gold and silver.[21]

Conflicts with Indigenous Peoples

The arrival of European and American trappers and, later, wagon trains crossing Idaho along the Oregon Trail, followed by the influx of prospectors, strained food and water resources essential to the survival of the Shoshone

19. E. S. Lohse, "Southeastern Idaho Native American Prehistory and History," in *Manual for Archaeological Analysis: Field and Laboratory Analysis Procedures* (Pocatello: Idaho Museum of Natural History, 1993), https://digitalatlas.cose.isu.edu/arch/Prehist/Pre_Summ/SE_Snake/Historic.htm.

20. Idaho Historical Society, *Fur Trade Posts in Idaho*, Reference Series no. 62 (Boise: Idaho Historical Society, 1970), https://history.idaho.gov/wp-content/uploads/2018/08/0062.pdf.

21. "Mining in Custer County," Custer County, Idaho: Genealogy and History, Genealogy Trails, accessed June 1, 2021, http://genealogytrails.com/ida/custer/history/history_mining.html; "McKay and Copper Basin," Custer County, Idaho: Genealogy and History, Genealogy Trails, accessed June 1, 2021, http://genealogytrails.com/ida/custer/history/history_mackay.html.

and Bannock peoples. Hostilities ensued as the tribes attempted to defend their traditional hunting and agricultural lands from the encroachment of white settlers. Following multiple skirmishes and battles with U.S. Army troops, the Shoshone and Bannock bands were relocated to the Fort Hall Reservation. By 1932, the reservation, originally 1.8 million acres in size, had been reduced by two-thirds. The tribes now live on the 540,000-acre Fort Hall Reservation, twenty miles north and west of Pocatello.[22]

The Growth of Custer County

Since the mid-1870s, mining in and around Custer County has undergone multiple boom-and-bust periods.[23] Ghost towns throughout the county reflect the changing fortunes of mining over the past 150 years. Rusted equipment, wooden cabins, and grave markers in Bayhorse, Bonanza, Boulder City, Custer, and Sawtooth City evoke once-thriving centers occupied by fortune-seekers and workers who came from throughout the world.[24] Today, the primary commodities mined in the county are silver, gold, and lead.

While mining drew the first significant influx of Euro-Americans to Custer County, new settlers soon became aware of the meadows along the county's rivers, and the abundant grasses in the lower reaches of the mountain ranges on Custer's eastern and western boundaries. Settlers began to import herds of cattle and sheep as ranching was viewed as potentially profitable activity, less subject to the boom-and-bust cycles of the mines.[25] By the 1920s,

22. "Shoshone-Bannock Tribes," Shoshone-Bannock Tribes, accessed June 1, 2021, http://www2.sbtribes.com/about/.

23. Cultural Resources Working Group of the YFTA Interdisciplinary Team, comp., *Appendix D: Cultural Resources of the Yankee Fork Tributary Assessment Area, North-Central Idaho* (Boise, Idaho: Bureau of Reclamation Pacific Northwest Region, 2011), https://www.usbr.gov/pn/fcrps/ce/idaho/uppersalmon/yf/; *History of the Challis National Forest: A Compilation* (Ogden, Utah: U.S. Forest Service Intermountain Region, 2009), https://www.fs.usda.gov/Internet/FSE_DOCUMENTS/fsbdev3_042166.pdf.

24. "Bayhorse, Idaho," Western Mining History, accessed June 1, 2021, https://westernmininghistory.com/towns/idaho/bayhorse/; "Custer, Idaho," Western Mining History, accessed June 1, 2021, https://westernmininghistory.com/towns/idaho/custer_id/; "Sawtooth City / Smiley Creek," Blaine County, accessed June 1, 2021, https://www.co.blaine.id.us/DocumentCenter/View/5958/Smiley-Creek-Historic-Page.

25. Bill Little, *A History of Early Livestock Grazing on Lands of the Sawtooth National Forest* (n.p.: U.S. Forest Service, 1991), https://www.fs.usda.gov/Internet/FSE_DOCUMENTS/fsbdev3_042090.pdf.

ranching became a centerpiece of Custer County's economy. Livestock grazing is now officially recognized as an activity of "historic and cultural significance" in the county and is listed on its register of cultural resources.[26]

Of Custer County's 4,300 residents, 10 percent now work in the mining industry; 13 percent work on ranches and farms; 29 percent work in travel and tourism; and the remainder work in government and service jobs. As a result, the health of the county's economy is critically dependent on access to federal land, and the regulations that govern this access.[27] The BLM and the U.S. Forest Service manage leasing of public lands for ranching and mining. The agencies determine where mining leases and grazing allotments are granted, how many livestock are permitted to graze during a given year, and what restrictions are placed on hunting, fishing, motorized and nonmotorized recreation, and camping on BLM or Forest Service lands.

County residents are thus keenly sensitive to proposed changes in the management of public lands, and are particularly skeptical about efforts to establish wilderness areas (where mining, grazing, and recreation opportunities are strictly regulated). To residents of Custer County, public lands represent their economic lifeblood, as well as places where they have for generations recreated, and drawn inspiration from their beauty and solitude.

With the coming of interstate highways (Interstate 80 to the south, Interstate 90 to the north, and Interstate 15 running north to south) and improved secondary roads, more visitors began to explore and became aware of Idaho's remote natural wonders. Starting in the 1960s, conservation groups interested in preserving the wildness and solitude of public lands in Custer County and elsewhere in Idaho began to lobby for their protection.

Mining Versus Conservation

The first major conservation battle in the postwar period was precipitated by a proposal from the American Smelting and Refining Company (ASARCO) to develop a large, open-pit molybdenum mine at the base of Castle Peak, the highest mountain in the White Clouds Range.

26. "Custer County, Idaho: Proposed Resource Management Plan," Custer County, Idaho (government website), uploaded February 15, 2018, http://www.co.custer.id.us/wp-content/uploads/1/Custer-County-Proposed-Resource-Management-Plan-Draft-2.pdf.

27. "Custer County, ID," Economic Profile System, Headwaters Economics.

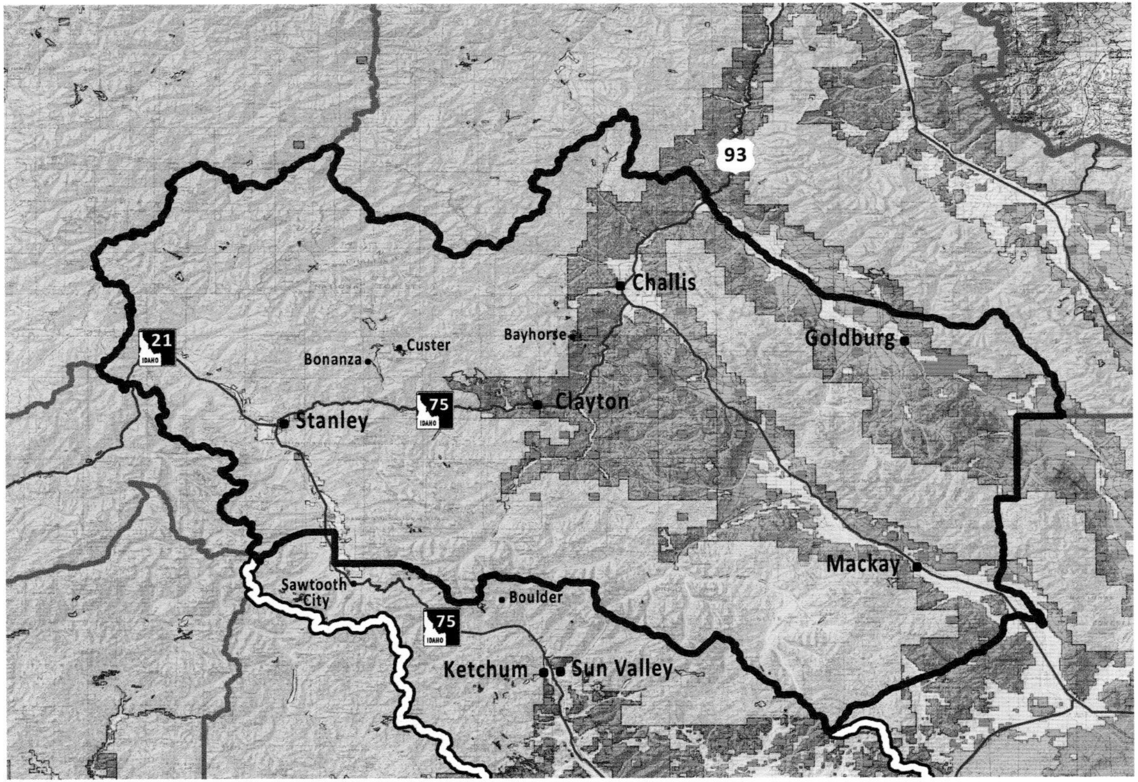

Custer County (*black outline*) and the northern part of Blaine County (*white outline*) in Idaho. The map indicates private land (*off-white*); school trust land (*purple*); and public land, managed by the U.S. Forest Service (*light green*) and the Bureau of Land Management (*dark green*). Locations of ghost towns are indicated in small font.

Castle Peak at sunset. Photo courtesy of Ed Cannady, https://www.edcannadyphotograph.com.

In 1970, the battle to stop the mine became the focus of the Idaho governor's race, in which the Republican incumbent, Don Samuelson, was challenged by Democrat Cecil Andrus. Buoyed by the support of conservation-minded Idahoans, Andrus was elected governor by a ten-thousand-vote margin and served until 1977, when he was asked by newly elected president Jimmy Carter to serve as secretary of the interior. Andrus often referred to Castle Peak as "the mountain that made a governor."[28]

Seeking Protection for the White Cloud Peaks and Sawtooth Valley

In Andrus's first years as governor, his lobbying for protection of the area around the White Cloud Peaks and the Sawtooth Valley led to Congress's declaring a national recreation area (NRA) in 1972. The legislative language designating the Sawtooth NRA stopped ASARCO from developing the mine, and precluded subdivision of land in the Sawtooth Valley into ranchettes. Even so, the Sawtooth NRA was a compromise: the new designation provided protections supported by many in Idaho, but it was not as strict as a national park, which was also considered at the time. The legislation provided for a Sawtooth Wilderness Area within the NRA, and designated the White Cloud and Boulder mountain ranges as wilderness study areas (WSAs).

However, conservationists believed that the protections offered by the recreation area were insufficient, as continued use by OHVs and snowmobiles were, in their view, detrimental to both wildlife and the wilderness qualities of the area. They continued to agitate for more stringent regulation of the Boulder and White Cloud regions: protection as wilderness areas.

Seeking Wilderness Protection for the Boulder and White Cloud Mountains

The battle to protect the region continued into the 1990s, when then representative Mike Crapo (R-Idaho), who would go on to serve in the U.S. Senate, initiated attempts to seek a solution that would balance the push for wilderness with the desires of Custer County residents to ensure that

28. Rick Johnson, "Experiencing Cecil Andrus' Legacy in the White Cloud Mountains," *Idaho Conservation League* (blog), July 19, 2018, https://www.idahoconservation.org/blog/experiencing-cecil-andrus-legacy-in-the-white-cloud-mountains/.

public lands would remain available for multiple uses: ranching, mining, and recreation.

In 1998, newly elected representative Mike Simpson (R-Idaho) seized the baton from Crapo and began what turned out to be a fifteen-year effort to resolve the conflict between those advocating multiple uses and those arguing for wilderness protection.

Representative Simpson recalled the many failures to formulate a land use bill for Custer County. "I know that [former governor Cecil] Andrus (D-Idaho) and [former senator James] McClure (R-Idaho) had tried to do it. Then [former representative Richard] Stallings (R-Idaho) tried to do it, and then Crapo tried to do it. There was just so much conflict between the counties and the ranchers and the conservationists, you couldn't get started."

Listening to Stakeholders

Not long after Simpson's election, Rick Johnson, then the executive director of the Idaho Conservation League, approached Simpson. "Rick said, 'you know, we in the environmental community have become very good at stopping things from happening, but we're not very good at making things happen,'" Simpson recalled. "'I'd like to try and make something happen.' I said, 'okay, this is a guy I can work with.'"

Johnson and Representative Simpson kept in close communication over the ensuing fifteen years, as each reached out to the broad range of stakeholders needed to forge an acceptable compromise regarding public lands use in Custer County: county commissioners, ranchers, hunters, fishermen, motorized vehicle users, mountain bikers, hikers, and climbers. "Simpson initially looked at the White Clouds and said there are four key constituencies—motorized recreation, wilderness advocates, the county, and ranchers—that have kept wilderness from happening," Johnson recalls. "Simpson said to me, 'I need to create a deal that is good enough for each of those four constituencies that they look at what they get rather than what everybody else gets.'"

Representative Mike Simpson (*left*) and Rick Johnson, then the Idaho Conservation League executive director, circa 2014. Photo courtesy of Katherine Jones.

"What we did was listen to each party very carefully," Simpson's chief of staff Lindsay Slater noted. "For example, in the case of motorized users we kept all their trails open. We didn't close a single trail. We set up a land use plan so that they don't have to worry for generations that the Forest Service is going to come in and close things. There was certainty. Everybody knew where everything stood. In the case of the county commissioners, we told them from day one, 'we'll keep you in the loop and if you don't like it, tell us.' We had a great working relationship with them."

Finding the Radical Center

In assembling what became the Boulder–White Clouds Wilderness Bill, negotiations among stakeholders took place according to what both Johnson and Simpson characterized as "shuttle diplomacy." Representative Simpson and Slater listened to the hopes, dreams, fears, and concerns of each party and developed draft language. They would then present the language, seek changes, and begin another round of drafting and discussion.

The challenge was finding what Johnson called "the radical center" (a term many have attributed to Malpai Borderlands founder Bill McDonald to describe a consensus-based approach to land management issues in the West).[29] In reflecting on his discussions with conservation groups and other stakeholders during the process, Johnson lamented that much of the conversation at first took place at the extremes: "Simpson and I, we spent all this time moving to the center and we

Members of the Idaho Conservation League assemble in Washington, D.C., to urge designation of Boulder-White Clouds as a wilderness area. Photo courtesy of Rick Johnson.

29. "The Radical Center," Resilience, December 16, 2013, https://www.resilience.org/stories/2013-12-16/the-radical-center/.

get there and we find that it's empty. This whole radical left and the radical right thing. The radical place is actually the center because there's nobody there!"

Between 2002 and 2013, Simpson introduced a number of bills aimed at satisfying stakeholder needs and desires. All foundered. "I look back at the first bills, and we tried to put into it everything that everybody wanted, knowing that that was not going to work but from [our failures, we'd learn what would work]. Little did I know it would be fourteen years of writing new bills and getting new compromises in it."

Overcoming Opposition to Protection for Boulder-White Clouds

Despite Representative Simpson's best efforts in Congress, it became clear by 2013 that legislative efforts to gain protection for the Boulder and White Clouds regions had stalled. At that juncture, Rick Johnson, along with former governor Cecil Andrus and a number of conservation groups, mounted a campaign to persuade the Obama administration to declare a region around the Sawtooth and White Clouds Mountains a national monument by using the power granted to the president under the Antiquities Act of 1906. Although a monument would provide less stringent protections than wilderness designation, Andrus believed that a national monument would represent a step forward from the NRA designation he helped forge in 1972.

Testimony to persistence: multiple versions of a bill were attempted before "the one" was passed in 2014. Photo courtesy of Rick Johnson.

"To build a serious, nationally recognized monument campaign that politically penetrated the [Department of the Interior and Department of Agriculture] and the White House was difficult, expensive, and required an entirely different set of assets and political work [than focusing on forging legislation]," Johnson says.

Andrus and Johnson's monument campaign gained momentum. It echoed the approach taken three decades prior by Andrus (during his tenure as secretary of the interior in the Carter administration) to protect vast tracts of wild lands in Alaska as national monuments. When President Carter declared the monuments, the Alaska congressional delegation worked with the administration to protect these public lands legislatively, hoping thereby to preclude additional monument designations. They succeeded in crafting the Alaska National Interest Lands Conservation Act, which was signed on November 12, 1980, two months prior to President Reagan's succeeding Carter.[30]

In September 2014, Rick Johnson worked with several people to arrange a meeting among Lindsay Slater, Representative Simpson, and Obama White House counselor John Podesta at a dinner celebrating the fiftieth anniversary of the Wilderness Act's being signed into law. It was by this time becoming increasingly likely that President Obama would protect a region around the Sawtooth and White Clouds Mountains as a national monument. However, presidential declarations of national monuments are nearly as toxic in Idaho as they are in Utah. Representative Simpson was keenly aware of the likely reaction of his constituents to a monument declaration, and he was eager to make one more try to effect the legislative solution he had been seeking for more than a decade. As Johnson recalls, "I had invited Simpson and Slater to sit at my table. Simpson asked Podesta to pause, and to give him six months to pass his bill. If he failed, the monument would go ahead."

Final Push to Draft a Land Use Bill

Following their meeting, Podesta announced publicly that the president "still has ink in his signing pen" for more national monuments, but he gave Simpson time to rally support for congressional passage of legislation enabling what became the Boulder–White Clouds Wilderness Area. Representative Simpson carried the message from the Podesta meeting back to Idaho, making it clear that Idahoans had a choice: an Obama-declared monument, or a compromise bill forged from the views of a broad range of citizens.

With the support of Senator James Risch (R-Idaho), Simpson went to work and drafted another bill. In parallel with Simpson's efforts, Rick Johnson, as Johnson explains, once again attempted "to build support, understanding, and room for the bill within the conservation community locally and nationally."

In the end, Simpson's bill garnered the support of a diverse group including East Fork of the Salmon River Ranchers, the Idaho Farm Bureau, the Idaho Cattle Association, Idaho Outfitters and Guides, the Pew Charitable

30. "Alaska National Interest Lands Conservation Act," National Park Service, last updated November 9, 2020, https://www.nps.gov/locations/alaska/anilca.htm.

Trusts, the Idaho Conservation League, the Wilderness Society, Backcountry Hunters and Anglers, the Sierra Club, and the Idaho Recreation Council, which represents motorcycle and snowmobile riders.[31]

Also important in forging the final version of the bill was the support of Blaine County, located on Custer County's southern border. Although only a small portion of the proposed wilderness area extended into Blaine, residents of the county—home to Ketchum and Sun Valley—are generally strong supporters of conservation efforts, and have both the resources and political clout to influence legislation.

Former Idaho governor Cecil Andrus (*left*) and Rick Johnson celebrate passage of the Boulder–White Clouds bill. Photo courtesy of Rick Johnson.

Representative Simpson then drew on his relationships with then Speaker John Boehner (R-Ohio) and Representative Rob Bishop (R-Utah), chair of the House Committee on Natural Resources Committee. With the help of Senator Risch's vigorous advocacy, the Sawtooth National Recreation Area and Jerry Peak Wilderness Additions Act was signed by President Obama on August 7, 2015. Rick Johnson witnessed the signing and then called Cecil Andrus. His message? "We finally got it done, Governor."[32]

To recognize Andrus's contributions to the protection of the Boulder–White Clouds region, Representative Simpson introduced a bill to rename the White Clouds Wilderness as the Cecil D. Andrus White Clouds Wilderness.[33] The bill was passed into law in 2018.

What the Bill Achieved

The act, typically referred to as the Boulder–White Clouds Wilderness Bill, designates three areas as part of the National Wilderness Preservation System:

31. Rich Landers, "Boulder–White Clouds Wilderness Passes U.S. Senate," *Spokesman-Review*, August 5, 2015, https://www.spokesman.com/stories/2015/aug/05/boulder-white-clouds-wilderness-passes-us-senate/.

32. Johnson, "Experiencing Cecil Andrus' Legacy in the White Cloud Mountains."

33. Rocky Barker, "Andrus Spent His Life Protecting This Iconic Idaho Wilderness; Now It Will Carry His Name," *Idaho Statesman*, March 22, 2018, https://www.idahostatesman.com/news/local/news-columns-blogs/letters-from-the-west/article206451719.html.

Jim McClure–Jerry Peak Wilderness (117,000 acres), White Clouds Wilderness (91,000 acres), and Hemingway-Boulders Wilderness (68,000 acres).

These protected areas preserve 276,000 acres of high mountain backcountry, home to crystal lakes and abundant wildlife. The U.S. Forest Service manages federal lands within the newly designated wilderness areas, with the exception of approximately 24,000 acres of the Jim McClure–Jerry Peak Wilderness and 450 acres of the White Clouds Wilderness, which are managed by the BLM.

The bill also releases four areas originally designated as wilderness study areas for multiple use activities such as ranching, mining, and recreation. Ranching is recognized explicitly for its place in the heritage of Custer County, and for its role in sustaining open spaces and unfragmented landscapes. Moreover, ranchers who retire grazing rights become eligible for compensation through a fund established by conservation groups. The bill also provides over $5 million in grants to the county and communities surrounding Boulder–White Clouds for a community center and county health clinic, as well as support for emergency medical services; and to the Sawtooth National Recreation Area for trail and other infrastructure improvements.

Reflections on the Significance of Forging the Bill

"Residents of Idaho loved the fact that [putting together the bill] brought people together," Rick Johnson says. "They saw [the benefit] if we portrayed it as something that was bringing diverse interests together to create an Idaho solution; people said 'yes, I support this, regardless of the size, regardless of where, regardless of the rules, whatever.'"

"I feel very strongly that conservation can complement the conservative values of the West very comfortably but to do that you have to ensure that you don't appear that you're trying to overthrow those conservative values," Johnson continues. "The Boulder–White Clouds bill represents one of the great achievements in Idaho. Mike Simpson, I know, walks down the street in Boise, Idaho, and people stop him and thank him for doing it. He and I have been given an award together for civility and [for our creation of] that radical center."

"The stars were so bright you didn't need a flashlight," Simpson says of camping in Quicksand Meadows, located in the White Cloud Mountains. "I was just sitting there contemplating [how] it's almost like you could grab

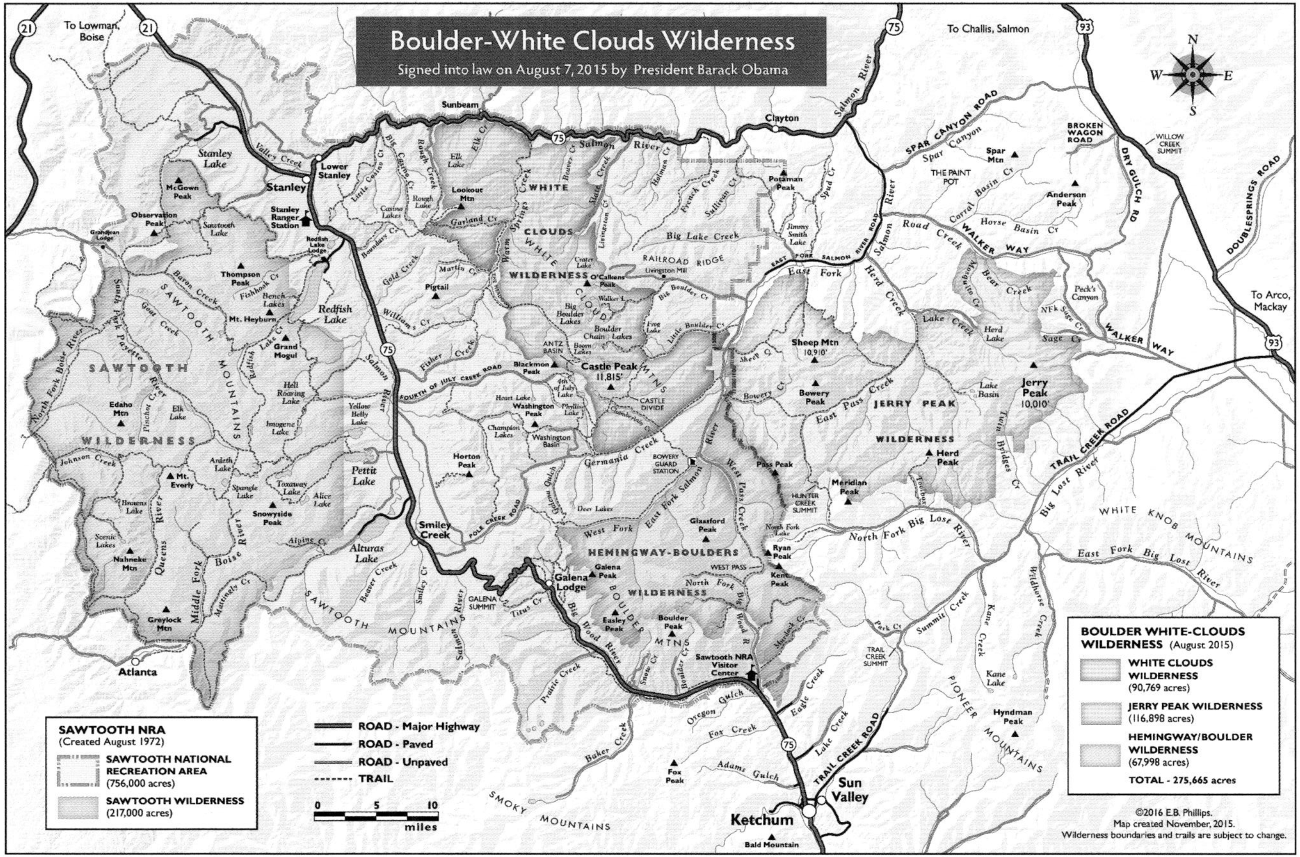

Map of the areas protected as wilderness in the Boulder-White Clouds bill: White Clouds Wilderness (*light purple*); Jerry Peak Wilderness (*light blue*); and Hemingway-Boulders Wilderness (*green*). The Sawtooth Wilderness to the west (*lime green*) had been protected by earlier legislation. U.S. Forest Service.

Dickshooter Creek cutting deep into Black Canyon. Photo courtesy of Mark Lisk, https://marklisk photography.photoshelter.com/.

them. And this goes on forever. I was trying to wrap my mind around infinity. . . . I kept thinking of one day, not 10 years, not 20, but 100 years from now some kid will lay there and look at those stars. That's why you do this."[34]

A Collaborative Approach to Conservation in Owyhee County, Idaho

Owyhee County, located in the southwestern corner of Idaho, is the second-largest county in the state, spanning 7,700 square miles (4.9 million acres), larger than the states of Connecticut and Rhode Island combined. Nearly the entire county is best described as a vast, high, intermountain desert, populated by sage, grass, and juniper, and incised with multiple canyons. The western part of the county is dominated by the Owyhee Mountain Range, a wild and rugged landscape that was one of the last areas explored in the continental United States. Hayden Peak, the tallest in the range, rises 8,400 feet above sea level.[35] The northern border of the county is defined by the Snake River, which passes through Owyhee as it courses westward to the Columbia River and the Pacific Ocean beyond.[36]

In the southwest corner of Owyhee, where Idaho, Nevada, and Oregon meet, lies a remote landscape of majestic beauty: the Owyhee Canyonlands. There, the Owyhee, Bruneau, and Jarbidge Rivers have carved deep, craggy canyons into the high desert plateau.[37] Rust-colored rhyolite cliffs rise above the riverbeds, bearing silent witness to the emergence of magma as the North American continental plate slid across the so-called Yellowstone hotspot.[38]

In other areas, deposits of rhyolite ash and pumice have been shaped into spectacular pinnacles and colorful hillsides.

---

34. Elizabeth Shogren, "How a Long-Sought Idaho Wilderness Bill Defies the Odds," *High Country News* (Paonia, Colo.), August 6, 2015, https://www.hcn.org/articles/how-a-long-sought-idaho-wilderness-bill-defies-the-odds.

35. "Hayden Peak," Summit Post, accessed June 1, 2021, https://www.summitpost.org/hayden-peak/196061.

36. "Snake River," American Rivers, accessed June 1, 2021, https://www.americanrivers.org/river/snake-river/; "Welcome to Owyhee County," Owyhee County, accessed June 1, 2021, https://owyheecounty.net/community/.

37. "Jarbidge Wild and Scenic River," Bureau of Land Management, accessed June 1, 2021, https://www.blm.gov/visit/jarbidge-wild-and-scenic-river.

38. "Geology: Continental Hotspot," National Park Service, last updated February 11, 2020, https://www.nps.gov/subjects/geology/plate-tectonics-continental-hotspots.htm.

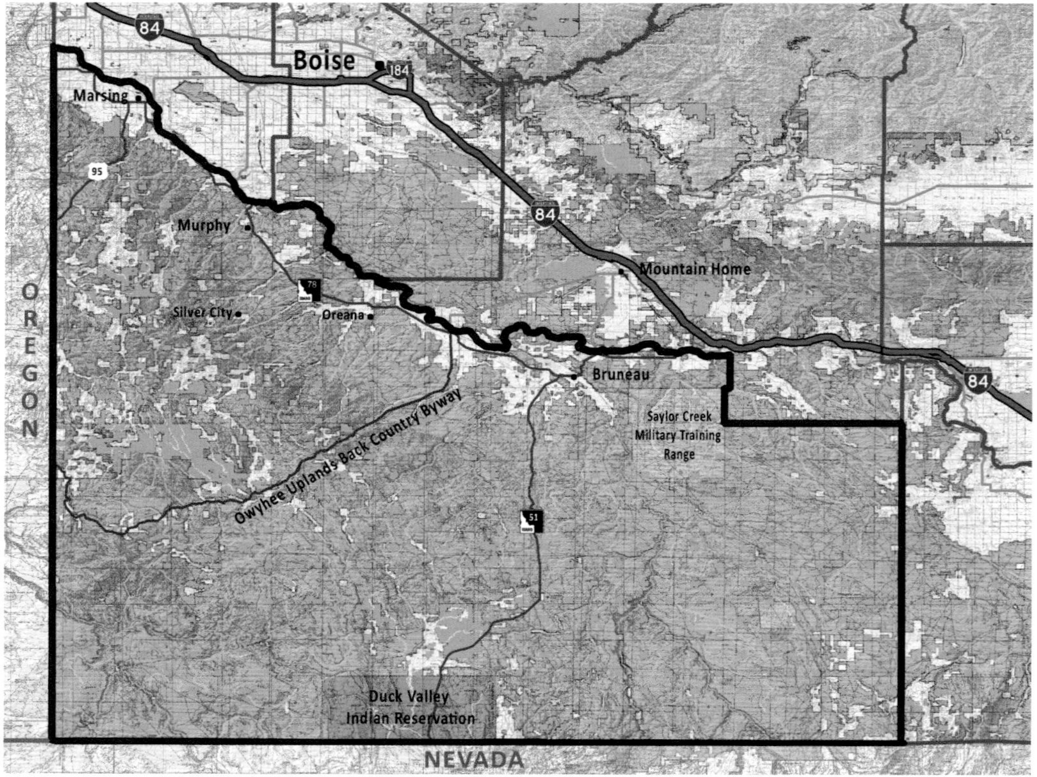

Map of Owyhee County, indicating public lands, held by the U.S Forest Service (*dark green*) and Bureau of Land Management (*chartreuse*); school trust lands (*purple*); and private lands (*white*). Public lands account for 78 percent of the total territory in the county.

County History

Artifacts from the first peoples to inhabit this area—ancestors of today's Paiute, Shoshone, and Bannock tribes—date back more than ten thousand years and include tools, weapons, and petroglyphs inscribed on canyon walls and talus slopes.[39]

The first Europeans to arrive in the area were part of Scottish Canadian Donald McKenzie's 1819 fur-trapping expedition along a major tributary of the Snake River. Three native Hawaiians were members of the McKenzie party. None of them survived, but they were honored posthumously by McKenzie, who named the tributary "Owyhee," the original Polynesian phonetic version of "Hawai'i."[40]

Later, during the mid-nineteenth century, thousands of pioneers passed through today's Owyhee County as they headed westward along the two-thousand-mile-long Oregon Trail, which linked Independence, Missouri, with Oregon City, Oregon.[41] In May 1863, near Silver City, gold was discovered in placer deposits, natural concentrations of heavy minerals like gold, silver, and platinum that are sorted from host rock complexes over time by streams washing soil down mountainsides. The Idaho gold rush that followed led to the establishment of the first three permanent settlements in Owyhee County: Booneville, Ruby City, and Silver City. At one time, the wealth in gold and silver extracted from Owyhee County brought worldwide fame to the area.[42] The year 1863 also witnessed the declaration of Idaho as a territory, and Owyhee County was the first county in Idaho to be organized.[43]

---

39. Douglas Beauchamp, "Rock Art in the Owyhee," Owyhee Canyonlands, June 17, 2014, https://wildowyhee.org/rock-art-in-the-owyhee/; "Idaho—History and Heritage," *Smithsonian Magazine*, November 6, 2007, https://www.smithsonianmag.com/travel/idaho-history-and-heritage-177411856/; "Shoshone-Bannock Tribes," Shoshone-Bannock Tribes, accessed June 1, 2021, http://www2.sbtribes.com/about/; "Our History," Shoshone-Paiute Tribes of the Duck Valley Indian Reservation, accessed June 1, 2021, https://www.shopaitribes.org/spculture/.

40. "Welcome to Owyhee County," Owyhee County.

41. "Oregon Trail—Facts, Information and Articles About the Westward Expansion," History Net, accessed June 2, 2021, https://www.historynet.com/oregon-trail.

42. A. H. Koschmann and M. H. Bergendahl, "Owyhee County Idaho Gold Production," 1968, Western Mining History, accessed June 2, 2021, https://westernmininghistory.com/articles/114/page1/.

43. "Owyhee County," Elmore County Press, accessed June 2, 2021, http://www.elmorecountypress.com/Owyhee%20News.htm.

The Owyhee River at the confluence of the West Little Owyhee River. Photo courtesy of Mark Lisk, https://markliskphotography.photoshelter.com/.

Petroglyph Panel, Owyhee Canyonlands. Photo courtesy of Mark Lisk, https://markliskphotography.photoshelter.com/.

Rhyolite Towers, East Fork, Owyhee River. Photo courtesy of Mark Lisk, https://marklisk photography.photoshelter.com/.

Multiple ghost towns, abandoned in the face of fluctuating prices for precious metal and played-out lodes, are found throughout Owyhee County. Today, these towns evoke Owyhee's early history: buildings line now-empty streets that once teemed with boisterous, intrepid fortune-seekers making their way to lively bars, gambling houses, and more notorious night spots.

The late 1860s witnessed the introduction of livestock into the county.[44] Ranching continues today, serving the market for livestock and representing a highly valued cultural link to the county's past. As in Emery County, Utah, semiarid conditions in the region (four to eighteen inches of annual precipitation) make farming challenging. Early farmers and their successors created extensive irrigation systems, drawing water from rivers and creeks to irrigate fields of beets, potatoes, corn, mixed grains, and, of course, potatoes.

Owyhee County Today

The county's estimated population as of 2017 was 11,400 people, nearly identical to that of Utah's Emery County. The demographics, however, differ from those of Emery: 68 percent white, non-Latino; 27 percent Hispanic or Latino; 4 percent Native American; and 1 percent mixed ethnicity.[45] Owyhee is home to part of the Shoshone-Paiute Tribe's Duck Valley Indian Reservation, the headquarters of which are located across the border from Idaho in Nevada. Murphy (population 97) serves as the county seat, while Homedale (2,700), Grand View (450), and Marsing (1,030) are the largest incorporated towns in a county whose population is highly dispersed. Jobs in agriculture (28 percent), timber (6 percent), travel and tourism (11 percent), and government (15 percent) account for the majority of Owyhee County's nonservice employment.[46]

The Economic and Cultural Significance of Public Lands in Owyhee County

Of the 4.9 million acres in the county, public land accounts for 78 percent.[47] As is the case in Utah's Emery County, any regulations or new protections con-

44. "Welcome to Owyhee County," Owyhee County.

45. "Owyhee County, ID," Economic Profile System, Headwaters Economics, accessed June 2, 2021, https://headwaterseconomics.org/apps/economic-profile-system/16073.

46. "Owyhee County, ID," Data USA, accessed June 2, 2021, https://datausa.io/profile/geo/owyhee-county-id.

47. "Owyhee County, ID," Economic Profile System, Headwaters Economics.

trolling use of and access to public lands can affect ranchers, the travel and tourism industry, and recreational activities. Moreover, cultural attachment to these lands runs deep among both members of the Shoshone-Paiute Tribe and citizens of Owyhee County, whose forebears ranched, tilled, and mined there for generations. The desire to protect lands of immense natural beauty and cultural significance runs strong as well. In particular, conservationists have long sought to protect the Owyhee Canyonlands both in Owyhee County and across the border in Oregon. And in counterpoint, many residents of Owyhee County are deeply skeptical of the federal government, and view attempts to protect public lands as an affront to their rights to use these lands as they see best.

Conservation Versus Ranching

Fears of a federal attempt to protect the Owyhee Canyonlands area reached a crescendo in the late 1990s as rumors swirled of a possible national monument declaration. In the end, no monument was declared. However, anxiety about future attempts to declare a monument or legislate wilderness protection spurred the Owyhee County commissioners to develop a long-term plan for the area.[48]

In early 2001, the County Commission approached Fred Grant to assist with these efforts. Grant is a former Maryland prosecutor who had grown up in Idaho and returned to the state to serve as a consultant to groups fighting for private property rights. The commissioners had witnessed his prior efforts in support of the rights of local ranchers and thus trusted them to represent their interests regarding grazing rights on BLM lands.

After accepting the commission's offer, Grant began to reach out to both ranchers and local conservation groups to see whether together they might be able to forge a long-term solution to public lands disputes. He found a counterpart in the Wilderness Society's Craig Gehrke, in collaboration with whom he approached other important stakeholders in Owyhee County.

Gathering Stakeholders to Seek Compromise

In October 2001 Grant and Gehrke formed the Owyhee Initiative Collaborative Committee, a working group that at its inception comprised ten groups

48. Steve Stuebner, "The Owyhee Initiative: An Idaho Success Story," Life on the Range, accessed June 2, 2021, https://idrange.org/range-stories/southwest-idaho/the-owyhee-initiative-an-idaho-success-story/.

Participants in the Owyhee Initiative (*from left*): Jerry Hoagland, Owyhee County commissioner; Chris Black, Bruneau rancher; Craig Gehrke of the Wilderness Society; Brenda Richards, Owyhee Initiative chair and Reynolds Creek rancher; and Grant Simonds, Idaho Outfitters and Guides Association. Photo courtesy of Steve Stuebner. Life on the Range, https://idrange.org/life-on-the-range/.

whose views regarding public lands use and protection spanned a wide range: the Nature Conservancy, the Owyhee Cattlemen's Association, the Wilderness Society, Idaho Conservation League, the U.S. Air Force, Idaho Outfitters and Guides Association, Owyhee County Soil Conservation Districts, the Owyhee County Commission, People for the Owyhees, and the Owyhee Borderlands Trust. Later, representatives from the Shoshone-Paiute Tribe also became involved with the initiative.

Former Idaho Conservation League executive director Rick Johnson recalls meeting with Grant and Gehrke in 2001. "In the annals of Owyhee land, it is recalled as 'the meeting in a bagel shop,'" Johnson says. He continues:

> That led to eight years of meetings where conversations would happen about places. Conversations would happen about county economics, how ranches work, how everything about Owyhee works. How recreation works, the conflict of people not closing gates, and motorized issues and cultural resources. There are a lot of cultural resources [from Indigenous Northern Paiute, Bannock, and Shoshone] in the Owyhee Canyonlands.
>
> The stakeholders were conservation groups, and in this case there was a reasonable diversity of folks, that included the Idaho Conservation League, where I worked; the Wilderness Society; the Sierra Club, primarily through active volunteers in the Boise area that had long worked on behalf of this country;

> and Idaho Rivers United, [which] focused on the river resources because these canyons are characterized by the rivers in them. There was motorized recreation, and that is really focused on the diversity of two-track dirt roads that cut through this country. Then really at the top of the heap was the ranching community. Ranching is what dominates Owyhee County above all else. Owyhee County is very big and very sparsely populated, and ranching is what the whole game is about.

Creating the Owyhee Initiative

In May 2006, members of the Owyhee Initiative Collaborative Committee arrived at a formal agreement to establish the Owyhee Initiative, a long-term plan for the county.[49] In a summary of the history of the Owyhee Initiative published as part of the online Life on the Range project, Bruneau rancher Chris Black—a member of the Owyhee Initiative Board of Directors—said, "no matter if we're humans or plants [or] animals, we're all on this earth together. . . . And what we have to do is do the best we can with what we have. And that's what we're doing with the Initiative. We're doing the best we can for management, and the disparate communities, what their needs are. All of the people in the Initiative are part of my community now. And I'm part of them. As long as we keep talking, as long as we keep working together, then we're successful."[50]

A key to the success of the Owyhee Initiative was building relationships among stakeholder groups over time, discovering what they had in common, and what they wanted Owyhee County to be. Their initial conversations were guided by a statement of goals that called for "preserving natural processes that create and maintain a functioning unfragmented landscape supporting and sustaining a flourishing community of human, plant and animal life."[51] The goal statement also made clear that any long-term plan would need to preserve ranching as an economically feasible activity.

The group met not only around tables and in conference rooms, but in homes and on ranches. "There were certain breakthrough moments," Johnson says.

> One of them being when local people, through one of their own voices, [realized that] the Wilderness Act, in the way that it's written and the way that it's

49. Owyhee Initiative Agreement, signed May 10, 2006, https://static1.squarespace.com/static/5950fe6b099c01a39eee4fb2/t/59517491440243892991d59f/.

50. Stuebner, "The Owyhee Initiative."

51. Stuebner, "The Owyhee Initiative."

Owyhee Initiative members meeting with congressional staff. Courtesy of Idaho Conservation League and the Owyhee Initiative. Life on the Range, https://idrange.org/life-on-the-range/.

> implemented, actually protects things the way they are, as opposed to throwing something on top of them. That reframed it mentally a little bit.
>
> If you can get a group of people who walk in with their own agenda to coalesce, if there's enough common spirit of trying to create something together, then they actually start working in concert. . . . "I've become a leader for a rural economy school district," or "I've become a leader for a timber project." You flip the game. Timber people become leaders for wilderness and vice versa. That creates this interesting oxygen.

Meeting with Community Members

As the effort proceeded, one-on-one meetings with members of the community took place, something that turned out to be particularly important in winning the support of the ranching community. "Ranchers are very independent, and they don't like somebody that speaks for the whole," Johnson says. "A lot of the work with ranchers, particularly with wilderness designations and things like that, required our team to meet one-on-one with individual ranchers all over the landscape. There were endless meetings of the group, but there were also endless meetings of a couple of conservation folks sitting around the kitchen table with maps with a rancher who was a permittee in the area. A lot of these were negotiated pretty much acre by acre with affected people."

Owyhee Initiative group photo with Senator Mike Crapo (R-Idaho) in the front, third from left. Photo courtesy of Rick Johnson.

Throughout much of the process, staff members representing Senator Mike Crapo (R-Idaho) participated as observers. Their presence and occasional intervention helped keep discussions on track. Interviewed by Steve Stuebner for Life on the Range, Craig Gehrke of the Wilderness Society was quoted as follows: "We needed an adult supervisor, if you will. We knew that whatever we got done, it would take an act of Congress. So we needed a sponsor from the Idaho delegation who could say, I can get that through, or good luck getting *that* through."[52]

"Congressional staffers were observers, not active participants," Rick Johnson says. "Senator Crapo made a commitment that assuming this collaborative came up with a final resolution, he would carry it to Congress. He basically just flat out said that he would do that."

Passing a Compromise Bill

With the May 2006 Owyhee Initiative agreement, the members came to an accord on a wide range of issues and developed both a legislative proposal and plans for the management of public lands in Owyhee County. The collaborative agreement they forged was able to meet the needs of conservationists, recreationists, and Native American tribes, while preserving ranching and the economic future of Owyhee County.

It was then up to Senator Crapo and his staff to bring the Owyhee Initiative's proposal to Congress and forge a bill that could win support. By the end of 2006, both the House and Senate had returned to Democratic control, which meant that Crapo needed to build bipartisan support. Working with members of the 111th Congress and the newly elected Obama administration, Crapo was able to include key elements of the Owyhee Initiative in the Omnibus Public Land Management Act of 2009, which protected millions

52. Stuebner, "The Owyhee Initiative" (emphasis added).

Former Idaho Conservation League executive officer Rick Johnson (*far left*). Photo courtesy of Rick Johnson. On the right is a press conference with (*left to right*) Senator Mike Crapo, Fred Grant, and Craig Gehrke. Photo courtesy of Craig Gehrke, the Wilderness Society. Life on the Range, https://idrange.org/life-on-the-range/.

of acres of public lands, established the National Landscape Conservation System, and funded a number of programs overseen by the Departments of Interior and Agriculture.[53]

What the Owyhee Initiative Achieved

The Owyhee Initiative resulted in the inclusion of the Owyhee Public Land Management Act in the 2009 public land omnibus bill. The act designated as wilderness 517,000 acres in and around the Owyhee Canyonlands; protected 316 miles of the Jarbidge, Bruneau, and Owyhee Rivers as well as their tributaries as wild and scenic rivers; released 199,000 acres of federal land originally designated as wilderness study areas for "multiple uses" including livestock grazing and motorized recreation; and enhanced protection for tribal cultural sites and resources. Importantly, the bill also provided ranchers with cash in exchange for private land and adjustments in grazing rights.[54]

53. Omnibus Public Land Management Act of 2009, H.R. 146, 111th Cong., sec. 1502 (2009–10); "National Conservation Lands," Bureau of Land Management, accessed June 2, 2021, https://www.blm.gov/programs/national-conservation-lands; *National Landscape Conservation System: America's National Conservation Lands*, 1:3,571,000 scale (Washington, D.C.: National Geographic Society, 2010), https://www.blm.gov/or/resources/nlcs/files/NLCS_NG_Map.pdf.

54. Bobby Atkinson, "517,000 Acres of Unspoiled Owyhee Wilderness Protected Under Act," *Idaho Press*, September 2, 2014, https://www.idahopress.com/members/517-000-acres-of-unspoiled-owyhee-wilderness-protected-under-act/article_4e86ad9a-3266-11e4-a621-0019bb2963f4.html; Office of Senator Mike Crapo, "Owyhee Initiative, Lands Bill Passed by Senate," press release, January 15, 2009, https://www.crapo.senate.gov/media/newsreleases/owyhee-initiative-lands-bill-passed-by-senate.

Big bend in Camas Creek, across from Avery Table in the Owyhee Wilderness. Photo courtesy of Mark Lisk, https://markliskphotography.photoshelter.com/.

Celebrating the Bill in Idaho

The signing of the bill was widely celebrated by participants in the Owyhee Initiative. Chairman Robert Bear of the Shoshone-Paiute Tribe, along with Owyhee Initiative Collaborative Committee chair Fred Grant and executive director of the Idaho Conservation League Rick Johnson, joined Senator Crapo in witnessing President Obama's signing of the bill. Chairman Bear commented, "This has been a very good collaboration. It took a team mentality to work together to complete this long overdue effort, but it brings us a step closer to protection of our cultural and natural resources."[55]

Fred Grant said, "Resolution of conflicts will help the economy in the West and preserve that which we all want to preserve. Some of the people in the private property rights organizations can use the same collaborative process. It works. Senator Crapo believed it eight years ago and he made it work."[56]

Rancher Brenda Richards watched the signing ceremony and offered congratulations on behalf of the ranching community. "Congrats and thanks to each and every one who worked so hard to get this through! Now the work continues," she said.[57]

Senator Crapo, whose leadership was essential in steering the bill through Congress, offered the following thoughts: "It took eight years, working stream by stream, trail by trail and parcel by parcel to evaluate how to best manage

55. Office of Senator Mike Crapo, "Owyhee Initiative Signed into Law," press release, March 30, 2009, https://www.crapo.senate.gov/media/newsreleases/owyhee-initiative-signed-into-law.

56. Office of Senator Mike Crapo, "Owyhee Initiative Signed into Law."

57. Office of Senator Mike Crapo, "Owyhee Initiative Signed into Law."

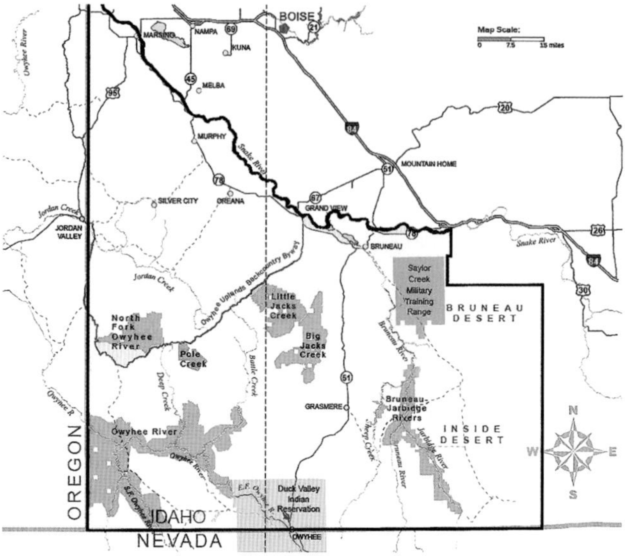

Map of Owyhee County (*left*) and of its location in Idaho. The county map indicates areas protected as wilderness (*dark orange*), the Duck Valley Indian Reservation (*light orange*), and the Saylor Creek Range (Air Force, *light purple*). This map was created by the Bureau of Land Management and has been modified for clarity.

and protect these lands while preserving the cultural heritage and multiple use opportunities for the people who live there. Everyone is better off under this legislation than they were under the status quo. I expect that this collaborative process will become a model for the nation on how to approach land management and decision-making."[58]

Ten years after the signing of the 2009 omnibus bill, some participants in the Owyhee Initiative reflected not only on the protections and economic opportunities it afforded but on the impact it has had on discussions throughout the West regarding the future of public lands. "A decade later, similar collaborative partnerships have spread throughout Idaho and the West," Senator Crapo said. "The Owyhee Initiative group still meets regularly and works together to support each other's interests."[59]

58. Office of Senator Mike Crapo, "Owyhee Initiative Signed into Law."

59. Rocky Barker, "Can a Decade-Old Owyhee Initiative Model Bring Peace Among Adversaries to Save Idaho Salmon?," *Idaho Statesman*, October 28, 2019, https://www.idahostatesman.com/article236654183.html.

Ribbon cutting at Bruneau Overlook, Owyhee Canyonlands. Courtesy of the Owyhee Initiative. Life on the Range, https://idrange.org/life-on-the-range/.

The Owyhee Initiative as a Model for Conservation Collaboratives

"The Owyhee was very much a model or perhaps an inspiration for conservation collaboratives throughout Idaho," says Rick Johnson, who retired as executive director of the Idaho Conservation League in 2019. "Idaho is becoming reasonably well known for having a lot of public land collaboratives," Johnson continues. "The conservation community in Idaho is now involved in perhaps a dozen formal collaboratives that meet on a regular basis. They have ground rules and named stakeholders, and they meet regularly to talk about public land management across the entire state, often based around a single national forest or BLM district. Those collaboratives unquestionably arose out of the Boulder–White Clouds' and the Owyhee Canyonlands' success(es)."[60]

60. Among these ongoing efforts is one to protect the part of the Owyhee Canyonlands to the west of Idaho's Owyhee Canyonlands Wilderness. In 2019, Senators Ron Wyden (D-Ore.) and Jeff Merkley (D-Ore.) introduced legislation to permanently protect the red rock canyons, rolling plains, and wild rivers of the Owyhee Canyonlands in Oregon. Office of Senator Ron Wyden, "Wyden, Merkley Introduce Legislation to Boost Economic Development in Malheur County," press release, November 7, 2019, https://www.wyden.senate.gov/news/press-releases/wyden-merkley-introduce-legislation-to-boost-economic-development-in-malheur-county.

Marsh Flat, north of Woodside, Utah. Aerial photo by Stephen E. Strom.

Finding Common Ground

Lessons for Approaching Public Lands Disputes

All ethics so far evolved rest upon a single premise: that the individual is a member of a community of interdependent parts. The land ethic simply enlarges the boundaries of the community to include . . . the land.

—ALDO LEOPOLD, *A SAND COUNTY ALMANAC*

Landscape in the San Rafael Swell, west of the Wedge. Aerial photo by Stephen E. Strom.

The stories behind the efforts to shape the future of public land use in Emery, Washington, Owyhee, and Custer Counties differ in the nature and alignment of opposing interests, the national political context, and the cultural outlook and economic needs of the counties. Nevertheless, their approaches to effecting constructive and civil resolution of seemingly intractable battles over public lands share a number of common elements. What follows represents a synthesis of lessons learned as gleaned from the testimonies of individuals whose commitment and persistence enabled compromise in the face of controversy.

Create Processes That Engage a Broad Range of Stakeholders

Many of the public lands that Americans treasure most were first protected by executive action. Think of the Grand Canyon: federal land that was declared a national monument in 1908 by President Theodore Roosevelt, using the powers granted to him by the Antiquities Act of 1906.[1] It is perhaps difficult to believe that despite widespread, grassroots support across the nation for Roosevelt's conservation agenda, his protection of the iconic canyon was met with fierce opposition by local miners and ranchers. They argued in the courts that Roosevelt had exceeded his authority under the Antiquities Act, and that as a result, they and those in the surrounding region would suffer economic harm. In the end, Congress chose to validate the broad support for Roosevelt's action by granting national park status to the Grand Canyon in 1918, and two years later the Supreme Court affirmed that Roosevelt's use of the Antiquities Act was appropriate.

President Bill Clinton's 1996 declaration of the 1.9-million-acre Grand Staircase-Escalante National Monument provides another example of how a president's use of the Antiquities Act can evoke powerful political opposition to a widely popular conservation effort, in this case one that had enjoyed national advocacy and some local support for more than five decades.[2]

---

1. Ken Burns, *National Parks: America's Best Idea*, six-episode series, premiered September 27, 2009, on PBS, http://www.pbs.org/nationalparks/parks/grand-canyon/; American Antiquities Act of 1906, 16 U.S.C. § 431–33 (1906).

2. Ann E. Halden, "The Grand Staircase-Escalante National Monument and the Antiquities Act," *Fordham Environmental Law Review* 8, no. 3, (2011), article 1, https://ir.lawnet.fordham.edu/cgi/viewcontent.cgi?article=1448&context=elr; Paul Larmer, "1996:

The extreme negative reaction to the monument declaration in parts of Utah was fueled in part by the growth of the Sagebrush Rebellion, which had its roots in the passage of the Federal Land Policy and Management Act (FLPMA) of 1976, as well as Utah's historically based wariness of federal intervention in state affairs.[3]

Following President Clinton's declaration of the monument, Utah's political establishment, along with citizens of Kane and Garfield Counties (where the monument is located), reacted furiously, characterizing the declaration as a "land grab" and a "midnight monument" that would undermine the economy of the two counties. In late 2017, in response to pleas from the Utah delegation, President Donald Trump reduced the size of Grand Staircase-Escalante by nearly half.[4]

A similar reaction followed President Barack Obama's declaration of the 1.3-million-acre Bears Ears Monument in 2016.[5] Although the declaration of Bears Ears was celebrated widely, opposition by the leadership of Utah's San Juan County and virtually the entire Utah political establishment resulted in President Trump's reducing the monument by 85 percent.[6] Trump acted despite considerable support for the monument among a majority of citizens in Utah; Native Americans in San Juan County, who trace their roots to the Bears Ears region; and conservation and outdoor recreation organizations across the United States.[7]

Clinton Takes a 1.7 Million-Acre Stand in Utah," *High Country News* (Paonia, Colo.), September 30, 1996, https://www.hcn.org/issues/90/2795; John Weisheit, "Escalante National Monument: A History of the First Proposal," On the Colorado, August 27, 2008, http://www.onthecolorado.com/articles.cfm?mode=detail&id=1219881501520.

3. Jonathan Thompson, "The First Sagebrush Rebellion: What Sparked It and How It Ended," *High Country News* (Paonia, Colo.), January 14, 2016, https://www.hcn.org/articles/a-look-back-at-the-first-sagebrush-rebellion.

4. Hannah Nordhaus, "What Trump's Shrinking of National Monuments Actually Means," *National Geographic Magazine*, February 2, 2018, https://www.nationalgeographic.com/science/article/trump-shrinks-bears-ears-grand-staircase-escalante-national-monuments.

5. Brian Maffly and Thomas Burr, "Obama Declares Bears Ears National Monument in Southern Utah," *Salt Lake Tribune*, December 29, 2016, https://archive.sltrib.com/article.php?id=4675012&itype=CMSID.

6. Nordhaus, "What Trump's Shrinking of National Monuments Actually Means."

7. Mike Matz, "New Poll: Utahans Support Protections for Bears Ears Area," Pew Charitable Trusts, press release, August 11, 2016, https://www.pewtrusts.org/en/research-and-analysis/articles/2016/08/11/new-poll-utahans-support-protections-for-bears-ears-area; Lori Weigel, "Utah Voters Support Protection of Bears Ears Area as National Monument;

As of the time of this writing, 2021, the fate of Bears Ears and Grand Staircase-Escalante rests with the courts, and with newly elected President Joe Biden, who has undertaken a review of both of Trump's monument reductions in preparation for potential executive action.[8]

The local resentment of the use of executive action under the Antiquities Act, along with President Trump's efforts to undo previously declared monuments, has led many conservation groups to place greater emphasis on seeking legislative protection of areas having high natural, scientific, or cultural value.

To do so requires finding a new approach to conservation efforts, one that involves working with public lands communities, with the goal of establishing a shared vision for the future of those lands that takes into account local economic and cultural needs. This approach requires establishing long-term partnerships with a broad range of local and national stakeholders who aspire to find mutually acceptable solutions to the use and protection of public lands.

Public lands counties, too, seek solutions that balance conservation goals with their economic needs, culture, and values. Negotiated legislation is to them far more palatable than what they regard as the arbitrary use of presidential power to change their lives with a stroke of a pen.

By all parties' choosing to work with sensitivity and mutual respect, conservation efforts can serve as a catalyst for bringing communities together

---

Place High Importance on Protecting Historic Sites and Artifacts in the Area," Public Opinion Strategies, press release, May 16, 2016, http://www.creationjustice.org/uploads/2/5/4/6/25465131/utah_national_monument_key_findings_memo.pdf; "Fact Sheet: A Majority of Residents in San Juan County Support Bears Ears," Utah Diné-Bikéyah, May 2019, https://utahdinebikeyah.org/wp-content/uploads/2019/05/Fact-Sheet-SJC-supports-Bears-Ears-5-2-19r.pdf; Dan Merica, "Native American Tribes, Conservation Groups Sue Trump over Monument Changes," CNN, December 5, 2017, https://www.cnn.com/2017/12/04/politics/monument-trump-utah-shrink-conservation-tribes-sue/index.html; Patagonia, "Hey, How's That Lawsuit Against the President Going?," press release, April 2019, https://www.patagonia.com/stories/hey-hows-that-lawsuit-against-the-president-going/story-72248.html; David Gelles, "Patagonia v. Trump," *New York Times*, May 5, 2018, https://www.nytimes.com/2018/05/05/business/patagonia-trump-bears-ears.html; Derek Franz, "Arc'teryx, Ibex and Polartec Join Patagonia's Movement to Pressure Utah over Bears Ears," *Alpinist*, February 10, 2017, http://www.alpinist.com/doc/web17w/newswire-arcteryx-ibex-join-fray.

8. Brian Maffly and Zak Podmore, "President Joe Biden's Order to Review Utah Monuments Leaves Options Open, but Expansion All but Certain," *Salt Lake Tribune*, January 25, 2021, https://www.sltrib.com/news/environment/2021/01/25/president-joe-bidens/.

and ensuring that the outcome of these efforts are beneficial to local as well as national interests. Such efforts are necessary in order that the fate of public lands counties not be subject to ping-ponging land protections as administrations in Washington change, and as ideologues often dictate policy.

Emery County, Washington County, and Owyhee County each developed processes that engaged broad groups of stakeholders, who worked for years or decades with local and national political leaders to seek legislative solutions to long-standing public lands disputes. They serve as examples of the power of "collaborative conservation," or what Ch'aska Huayhuaca and Robin S. Reid define as

> a way of working together, over significant periods of time, to conserve and manage the natural resources that people depend on and care about. People representing government agencies, nonprofits, businesses, or just themselves work together to decide how to use and manage land and water, wildlife, forests, and more. . . .
>
> The promise of collaboration is that it can generate new and creative solutions, and ensure that solutions to problems are owned by stakeholders and fit local situations. Collaboration among diverse participants can ensure buy-in to solutions that are less vulnerable to political change and thus more long-lasting. Successful collaboration can also build community spirit and strength, and ensure that participants collaborate more often on new problems in the future.[9]

Over the past decade, the collaborative conservation movement has taken root throughout the West.[10] The breadth of the growing movement is appar-

---

9. Ch'aska Huayhuaca and Robin S. Reid, *The Atlas of Collaborative Conservation in Colorado* (Fort Collins: Colorado State University, 2019), 5, https://collaborativeconservation.org/media/sites/142/2019/02/Atlas-Report-v.8-Feb-26-Final.pdf.

10. "Center for Collaborative Conservation," Colorado State University, June 2, 2021, https://collaborativeconservation.org/; R. Randall Schumann, "The Malpai Borderlands Project: A Stewardship Approach to Rangeland Management," U.S. Geological Survey, last modified December 9, 2016, https://geochange.er.usgs.gov/sw/responses/malpai/; "Community-Based Collaborative Conservation," Center for Natural Resources and Environmental Policy, accessed June 2, 2021, https://naturalresourcespolicy.org/projects/Community%20Based%20Collaborative%20Conservation.php; Joni Carswell, "The Future of Conservation is Collaboration," *Catalyst*, Spring 2019, https://www.bushcenter.org/catalyst/environment/carswell-conservation-and-collaboration.html; Nevada Collaborative Conservation Network (home page), accessed June 2, 2021, https://www.nvccn.org/.

ent from the number and diversity of groups hosted during a March 2020 meeting organized by the Center for Collaborative Conservation at Colorado State University in Fort Collins: meeting participants included representatives of collaborative conservation groups from Montana, Idaho, Wyoming, Utah, Colorado, Arizona, and New Mexico, working in forests, rangelands, and watersheds.[11]

Organize Broad-Based, Multistakeholder Groups That Meet Regularly over Years or Decades

Former Emery County commissioner Randy Johnson emphasizes the essential role played by the Emery County Public Lands Council, which met monthly with a broad range of stakeholders, along with representatives of state and federal agencies. "There were a number of important factors that needed to be in place to give us sort of a perfect storm, as it were, to get this passed," Johnson says. "Number one, among them I think, is that the Public Lands Council and the hundreds of people involved, and the hundreds of tours on the San Rafael Swell, and the hundreds and hundreds of meetings, was a process that gathered people in."

Ray Peterson, also a former county commissioner, notes that the Public Lands Council worked for decades to engage the citizens of Emery County in the drafting of a viable public lands bill:

> We [made] earlier attempts in 1998 and 2000 to [pass a bill] legislatively, but lessons were learned when they weren't successful. When we started in 2009, we cast a broad net. Who are all the stakeholders? Let's talk to them. Let's invite them to come and talk to us and be part of this. We created subcommittees out of the Public Lands Council, and they held public meetings for the people that they represented: water users, livestock grazers, recreation folks, etc. For most meetings, the first question was, does Emery County want to pursue something legislatively? Do we have support to do that? And if we do, what are your thoughts? What do you want to tell us as we proceed?

11. The meeting, dubbed Confluence 2020, was hosted by the Western Collaborative Conservation Network and held at Colorado State University, March 10–12, 2020. See the conference website: "Western Collaborative Conservation Network: Confluence 2020," Colorado State University, accessed June 2, 2021, https://collaborativeconservation.org/confluence_2020/.

"Piece one was developing this inter-coalition of allies that wanted to see something get done, and weren't going to let the perfect be the enemy of the good," says Jessica Wahl of the Outdoor Recreation Roundtable, a participant in the Emery County process.[12]

John Sterling of the Conservation Alliance was one of the key stakeholders engaged in the efforts to create the Emery County bill. In his opinion, "There's got to be this interplay between local elected officials, the conservation community, and in our case, the outdoor recreation business community, coming together with mature and thoughtful congressional staff who can get past the old [entrenched] positions we all take and say, 'Yes, we all want to get something done, so what's that going to look like?'"

"I do think there's a case study in Emery [County]," Sterling adds. "It's unheard of to move a bill of that size in one year. That never happens. [There is] a magic formula: You've got a county that wants some issues resolved. You've got a wide range of stakeholders who care enough to spend the time to engage, and you have willing members of Congress with smart staff."

Through these efforts, a diverse group of stakeholders found common ground. "It was really encouraging to discover as we went along that there were conservation groups that were interested in some of the things we were, and could understand our interests," Emery County historian Edward Geary says. "That's probably what kept us going is this sense that it might be possible to reach some kind of resolution."

In Idaho, Rick Johnson, the former executive director of the Idaho Conservation League, attributes the success in passing the Owyhee Canyonlands and Boulder–White Clouds bills to their proponents' reaching out and engaging citizens of Owyhee and Custer County, along with other individual stakeholders and groups. In turn, those successes led to the creation of a significant number of what he calls "public land collaboratives" (another moniker for conservation collaboratives) in Idaho that continue to address and resolve public lands issues.[13]

12. See also Outdoor Recreation Roundtable (home page), accessed June 2, 2021, https://recreationroundtable.org/.

13. See also Shevawn Von Tobel, "Taking Care of Our Public Lands the 'Idaho Way,'" Conservation Voters for Idaho, January 3, 2020, https://cvidaho.org/taking-care-of-our-public-lands-the-idaho-way/; Keith Schneider, "Trump Called for a 'Truly Representative Process' for Managing Public Land. One Already Exists in Idaho," *Los Angeles Times*,

Make Sure to Involve Federal and State Agencies and Tribal Representatives

Federal agencies—the Bureau of Land Management, the U.S. Forest Service (USFS), the National Park Service, and the Fish and Wildlife Service—are responsible for managing public lands. The framework within which they do so is set by legislation, while more detailed decisions regarding how public lands are managed are made by local agency field offices. Management plans developed by field offices are reviewed periodically and are open to public comment prior to their formal adoption.

In some parts of the rural West, field agents are viewed as hostile representatives of a distant, overbearing federal government. Relationships between local communities and the agencies can sometimes be challenging, particularly if the field offices propose management changes that are developed absent much dialogue with the community, and later presented for public comment as mature plans.

Some field offices and communities have taken proactive steps to initiate ongoing collaborative discussions regarding the management of public lands. In such cases, community residents come to recognize that individuals working in agency field offices possess a wealth of on-the-ground knowledge regarding the land resources they manage and are well positioned to provide informed insight into the challenges posed by proposed changes in land designation or management protocol. In parallel, agency representatives become cognizant of local expertise, often gained over generations spent working in and with the land, as well as potential cultural flash points.

Collaboration among stakeholder groups and agency representatives was essential to shaping positive outcomes in the case of the four wilderness bills discussed in the previous chapters. Their successes serve as models for stakeholder-agency collaboration.

Former Emery County commissioner Randy Johnson notes the important role played by representatives of state and federal agencies in working with the Public Lands Council to develop the framework for the Emery County Public Land Management Act:

December 28, 2017, https://www.latimes.com/nation/la-na-public-land-collaborate-2017-story.html.

> We determined there's just no way for us to do justice to all the public lands issues without some help. Our Public Lands Council created and signed MOUs [memoranda of understanding] with all of the agencies and entities that do business on public lands: state parks, School and Institutional Trust Lands Administration (SITLA), [Utah's] State Department of Mining, and the BLM, the Forest Service on the federal side. We created an MOU with [each of] them, and since 1995, every single month, until now and continuing, the Public Lands Council [has] sat down and met with all of those various agencies. . . . They come and they report their activities, and they have discussions in a friendly atmosphere. All of the surprise, all of the indignation, and all of the upsets that normally exist between agencies and counties melted in this process; it's worked extremely well since 1995. In both our early efforts and in the recent effort that led to our success [in bringing about the Emery County Public Land Management Act], the Public Lands Council was used as the core entity for the collaborative process.

Robert Bonnie, who served from 2013 to 2017 as undersecretary for natural resources and environment at the U.S. Department of Agriculture, commented on the growing importance of collaboratives in shaping the management of public lands:

> In making slide presentations to local citizens groups, I always projected images of twenty or thirty people standing in the forest in a big circle—talking to each other, [surrounded by] pickup trucks. I have hundreds of these pictures. These collaboratives are groups of people that are working together on [public lands issues]. There are agency people and foresters and range managers and environmentalists, [talking with local stakeholders]. Those groups, that's how conservation is done now. You have to go out into the woods and meet with people. People are out there, and they talk about things with one another, [and someone will say for example] "what if we looked at an alternative in the Environmental Impact Statement?" It takes work and people, and it takes a set of skills that they don't teach in range management or forestry school: people skills.

Karen Simms, who until recently worked in the Tucson BLM Field Office, brought together a broad range of stakeholders to develop the management plan for Las Cienegas National Conservation Area, south and east of

Tucson, Arizona.[14] Simms believes in the value of a robust collaborative group to discussing land management challenges in a collegial environment:

> I definitely think that you're seeing the value and the power of having these local collaborative groups working on land use issues, and the value or importance of having a manager or a leader in the local government agency being willing to engage with those groups to get something of mutual benefit done. During my thirty-year federal career, I've seen different managers come and go. Some of them are much more effective in engaging with a collaborative group or using that collaborative input than another leader might be. There's definitely that influence that comes into play. So far in the collaboratives that I've worked in, they've been strong and resilient enough that they've been able to continue to exist and do good work when those leaders change.

Tailor Efforts to Specific Attributes of Both the Land and the Local Community

The political landscape for protecting large tracts of land as wilderness or a national monument is far different in conservative areas such Utah or Idaho than it is in liberal western states like California. As a result, the approach to conservation efforts needs to reflect that political reality. Athan Manuel, director of the Lands Protection Program for the Sierra Club, who advocated for passage of the Emery County Public Land Management Act, notes the importance of setting realistic goals and adopting approaches tailored to states and localities:

> We need to be practical, and not demand too much. When we're working on these bills in Idaho or Utah or any state frankly, we know that those bills are going to look different based on which state you're in. If you're doing a public lands bill in California you're going to shoot for the moon. We know we can't

14. "Las Cienegas National Conservation Area," Bureau of Land Management, June 2, 2021, https://www.blm.gov/visit/las-cienegas-national-conservation-area; Jessica Hitt, Gita Bodner, and Karen Simms, "From Adaptive Management to Climate Adaptation at the Las Cienegas National Conservation Area: Starting Where You Are," Climate Adaptation Knowledge Exchange, November, 1, 2011, updated March 2, 2020, https://www.cakex.org/case-studies/adaptive-management-climate-adaptation-las-cienegas-national-conservation-area-starting-where-you-are.

have that same standard when we're lobbying for a bill in Idaho or Wyoming or Montana. So we try to be practical when we're dealing with different states to make sure those things work for that state, and that we don't go too far, but don't ask for too little either.

Rick Johnson of the Idaho Conservation League thinks conservation groups need to recognize that political realities define the contours of a successful approach. In places like Idaho and Utah in particular, he argues for conservation efforts that recognize the conservative values of the majority of citizens living in those states:

> The radical place in today's politics is actually the center because there's nobody there. I care deeply about the substantive reasons of why you protect these places, cultural, biological, ecological, and other values, but in the end it's all politics, and that's how my head works. I'm unapologetic about that. In politics, it's strictly the art of the possible, and it's a deal, and you're going to have to compromise.[15]

Find the Right Balance Between Nationally and Locally Focused Conservation Efforts

Large-landscape, multicounty conservation efforts face the dual political challenges of accounting for a wide range of interests and gaining the support of counties whose economic and political interests may not be fully aligned. Such efforts also tend to draw the interests of national conservation organizations, which depend on nationwide contributions to support their work. Nationalizing a conservation effort has the advantage of assembling greater lobbying power, but the disadvantage of sometimes inciting ideologically based opposition.

America's Red Rock Wilderness Act is one notable example. The act, first introduced in the 101st Congress by Representative Wayne Owens (D-Utah)—and reintroduced in every congressional session since 1989—aspires to protect

15. The term "radical center" is generally attributed to Bill McDonald of the Malpai Borderlands group; see Courtney White, "The Radical Center," Resilience, December 16, 2013, https://www.resilience.org/stories/2013-12-16/the-radical-center/.

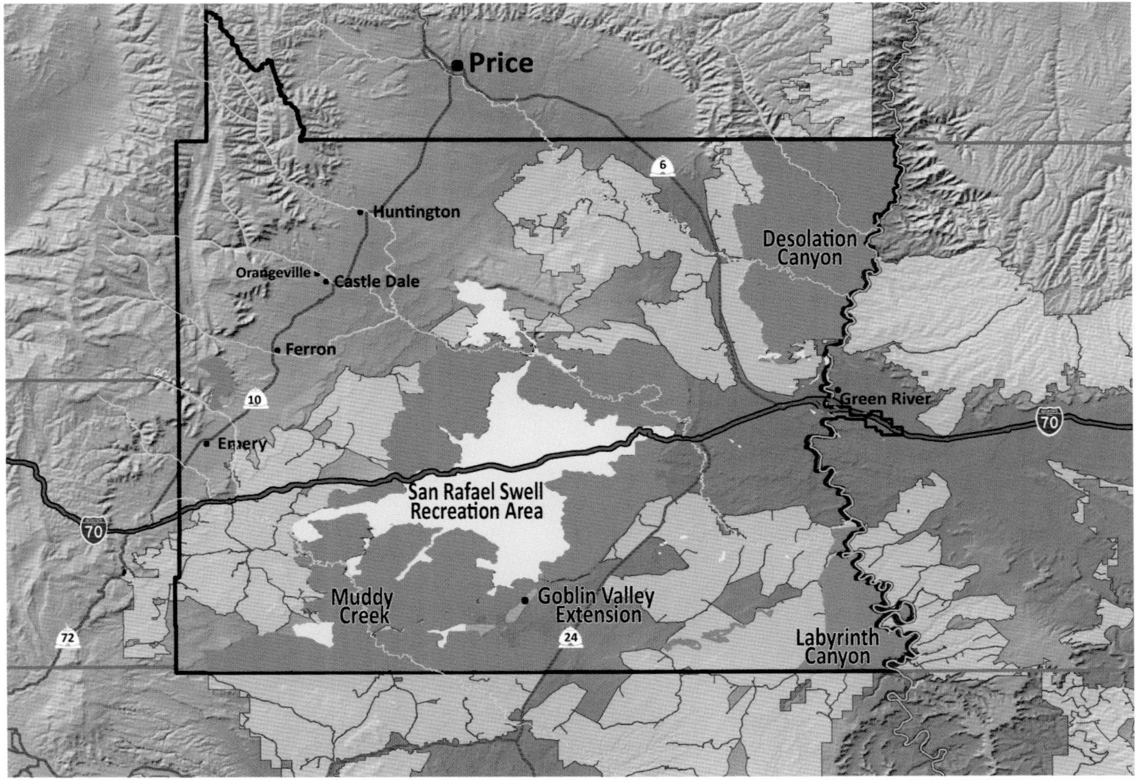

This map shows the areas proposed for wilderness protection in the 2020 version of America's Red Rock Wilderness Act (ARRWA), following the 2019 passage of the Emery County Public Land Management Act. Earlier protected areas include the lands protected as wilderness in the Emery County bill (*brick red*), the San Rafael Swell Recreation Area (*light blue-green*), and the extension of Goblin Valley State Park (*dark green*). The areas now proposed for wilderness protection (*yellow*) span multiple counties.

8.2 million acres of Utah's iconic red rock country.[16] The proposed wilderness spans multiple counties and would protect land equal to 12 percent of the total land area of the state of Utah. Thus far, this ambitious effort has failed, though its authors attribute multiple conservation successes to its existence.

Achieving large, landscape-scale protections is politically challenging, and wins can be infrequent. Some argue that choosing more modest approaches—long-term collaborative efforts with a broad group of stakeholder groups—may lead to more conservation successes. John Seebach and Anders Reynolds of the Pew Charitable Trusts, who worked together on the Emery County effort, point out the potential political liability of trying to protect 8.2 million acres of red rock country in Utah and nationalizing the campaign. "The larger a bill becomes, the easier it is to become nationalized," Seebach says. "Once it's nationalized, people retreat to their corners pretty fast. I think of America's Red Rock Wilderness Act as an example. As long as that covered as much of the state [as] it did, it was such a big-ticket item that it attracted funders and those interested from other states that really, really wanted to push it even though it wasn't a politically viable option."

"Having a hard jurisdictional boundary like a county saved us from mission creep a couple of times," Manuel adds. "There were stakeholders who insisted, 'well if you're protecting one side of the river you need to protect the other side of the river.' That's true. Those people aren't wrong. The conservation ethic would agree with that. But because we had these hard county boundaries we were able to say, 'we can't.' We can't go beyond the edges of this jurisdiction. I think that kept us from getting into larger issues."

On the other hand, Ray Bloxham of the Southern Utah Wilderness Alliance (SUWA) sees advantages in large, nationalized bills: "In my [view], when you do get conservation—and this is a nationwide issue, not just a

---

16. "The Story of America's Red Rock Wilderness Act," Southern Utah Wilderness Alliance, accessed June 2, 2021, https://suwa.org/issues/arrwa/the-story-of-americas-red-rock-wilderness-act/; Office of Representative Alan Lowenthal, "Congressman Lowenthal Introduces Bill to Protect Federal Lands in Utah as Wilderness," press release, February 6, 2020, https://lowenthal.house.gov/media/press-releases/congressman-lowenthal-introduces-bill-protect-federal-lands-utah-wilderness; Office of Senator Dick Durbin, "Durbin Introduces Bill to Protect America's National Parks and Monuments," press release, December 16, 2019, https://www.durbin.senate.gov/newsroom/press-releases/durbin-introduces-bill-to-protect-americas-national-parks-and-monuments.

local Utah one—it takes another twenty or thirty years to ever come back and gain more conservation. That's sort of where SUWA's been over its history. We don't want to take some piecemeal bill where we lose the political momentum to ever come back and get more conservation."

Involve the Recreation Community in Stakeholder Discussions

Public lands draw visitors seeking a wide variety of experiences: hiking, hunting, fishing, mountain biking, off-highway vehicle (OHV) trekking, boating, and climbing, to name but a few. The interests of those who might broadly be called "recreationists" and those who seek the quiet solitude of a wild landscape can both overlap and conflict. The sound of OHVs and their sometimes harmful damage to sensitive lands offend many conservationists. And proposals to restrict some areas solely to backpacking distress many recreationists.

In the past, recreation and conservation groups have not always worked together harmoniously. However, in recent years, both groups have begun to recognize the significant overlap in their goals for protecting public lands, and the political advantages of combining their advocacy efforts.

John Seebach of the Pew Charitable Trusts notes the important role that the recreation community played in efforts to shape and pass the Emery County bill:

> [The coalition that we worked on for the Emery County bill] was right at the nexus of conservation and recreation. It was a little bit more challenging for some of the more traditional conservation groups to see the value in taking the risk [of collaboration]. I think the recreation groups saw an opportunity to do conservation which would also benefit recreation. We worked quite a bit with recreation groups at some level or another.
>
> It's not always a perfect marriage. Sometimes there are particular types of recreation that might not be compatible with particular levels of conservation, but working together and engaging is the way that you avoid those kinds of problems.

Jessica Wahl of the Outdoor Recreation Roundtable sees the opportunity to develop land use protocols that provide for recreation-dominated activities in areas just outside lands protected as wilderness:

The family of Jason Keith, senior policy advisor for Access Fund, hiking in Little White Horse Slot Canyon, San Rafael Swell (*left*); and a hiker, navigating a slot canyon in the San Rafael Swell. Photos by Jason Keith and Whit Richardson (https://whitrichardson.com), respectively.

> I think the recreation community has felt, as a whole, conservation is the backbone of recreation. We [often talk] about the economic opportunities in the gateway communities [those close to wilderness or other protected lands], if the surrounding area were really marketed and managed for recreation. We think that in some areas [recreation] can almost be a buffer [between a gateway community and wilderness]. For example, where you see an area poised for development next to a wilderness study area [for potential wilderness designation], maybe that's a good area for mountain biking or RVs or a campground or boats. And we're hopeful that [recreation and conservation] can go hand in hand, that they can complement each other.

Ashley Korenblat of Public Land Solutions has witnessed the harm that can follow if the recreation and conservation communities fail to find common ground in efforts to protect public land. She, too, sees the value of "buffer" recreation areas near more heavily protected conservation areas. "Every time the conservation and recreation communities fight, the oil and gas industry laughs all the way to the bank," Korenblat says. "So it's sad when we fight. If you do a good job of organizing, or [do] the right type of mapping, a lot of recreation can happen on what is essentially front-country landscapes [proximate to more populated areas]. You can use those front-country recreation areas to protect, to buffer wilderness and national parks and other [remote, backcountry] places that are more sensitive."[17]

Drew McConville, senior managing director at the Wilderness Society, where he leads the organization's government relations team, points to the contributions of outdoor industry giants in lobbying for public lands protection alongside the conservation community. He emphasizes that recreation voices speak to business opportunities in public lands counties: "They implicitly answer the question 'what can public land protection do other than harm our economic prospects?'" He continues:

> [Recreation groups are now] leading more than they have been in conservation history. I think you see it at the company level. You've got companies like Patagonia, Keen, REI, and others that really stepped up into the advocacy space just in recent years, in a way that companies hadn't been before. Those guys are not just working with the big national groups but working at funding local conservation organizations to partner with. I think we have really good relationships across the conservation community with Outdoor Industry Association, with Outdoor Recreation Roundtable, and [with] Outdoor Alliance.
>
> Recreation voices have sway. They're business voices in their communities. They have a different message, and command respect and the attention of county officials and other elected officials at higher-level offices, that to a big degree the environmental groups just don't.[18]

Commit to Win-Win Outcomes

Virtually no piece of legislation ever results in full satisfaction for all affected parties. However, accepting that reality is often difficult, and in this society in particular, negotiations often evolve into battles not only over outcomes

17. See also Public Land Solutions (home page), accessed June 2, 2021, https://publiclandsolutions.org/.

18. See also Outdoor Industry Association (home page), accessed June 2, 2021, https://outdoorindustry.org/; Outdoor Alliance (home page), accessed June 2, 2021, https://www.outdooralliance.org/.

but over institutional or personal prestige. The evidence from our four case studies suggests that conversation among stakeholder groups, trust-building in living rooms, in meeting rooms, and in the landscape, and long-term commitment to finding common ground can lead to outcomes in which all interested parties leave with something they might not have achieved in a winner-take-all negotiation.

Former Emery County commissioner Ray Peterson notes that engagement with individuals and groups with different perspectives can often lead to better outcomes than any of them might have achieved individually:

> I go back to [Representative John Curtis's] metaphor: "get everyone into a box and play together." Some will say "well I can't, or I won't." They really don't want to [find compromise]. It's not easy. It's hard. This is the hardest work I've ever done, working with people who [have different] perspectives. Guess what? We all do. My perspective is different from yours. Yours is different from [that of] your loved ones. We all have our own perspectives. If we can't realize that everybody coming to the playground has a different perspective, and honor that, and expect that, we're not going to get anything done. The challenge is to allow everyone to have their voice, and also to educate people to the fact that we need to listen to everyone, and out of the collective efforts of the whole body, the end product is going to be better.

Recognize That the Path Toward Compromise Is Long and Winding

Efforts to assemble what became the Emery County Public Land Management Act spanned almost twenty-five years. Negotiations that led to passage of the Boulder–White Clouds Wilderness Bill spanned fifteen years. Establishing the Owyhee Canyonlands Wilderness took almost a decade's work, while crafting and passing the Washington County bill required six years. Bringing together stakeholders, building trust through numerous meetings, developing the political coalitions needed to pass a complex bill, and finding an optimal window for passing the bill take time—and lots of it. But investing that time can lead not only to mutually favorable outcomes, but to relationships that extend far beyond the issue that precipitated discussion: it can lead to a potential foundation for community understanding and growth.

"[Negotiating public lands bills] takes time," says Tyler Owens, who, as a member of the late senator Robert Bennett's staff, played a key role in building consensus for the Washington County bill. He continues:

> And when you put one fire out, something else happens. It's very, very, very complicated. When you're dealing with all that, you've got to have people who are willing to sit there and be honest with you, and you've got to devote time to process. And a lot of people don't like process. But the *process* [that culminated in the Washington County Bill] was the one thing that got us through. We could go back and say, "we examined this, here's what we talked about. We did a map, we exchanged papers, and we were able to do this methodically for all of these areas." We had a very broad group engaged, and we had the leadership at the highest levels engaged. I think that's really important for these efforts to work.

And Jason Keith, senior policy advisor for the Access Fund, pointed to an important ancillary benefit of spending time with individuals determined to seek a compromise solution to complex public lands issues: "The more time you spend with anybody, you see them as people instead of just some devil with a political ideology."[19]

Involve Local, State, and Congressional Leaders Early in the Process

Effective compromise starts with buy-in from citizens living adjacent to public lands, who share strong cultural ties to those lands, and whose economic future is interwoven with how those lands are used and managed. Emery County's Public Lands Council provided a forum for discussion among representatives of state and federal agencies, a variety of stakeholders both local and national, and the citizens of the county. The council's effort over twenty-five years to seek certainty regarding the future of nearby public lands—which make up 92 percent of the county—was essential to passage of the Emery County Public Land Management Act in 2019.

19. See also Access Fund (home page), accessed June 2, 2021, https://www.accessfund.org/.

Meeting of the Emery County Public Lands Council. Courtesy of ETV News.

"Those guys worked on this thing for a quarter of a century," Ron Dean, formerly a key member of Senator Orrin Hatch's (R-Utah) staff recalls. "They were determined that they were going to leave it all on the field, so to speak, and do everything they could to get some resolution. Along the way, you had commissioners who were skeptical of proposals, but were willing to kind of put their hands in their pockets and keep listening and keep taking the temperature of their constituents, sometimes knowing they were going to take a lot of political heat, but were willing to do the right thing."

Develop Trust Between Congressional Leaders and Stakeholders

Ray Peterson, former member of the Emery County Commission, commented on the importance of the trust relationship that quickly developed between county political leaders and then newly elected representative John Curtis (R-Utah). "When [Representative] John Curtis came on board, he was, from the get-go, very interested in what we were doing. When we told him what we were trying to do, he said 'I'm with you and I'm game. I'll run this bill for you.' And about the same time, Senator Hatch really became supportive. His staff took it on at his request."

"Having Senator Hatch and Representative Curtis be intimately involved personally, and Representative [Rob] Bishop (R-Utah), who was the chairman of the [House Natural Resources] Committee and could get it through the committee very quickly" was essential to the Emery County bill's success, Outdoor Recreation Roundtable executive director Jessica Wahl says. She

Representative Curtis's meetings with stakeholders. *Left photo*: Representative Curtis (*left*) and Friends of Cedar Mesa executive director Josh Ewing meet under a sandstone alcove adjacent to an Ancestral Pueblo structure. *Right photo*: Representative Curtis (*left*) meets with Hopi vice chairman Clark Tenakhongva. Photos courtesy of Jake Bornstein.

also tips her hat to congressional staffers. "I think the passion and work ethic and honesty of the staff cannot go unspoken about. If there were a different staff in either of those offices, I'm not sure you'd get to where you are today. Literally we talked to the staffers several times a week, if not several times a day, when it was getting down to the [finish] line. I know they were working overnight. I know that they were working every hour of every day. They were flying back to Utah, talking to commissioners. They were trustworthy, and they were passionate about getting a good deal."

Discuss Conservation Goals in Larger Cultural and Economic Contexts

Discussion about the future of public lands requires recognizing both the economic needs of local citizens as well as their cultural connections to these lands, and the importance of protecting areas of significant scientific, cultural, and spiritual value. Complicating these discussions on two extremes are those in the rural West who are skeptical of or hostile to the role of the federal government in public lands management, and individuals or groups who see only wilderness designation as a valid form of land protection. Finding constructive paths toward civil compromise requires reframing the terms of the conflict, and seeking solutions that achieve both conservation goals while enhancing the economic and cultural health of communities adjacent to public lands.

Recognize the Connection of Local Citizens to Surrounding Public Lands

Residents of public lands counties, over decades and sometimes centuries, have developed enduring connections to those lands. Many have grown to depend on the lands for economic sustenance, and believe sincerely that they have served as good stewards. Campaigns to protect public lands are sometimes seen as existential threats to "traditional" uses—ranching, mining, and oil and gas extraction—of public lands.

Gaining the support of local citizens and their representatives in Congress is essential to creating the context for legislation that advances both conservation goals and the interests of those who live closest to public lands.

"I think the conservation groups that were able to work best with the [county] commissioners were the ones who acknowledged on the front end that the commissioners and the locals in Emery County care about protecting the San Rafael Swell too," says Jake Bornstein, a staffer for Representative Curtis who was deeply involved in efforts to pass the Emery County bill. Bornstein adds:

> Representative Curtis has spent a great deal of time listening to his constituents in Emery County. He has come to realize that locals love the land and believe that, from their perspective, they have been good environmentalists.
>
> [Conservation groups sometimes argue that] "we have to come in and do this because you can't be trusted [to protect public lands]." The county commissioners will look around and say, "well, you know what: we've protected these lands for decades, for generations. We think we've done a pretty good job." They love the land, they love the beauty of the land, and they love the natural state of the land, and so the narrative that they can't be trusted with it just kills [efforts to negotiate].

Representatives from many conservation groups have come to understand that listening to the concerns of residents in public lands counties is an essential precursor to building trust and developing mutually beneficial outcomes. Paul Spitler, director of wilderness policy at the Wilderness Society, reflects on his longtime efforts to work with the citizens of Emery County as they developed multiple iterations of their public lands bill: "I've been to Emery County more times than I can count. I personally have come to know people there, and have had a relationship with them for over a decade."

Recognize the Economic Needs of Local Communities

Many counties that contain public lands worthy of wilderness or other protections are small, with populations under twenty thousand, and have until recently been primarily dependent on mineral extraction, logging, or ranching. Conservation efforts that change the management of nearby public lands are viewed by some residents of these counties as threats to local economies. At a less quantifiable level, such efforts are seen as having the potential to sever deep cultural connections to ranching, mining, or logging jobs. Urging large-scale conservation efforts when such "legacy" occupations are phasing out can further complicate a fraught situation.

Taking into account the current and future economic health of rural public lands counties is both critical in its own right and essential to achieving conservation goals. An important element of recent successful compromises regarding the use of public lands has been the involvement of the conservation and recreation communities in local stakeholder discussions on the future of public lands, and also as visible partners in community-based efforts to enhance the use of public lands protected as wilderness areas, national monuments, national conservation areas, or national recreation areas.

Jessica Wahl, executive director of the Outdoor Recreation Roundtable, recognizes the importance of working collaboratively with communities and counties adjacent to public lands in order to achieve recreation and conservation goals. "How do we work with those communities to supplement and not supplant what they already know and care about, and [to not undermine] their economy that has been there for a long time? I think that's the key. Recreation isn't probably going to take over all those full-time jobs tomorrow, but what it can do is allow there to be other areas of economic growth when some of the more traditional economies are not as stable or as certain."

Hunter Power Plant, south of Castle Dale in Emery County. The power plant is a major employer in the county, but it is scheduled to cease operations in the mid-2030s. Courtesy of Tricia Simpson, Wikimedia commons.

Paul Spitler of the Wilderness Society emphasizes the importance of conservation groups' willingness to work with communities to help them create sustainable economies that build on their proximity to protected public lands. "In order to secure the local support for wilderness, and in order to maintain local economies adjacent to the areas that we're seeking to protect, we need to be [cognizant] of the economic realities. We need to be working with local communities to build up their economies in a way that is tied to the health of the land."

The budgets of public lands counties are typically stretched to the limit. Yet they have obligations not only to county residents, but to visitors to the public lands within county boundaries, some of whom may require rescue from remote backcountry or, in some cases, emergency care. Conservation groups can work with the counties to advocate for federal or state funding to support the services they render to visitors from elsewhere in or outside the United States, and more generally for investments aimed at establishing a sustainable economy in the face of significant economic challenges.

Mountain biking (*left*) and bouldering in red rock country. Tourism, travel, and recreation brought $8.2 billion to Utah's economy in 2015, and contributed $1.1 billion in state and local tax revenue. Photos courtesy of Whit Richardson, https://whitrichardson.com.

Rick Johnson, former executive director of the Idaho Conservation League, emphasizes this point. "As I started working with [Representative Mike] Simpson (R-Idaho) in the early days [of the Boulder–White Clouds bill], I became as concerned as he was that Custer County schools would only open four days a week because they had no money, or that emergency services, one bad [tourist] rescue [in the backcountry], could kill a budget for a county for a whole year, or any number of different things that I'd never even thought about."

Work Locally to Allow Person-to-Person Involvement "On the Ground" and "In the Land"

One of the challenges in reaching a compromise regarding protection and use of public lands is gaining a deep understanding of the land in question. Discussions carried out around conference tables by participants staring at paper or projected maps encourage abstract rather than practical argument. Sketching the boundary of a protected region with a marker may obfuscate facts on the ground: a storage tank, a fence, an access road, or an important group of cultural sites. Meeting in the land, and "feeling" whether it merits wilderness or another form of protection, or whether it might instead be suitable for motorized recreation, can lead both to common-sense decisions and to building trust among individuals holding very different views regarding public lands use.

Former Emery County commissioner Ray Peterson describes the process of engaging stakeholders in efforts to "get to yes" on what became the Emery County Public Lands Management Act. "We did three dozen field trips with stakeholders," Peterson recalls. "All of the local knowledge of the [Public] Lands Council brought stakeholders to the table. When we were out on the ground, looking at maps, we asked 'OK, what makes sense?' We spent a lot, a lot, a lot of time. There's no substitute for being out on the ground. You can't make decisions while looking at a map in an office. [When you're on the ground you can] see the light go off in peoples' eyes . . . there's no substitute for that."

Ron Dean, a member of former senator Orrin Hatch's (R-Utah) staff, emphasizes the importance of having stakeholders meet in the landscape:

> [It's important to go] out on the ground—actually seeing it, and having all the stakeholders present looking at it at the same time. [That way] a stakeholder

> can say "I look at this ground through this prism." And another stakeholder says, "well I look at the ground through this prism." And another stakeholder says, "I look at the ground through this prism." It does several things. First, it becomes more [tangible] as to what's actually there, but it also provides an opportunity for all stakeholders to see the world through the eyes of someone else, and to then either decide at that point whether that view is a valid way to look at the public lands that they're talking about, or not. In most cases, it increases the collaborative spirit by leaps and bounds, to get all the stakeholders in the same place at the same time, talking about the same thing and the same issues.

Rick Johnson, former executive director of the Idaho Conservation League, makes an important, complementary point: meeting face-to-face on the home turf of nominal opponents of conservation is crucial to building an understanding of their viewpoints and needs, and creating the trust needed to forge compromise. "[To shape and pass a conservation bill] you have to have the support of the congressional delegation, and to have the support of the congressional delegation you have to have the support of other elected officials, and Chambers of Commerce, and businesses, and all these different constituencies that I would say conservation folks generally are not very good at talking to."

Representative Mike Simpson (R-Idaho) recalls the time he spent with Johnson in Custer County, where fifteen years of on-the-ground conversation in a county with four thousand residents built the trust needed to create and pass the Boulder–White Clouds Wilderness Bill. "I'd say half the time the environmentalists thought I was representing the cattlemen and the recreationists, and half the time [the cattlemen and recreationists] thought I was representing the environmentalists," Simpson says. "I told Rick [Johnson] one time, even if we never get this bill done, it's really been successful because we've got people sitting at the table that would not be seen in the same room with one another, and they actually sat and talked to one another. Now they actually consult with one another when they're going to do something, or they want to do something or whatever. That's a whole different and probably more important form of success than the Boulder–White Clouds itself."

"Where we have found a lot of success has been with building solutions with a very broad tent of community members," says Drew McConville of the Wilderness Society. "It takes a long time, but it's how you build durable conservation outcomes: by working together and sitting down with the local community, with the local economic interests, with recreation interests, and across the whole spectrum."

Be Creative in the Use of Public Lands Designations for Protected Areas

Individuals and groups seeking protection of public lands often focus first on the "gold standard" of protection: wilderness. Passing wilderness bills is difficult, and perhaps should be, given the finality of preserving large tracts of land in perpetuity. Conservationists often turn next to national monument designations, which offer significant protections, though not so strict as those that obtain in wilderness areas.

National monuments have the seductive advantage of their supporters' needing to convince only one individual: the president of the United States, who can declare a national monument with the stroke of a pen using powers granted under the Antiquities Act of 1906. Indeed, while Congress does have the power to create a monument legislatively, most have been created by executive action.[20] This executive action may evoke strong support nationally and even from some residents of public lands counties, but it can also evoke powerful negative reactions among local and state residents and political leaders.

Over the years, Congress has developed a variety of other land protection designations: national conservation areas, national recreation areas, national historic districts, and so on. In these cases, the management framework is established in the enabling legislation for a particular designation. Doing so allows protection tailored to the characteristics and value of the landscape and also makes space for purposes other than conservation as may be specified and constrained by the legislation.

The Emery County Public Land Management Act suggests the possibility of using a hybrid mix of public lands designations to effect both conservation and community goals. The act protects three large areas as wilderness, and another as the San Rafael Swell Recreation Area, a new designation created in the bill. The language creating the recreation area is similar in many respects

20. U.S. Library of Congress, Congressional Research Service, *National Monuments and the Antiquities Act*, by Carol Hardy Vincent, R41330 (2018).

Left photo: Representative Mike Simpson (*third from left*) visits Marsh Creek in Idaho to discuss endangered salmon runs. *Below photo*: Representative John Curtis (*left*) visits with Hopi vice chairman Clark Tenakhongva to discuss the importance of protecting cultural resources in Bears Ears. Photos from the representatives' pages at the U.S. House of Representatives website, https://www.house.gov.

to a "typical" national conservation area, but its name conveys other advantages to proximate communities as well as to the recreation community.

Jake Bornstein, of Representative John Curtis's staff, noted the value of being flexible in choosing acceptable nomenclature for protected areas:

> Everybody wants to preserve and protect. We spend so much time focusing on the names for [public lands designations]. If we could just change the name and have the same intent, you could accomplish the same thing. It's a shame that we don't do it more often. It's basically what we did in Emery County. We went through every potential name in the book. [We tried] a national heritage area. We tried national conservation area, a national conservation and recreation area, a national recreation area, and we ended on recreation area. We tried everything. We eventually just found one that worked for the locals.

Brandon Bragato is the Democratic staff director of the House Committee on Natural Resources, which is central to forging public lands legislation. He was frank in pointing to the toxicity of national monuments or national conservation areas in some communities, and emphasized the importance of the management language in a land use bill, as opposed to the name adopted for the protected area. "Impressions matter," Bragato says. "In many communities the term national monument or national conservation area is a lightning rod. So if calling it something else makes certain stakeholders feel better about it then [I think there can be a willingness] and an openness to do it. I think from our perspective the key there is to ensure that we get the management language right and that there aren't inconsistencies with how things are managed, or a loosening of standards when we advance designations of any kind."

The Wilderness Society's Paul Spitler echoes Bragato's view. "I couldn't care less what the area was called," Spitler says. "I care much more about how it's managed. Designations such as national conservation area, national scenic area, national recreation area—I could list another half dozen others—are pretty common and pretty standard ways to protect the ecological, recreational, and cultural values of a place that isn't suited to wilderness designation due to some noncompatible use. So organizationally we strongly support using such designations to protect places that aren't appropriate for wilderness."

Former Emery County commissioner Ray Peterson noted that county citizens wanted control over the process leading to public lands protection, and hoped at all costs to avoid a national monument declaration: "[The citizens of Emery County and other stakeholders said] 'We better try and do something, otherwise a national monument might be declared. We can be proactive and try and attempt to get some certainty through legislation before we have a process that takes place where we don't have any control.'"

Stuart Gosswein of the Specialty Equipment Market Association, a group that represents the interests of OHV groups and other specialized motorized recreation advocates, mentioned the preference of their group for legislative rather than executive action in protecting public land. "One of the things that was important to us [about Emery County] was that we had concerns that this area was going to be subject to a national monument designation," Gosswein says. "With that designation you [might have] a lot more land being effectively locked up than what you could negotiate through this legislation. So it was a balancing act of how much can you get through legislation—you might not get everything—but at least you're precluding the national monument designation. So that was a big success."[21]

21. See also Specialty Equipment Market Association (home page), accessed June 2, 2021, https://www.sema.org/.

Scott Groene of SUWA acknowledges that the recreation area designation advanced conservation goals for the San Rafael Swell region. But he worries that the recreation area designation and others like it might lead to legal fights over the meaning of the management language in the enabling legislation. "The nice thing about wilderness designation is that everybody knows what it means. There's a history to it. There are clear rules. There is certainty. When you step off into the national conservation areas and national recreation areas, you make up new rules each time, and you're probably going to end up fighting about details later. The [national recreation area] is far better than the status quo for the San Rafael Swell. It's a step forward, although it's not nearly as good as wilderness."

Give Communities and Tribes a Voice in Managing Public Lands

One of the important outcomes of the Emery County Public Land Management Act was the legislative requirement to create a seven-person advisory council to work with the BLM to develop a management plan for the San Rafael Swell Recreation Area. The council will be composed of representatives drawn from the Emery County Commission, the motorized recreation community, the nonmotorized recreation community, individuals holding grazing permits in the swell, the conservation community, and a federally recognized tribe. In addition, the council will include a representative with expertise in historical uses of the recreation area.

The advisory council will provide the community with a significant voice in shaping the future of an area that has played an important cultural and historical role in the county. This seat at the table for the local citizenry represented an important element in gaining community support for the Emery County bill.

Brock Johansen, a rancher, as well as the CEO of the highly visible local company Emery Telcom, commented that "one of the reasons that ranchers supported the Emery County bill is that they will have a voice in setting the management plan for the San Rafael Swell Recreation Area via the advisory council specified in the enabling legislation."

Former county commissioner Randy Johnson hoped that that council would continue to work with the BLM following formal completion and adoption of the management plan for the San Rafael Swell Recreation Area.

"I speak for Emery County on this in the sense that we felt that the [advisory council] should have as much time as they needed to [create a successful management plan]," Johnson says. "We would like the council to continue to function afterwards in an advisory role [to the BLM]."

Former undersecretary in the U.S. Department of Agriculture Robert Bonnie believes that increased collaboration between federal agencies like the USFS and communities would enable management of public lands that is both more effective and more accepted by local citizens. The challenge, however, is not only engaging local citizens, but changing the culture of the agencies so that they are more accepting of input from broad groups of stakeholders. "[In many places] communities are asking to have more control, and for some folks in the Forest Service, that's not easy," Bonnie says. "But I think for the most part the agency has recognized that if [you] want to have value as an agency, if you want to be successful, if you want to get projects done, it's way easier to do it if you've got a bunch of local people that are right there with you and you're linking arms with them."

Make Creative Use of School Trust Land Transfers and Congressionally Directed Spending

As each state entered the union, Congress granted it a fraction of the public lands included within its borders, with the goal of providing the state with a resource base to support public institutions.[22] Examining land use maps in many western states reveals vast tracts of public lands, which include within their boundaries a checkerboard pattern of one-mile-square (640-acre) "sections" of school trust lands.

In Emery County, school trust lands amounting to more than one hundred thousand acres were located within the three wilderness areas identified in the Emery County bill (Labyrinth Canyon, Desolation Canyon, and Muddy Creek), as well as inside the boundaries of the San Rafael Swell Recreation Area. A key part of the Emery County legislation involved establishing a framework for trading the school trust land embedded within newly protected areas for federal lands elsewhere in the state that have potential

22. Andy Laurenzi, "State Trust Lands: Balancing Public Value and Fiduciary Responsibility," Lincoln Institute of Land Policy, July 2004, https://www.lincolninst.edu/publications/articles/state-trust-lands.

for significant economic return. The expected payoff to SITLA and to Emery County from these trades is likely to be significant, a factor that played an essential role in gaining the acceptance of Emery County and the state of Utah.

The SITLA trade will serve the interests not only of Utahns, but of all Americans who stand to benefit from the new protections gained for public lands. The question arises whether developing mechanisms to facilitate similar school trust land trades might incentivize more conservation agreements similar to Emery County's.

Adam Sarvana, who serves as communications director for the House Committee on Natural Resources Democrats, discussed a legislative step that might facilitate land exchanges beneficial to both conservation and state interests. "If the state owns land inside an area of high conservation value, we want to transfer that ownership to the federal government and allow the state to acquire land that doesn't have high conservation value, but may have resource values that [the state] can then turn around into a line of revenue for the school trust portfolio. Such an approach could provide a win-win from both the conservation and state/county education perspective."

"The amount of revenue that Emery County is going to generate through SITLA land exchange is going to be significant [over the years]," the Wilderness Society's Paul Spitler says. "It's not a one-time thing. I think Emery County will do well. We have attempted in the past to work with the county on economic development, and really had some good conversations with county commissioners about their economic development needs and interests."

Outright purchase rather than trade of SITLA lands could be another avenue for providing compensation to the state and to counties adjacent to public land containing significant numbers of SITLA sections. The 1996 declaration of the Grand Staircase-Escalante National Monument included a provision that ultimately enabled both trades and purchases of school trust land within monument boundaries.

Cody Stewart, former director of federal affairs for Utah governor Gary Herbert, a Republican, reflected on the value of having the option to purchase school trust lands outright in the past, and lamented that such purchases would probably be precluded by current congressional rules. "[Today] those [sorts of] land purchases would be described as an earmark, which [as of 2015] violates House rules. Hence, [purchasing school trust lands] as an option is procedurally off the table. I think you could fix that, but you'd have to change the definition of earmarks."

Representative Mike Simpson (R-Idaho) reflected on the importance of such earmarks, known more formally as congressionally directed expenditures, in providing resources for communities in Custer County, Idaho, adjacent to the Boulder–White Clouds Wilderness. "We did economic development earmarks for the county," recalls Simpson. "The best example is [one that funded] the Forest Service to build a bike trail from Redfish Lake to Stanley, a four-mile bike trail. That's going to be for economic development. They're building a community center in Challis that we got earmarks for, back when we could earmark. We got money for roads."

Economist Ben Alexander of the Resources Legacy Fund—an organization that facilitates partnerships aimed at protecting ocean, land, and water resources—argued that conservation groups should support legislative efforts aimed at providing rural communities with tools to diversify their economies. Acting as partners with those communities might, over time, create an environment more conducive to collaborative discussions regarding the future of nearby public lands. Alexander says:

> Many conservation groups see the practical advantages of working with rural constituents—who live in states that have disproportionate influence in the Senate—on how public lands policy is legislated and governed. I don't know if there's one set of conservation viewpoints on this, but clearly some do see the value of consistent appropriation and reform proposals which would help solve rural problems. [Those groups] have political power that could help and enable that change. If those interests could [help] enact that change—and there are members of the conservation community working on that right now—and they could do that in common cause with some of the representatives of rural places, then all of a sudden you have a really interesting politics.

Use Public Lands Transfers and Purchases to Advance Conservation and Rural Economies

Outright sale of less-sensitive public lands can provide funds for communities while simultaneously incentivizing efforts to protect conservation-worthy public lands. An example was provided by Allen Freemyer, a former senior staff member on the House Committee on Natural Resources.

Freemyer recalled that revenues from a sale of public lands to the city of Yerington, Nevada, were then made available for acquisition of conservation-worthy lands. The sale, which provided Yerington with needed land for development, also helped build support for the 1998 Southern Nevada Public Land Management Act, which also designated wilderness. "[The revenues from that sale] were made available for land acquisition and other activities in the Southern Nevada Public Land Management Act, where we also were able to designate some Forest Service wilderness. That bill was supported by the conservation community."[23]

Red Rock Canyon National Conservation Area Visitor Center, near Las Vegas, Nevada. Funds for the center were made available through the sale of nonconservation-worthy public lands as designated in the Southern Nevada Public Land Management Act of 1998. Bureau of Land Management.

Prior to the legislation creating the Boulder–White Clouds Wilderness, Representative Mike Simpson (R-Idaho) was able to pass a bill that benefited its home county, Custer County, Idaho, in two ways. First, the bill enabled transfer of nonsensitive public lands to the community of Stanley, Idaho, so that the community could build low-income housing. In addition, Simpson earmarked funds for several projects aimed at supporting economic development in the area. Were earmarks to return sometime in the future, they offer another avenue for providing economic assistance to rural communities adjacent to public lands, perhaps with the ancillary benefit of making the path toward negotiated public lands protections far less fraught.

23. The referenced bill is 144 Cong. Rec. S12735–36 (1998) (enactment of the Southern Nevada Public Land Management Act).

Develop Public-Private Partnerships to Advance Conservation and Economic Goals

In addition to participating in conservation collaboratives and similar mechanisms for stakeholder-driven discussions around the future of public lands, many conservation groups are expanding their efforts to serve as partners in advancing community projects. Doing so over time not only brings expertise and additional hands to meeting community challenges but creates an environment in which conservation groups are viewed as partners rather than antagonists. Paul Spitler of the Wilderness Society describes two such efforts:

> One of the [collaborative] efforts that we [the Wilderness Society] have been involved in in Montana is a multifaceted land management proposal. It includes some wilderness designations, which are additions to the Bob Marshall Wilderness and Scapegoat Wilderness.[24] It also includes some forest restoration pieces which restore national forest lands that have been degraded due to past management and fire suppression. And it includes some pieces which are in support of motorized and nonmotorized recreation. Part of that proposal will be implemented through legislation (which has been introduced by Senator Jon Tester [D-Mont.] and is currently pending before Congress), and part will be implemented through other actions outside of legislation.
>
> In addition, the Wilderness Society worked with the local timber company and a really diverse group of stakeholders in Montana to develop what's known as the Southwestern Crown of the Continent Collaborative.[25] This is a collaborative effort with very diverse stakeholders that seeks to advance forest restoration on the national forest. Through that effort, we were able to successfully write a proposal that was ultimately selected as one of the, at the time, ten national projects to be funded through a program called the Collaborative Forest Landscape Restoration Program.[26] . . . The proposal has, over the course of the past seven or eight years now, it's received tens of millions of dollars. It

---

24. Tristan Scott, "Tester Announces Legislation to Expand Bob Marshall Wilderness," *Flathead Beacon* (Kalispell, Mont.), February 22, 2017, https://flatheadbeacon.com/2017/02/22/tester-announces-blackfoot-clearwater-stewardship-act/.

25. Southwestern Crown Collaborative (home page), accessed June 2, 2021, https://www.swcrown.org/.

26. "Collaborative Forest Landscape Restoration Program," U.S. Forest Service, accessed June 2, 2021, https://www.fs.fed.us/restoration/CFLRP/.

has restored tens of thousands of acres of forest, aquatic habitats, streams, and yet provided about 150 jobs per year in [rural] Montana.

That effort was funded through a specific program that's focused on collaborative forest restoration that Congress had funded at $40 million a year. The 2018 Farm Bill extended and expanded the funding authorization for that program, one of the most successful forest restoration programs ever.[27]

Build Political Support in Washington

Creating consensus agreement regarding the future of public lands at a local level represents but a first step in advancing successful legislation. The next steps require creative leadership, relationships that transcend party and ideological lines, a unique political opportunity, or a vehicle that draws the support of a diverse cohort of legislators.

Passing the Emery County Land Bill in the 116th Congress required that Representative John Curtis (R-Utah) work with the Democratic majority in the House, and that Senator Orrin Hatch's (R-Utah) successor, Senator Mitt Romney (R-Utah), seek the support not only of majority leader Mitch McConnell (R-Ky.), but of key Democratic senators such as Richard Durbin (D-Ill.). "A key component of success [on the Emery County bill] was getting [now-former] Congresswoman Colleen Hanabusa (D-Hawai'i) to cosponsor the bill with me," Curtis recalls. "It was huge to have the Democratic cosponsor on the committee of jurisdiction. It made all the difference in the world."

The Owyhee Public Land Management Act was passed in 2009, when Democrats controlled both houses of Congress, as well as the presidency. As a result, Senator Mike Crapo (R-Idaho) needed to seek partners among his Democratic colleagues, and to work as well with Ken Salazar, his former Senate colleague and the newly appointed secretary of the interior.

Rick Johnson, formerly of the Idaho Conservation League, recalls that "there was a process of negotiation that went on for years to create the agreement on the Owyhee County bill that Senator Mike Crapo brought to D.C. Then there was a key negotiation process where the Democrats took that draft bill, massaged it a bit, and said 'this is what we can do,' to which Crapo agreed."

27. See also "Farm Bill," U.S. Department of Agriculture, accessed June 2, 2021, https://www.usda.gov/farmbill.

The impending retirement of Senator Hatch after forty-two years in office—the longest tenured Senate Republican in history—presented a unique window for passing the Emery County bill. Hatch's seniority, and the respect he had earned over more than four decades, meant that his colleagues were inclined to support legislation in recognition of his legacy. His support for the public lands legislation that included the Emery County bill was critical to attracting support from Republican senators, many of whom normally view such bills with considerable skepticism.

Jessica Wahl of the Outdoor Recreation Roundtable believes that the Emery County bill would not have become law without Hatch's support:

> There was a senator who was powerful and was leaving. [In fall 2018], there was momentum, because the Republicans knew that they might lose at least one or maybe both majorities in the House and Senate. So that's the perfect policy window opening. In any other circumstance, if it wasn't a lame duck year for Congress, if the Congress weren't flipping, if we didn't have a senator like Hatch leading, you might have gotten a deal, but you might not have gotten it across the finish line. I think policy windows are very little talked about but can be a very important component for how these bills actually pass.

Brandon Bragato, the Democratic staff director for the House Committee on Natural Resources, agrees with Wahl. "Having Senator Hatch identify the Emery County bill as a priority for a 'retirement present' is definitely one of the things that enabled [Senator] Mitch McConnell to prioritize the package and move it through some of the opposition within his party including from Senator [Mike] Lee [R-Utah]."

In the recent past, most large-scale public lands bills have been included in packages comprising multiple pieces of legislation. Often referred to as "omnibus legislation," these bills gain support as members of Congress see an opportunity for having one or more of their stalled bills included in a larger package that might pass. A member might not like some or even many bills that find their way into the omnibus, but they will nevertheless agree to support it in order that their legislation pass. Of the four conservation efforts discussed in the previous chapter, only Boulder–White Clouds passed as stand-alone legislation.

Bragato emphasized the advantages of using omnibus bills as a vehicle for public lands legislation:

> [Most of the public lands] bills that we work on don't get enacted into law outside of an [omnibus] lands package. They come up in two- to five-year cycles. Individual bills typically can't make it to the Senate floor. They get reported out of Senate Energy and Natural Resources, and because of opposition from individual senators that are able to put holds on bills, they don't get brought up. That's the dynamic that requires us to find a vehicle and negotiate a package. The majority and minority in both the Senate and the House side identify tentpole pieces for each party that makes a package of bills interesting from each [party's] perspective.

Jessica Wahl notes that including reauthorization and funding for the Land and Water Conservation Fund (LWCF) in the omnibus bill was important to legislators in both parties, while the Emery County bill and Hatch's support for it were essential to gaining Republican support. "A lot of groups were in the public lands package, partly because the Land and Water Conservation Fund was part of it," Wahl says. "There is really good bipartisan support for LWCF, and a lot of people wanted to see that get done. But I think Emery County being part of the package really brought Republicans to the table, along with Senator Hatch, who was on his way out. His interest in getting this over the finish line was monumental—with his leadership position and the access to Senator McConnell and others."

Athan Manuel of the Sierra Club believes that inclusion of the Emery County bill was sine qua non for passing the omnibus legislation. "That [omnibus] package would not have gotten done without Emery County's being the centerpiece of it," Manuel says. "It had to be something big, and it had to have bipartisan support."

"As important as our bill was, and as complex as it was, I still believe that the workload of taking that through on its own would have been tremendous," former Emery County commissioner Randy Johnson says. "We might still be at it if we had not packaged it with the larger lands bill."

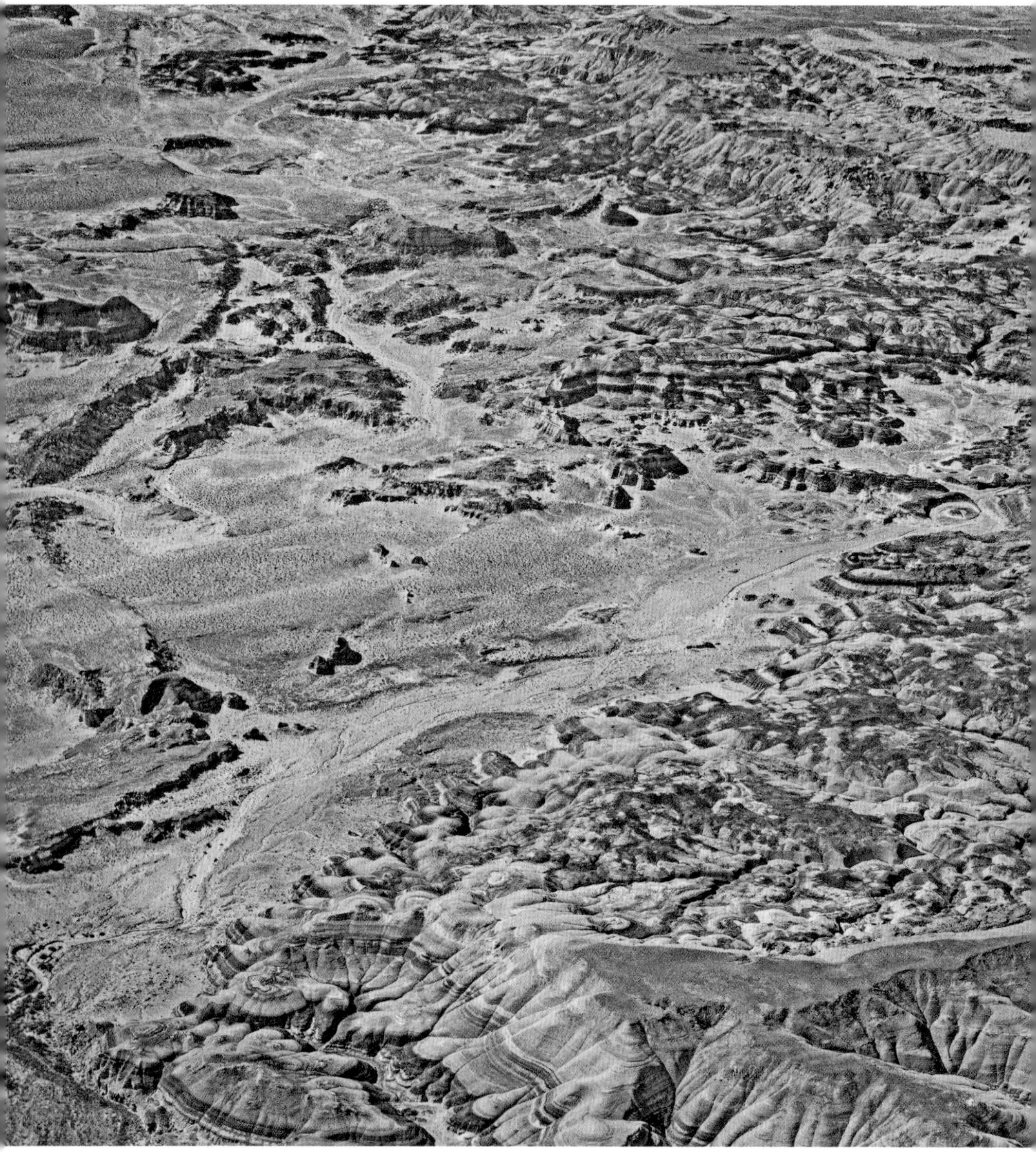

Red Desert, west of North Caineville Reef. Aerial photo by Stephen E. Strom.

Aligning Conservation Goals with the Economies and Cultures of Public Lands Counties

Citizens of many rural counties in the West have long looked to public lands as central to their livelihood: cattle and sheep graze on public lands, timber is harvested in national forests, and minerals are extracted on either Bureau of Land Management (BLM) or U.S. Forest Service (USFS) land. Moreover, jobs that depend on ranching, mining, or logging have provided not only income, but dignity and a link with generations past.

Over time, however, the role of ranching and resource extraction has decreased, as automation has reduced the demand for labor, and as the need for fossil fuels has diminished in response to the requirement that more energy be generated by renewable sources.

To cite one particularly dramatic example, S&P Global Market Intelligence notes that over the period from 2011 to 2019, the number of tons of coal produced annually in the United States dropped by nearly a factor of two, from almost 300,000 tons at the beginning of 2011, to 150,000 tons at the end of 2019. During that same period, the number of employees involved in coal production dropped from approximately 95,000 to 50,000.[1]

Throughout the West, rural counties are facing the need to chart a future in which a sustainable economy is likely to depend increasingly on attracting jobs in services (health care, education, sales, restaurants, and hotels); recreation and tourism; the knowledge industries; and income both from retirees who choose to move into these areas and from younger workers who choose to work remotely in amenity-rich communities located near public lands, "Zoom towns."[2]

Some rural counties having large shares of public land—"public lands counties"—have already embraced plans to develop a more diverse economic base. Others are more skeptical of change, as their citizens face the cultural challenges of transitioning from "real" jobs in ranching and resource extraction, as well as the likelihood that "outsiders"—tourists, permanent retirees, and remote workers—will effect lasting, and not necessarily welcome,

---

1. Taylor Kuykendall and Gaurang Dholakia, "US Coal Mining Employment Hits New Low at the End of 2019, May Go Lower in 2020," S&P Global Market Intelligence, February 19, 2020, https://www.spglobal.com/marketintelligence/en/news-insights/latest-news-headlines/us-coal-mining-employment-hits-new-low-at-the-end-of-2019-may-go-lower-in-2020-57173047.

2. Jonathan Thompson, "How the Zoom Boom Is Changing the West," *High Country News* (Paonia, Colo.), January 1, 2021, https://www.hcn.org/issues/53.1/infographic-how-the-zoom-boom-is-changing-the-west/.

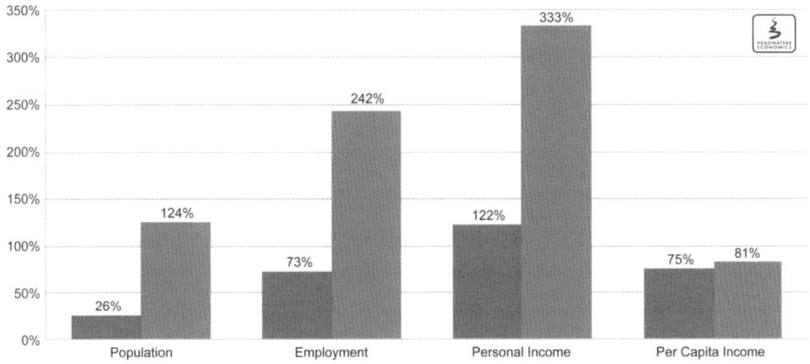

Changes from 1970 to 2015 in population, employment, personal income and per capita income for rural counties with the highest proportion (upper quartile, *blue*) and lowest proportion (lower quartile, *orange*) of both protected and unprotected federal lands. Rural counties with higher proportions of federal lands score higher on all metrics. Data are from a Headwaters Economics study.

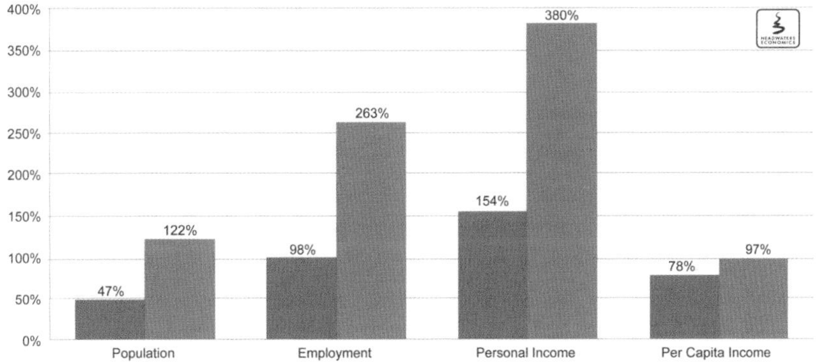

Changes from 1970 to 2015 in population, employment, personal income and per capita income for rural counties with the highest proportion (upper quartile, *blue*) and lowest proportion (lower quartile, *orange*) of protected federal lands. Rural counties with higher proportions of protected federal lands score higher on all metrics. Proximity to protected public lands neither enhances nor diminishes economic or demographic performance when compared with counties with unprotected Bureau of Land Management or Forest Service land. Data are from Headwaters Economics.

cultural changes to their communities. In light of the tensions that inevitably accompany change, how are public lands counties faring during this era of inevitable transition?

The good news is that rural public lands counties show significant demographic and economic advantages when compared with rural counties in the

West lacking large amounts of public land.[3] This conclusion holds both for public lands counties having protected lands (national parks, national monuments, national conservation areas) and for those that do not. Their natural amenities—the grandeur of the scenery, the chance to find solitude in rugged canyons or forested mountains, the opportunities for outdoor recreation—can, and often do, attract entrepreneurs, tourists, and retirees, as well as younger individuals willing and able to work remotely.

The changes in the economies of public lands counties are reflected in the decline in ranching, agriculture, and natural resource extraction, and the growth of tourism, the service industry, government jobs, and what economists refer to as "nonlabor income": income from investments, Medicare and Social Security payments, and payments associated with economic hardship.

The recent economic history of Emery County provides a vivid example.[4] In 1980, nonservice income (from ranching, mining, and construction) was dominant in the county, accounting for twice the income as that derived from service income (health care, retail, food services, education), and six times that from nonlabor sources. By 2017, nonlabor sources represented the major income source in the county, accounting for nearly three times as much as either service-related, or nonservice income.

However, despite the advantages that proximity to public lands confer on rural public lands counties relative to comparable counties lacking significant public lands, median income in public lands counties lags behind that characterizing the rest of the country. Custer (92 percent federal land), Emery (80 percent), Owyhee (78 percent), and Washington County (75 percent) exemplify the disparity: per capita income in those counties is only two-thirds that of the United States taken as a whole. Rural public lands counties have not as yet been able to capture as large a portion of the jobs that are driving the "new economy" both in the West and, more broadly, around the United States.[5]

3. Megan Lawson, "Federal Lands in the West: Liability or Asset?," Headwaters Economics, February 21, 2017, https://headwaterseconomics.org/public-lands/federal-lands-performance/.

4. "Emery County, UT," Economic Profile System, Headwaters Economics, accessed June 2, 2021, https://headwaterseconomics.org/apps/economic-profile-system/49015.

5. All statistics from the Economic Profile System of Headwaters Economics, accessed June 2, 2021: "Custer County, ID," https://headwaterseconomics.org/apps/economic-profile-system/16037; "Emery County, UT," https://headwaterseconomics.org/apps/economic-profile-system/49015; "Owyhee County, ID," https://headwaterseconomics.org/apps/economic-profile

Tourist facilities in Escalante, Utah: Escalante Outfitters (*left*), Utah Canyon Guides (*middle*), and Canyon Country Lodge (*bottom*). The town of Escalante is adjacent to the Grand Staircase-Escalante National Monument. As the economic impact of traditional activities—mining and ranching—decreases, towns like Escalante that are proximate to protected lands look to diversify their economies. Growth of tourism and recreation can represent one element of an evolving economic mix. Photos by Stephen E. Strom.

Advancing the economic health of rural public lands counties should be a shared national goal. Wallace Stegner challenged us to "create a society to match its scenery."[6] How can we meet his challenge and work with rural public lands counties to develop robust, sustainable economies while respecting local culture and protecting valuable public lands?

In what follows, we suggest some tangible actions that might be taken to support the economic health of rural communities in public lands counties.

Develop a Community Vision for a Sustainable Economic Future

The first step toward building a sustainable economic future for a public lands county is to recognize that the rural West is changing, and with it the mining and ranching jobs that have been the economic and cultural foundation for many communities located in such counties. The next is to develop a consensus vision for the county's future, and a plan for achieving that vision.

"Visioning for a community is so critical," Representative John Curtis (R-Utah) says. "If you can evaluate something from the thirty-thousand-foot level, then you can get people to agree on the end outcome twenty years from now. If you focus on a week from now or a year from now, it's really hard to get people to agree on the end outcome. I know as mayor [of Provo, Utah] we were able to do that."

The case studies in prior chapters demonstrate how Emery and Washington Counties in Utah and Custer and Owyhee Counties in Idaho came together to develop and implement long-term visioning plans.

Support Communities in Meeting the Challenges of Economic and Cultural Change

In order for rural public lands counties to flourish, their economies will need to evolve. Change, even in the form of carefully thought out and sensitively implemented transition, is challenging, particularly in counties where there

-system/16073; "Washington County, UT," https://headwaterseconomics.org/apps/economic-profile-system/49053.

6. Wallace Stegner, *The Sound of Mountain Water: The Changing American West* (1946; New York: Vintage Books, 2017), 32.

is fierce cultural attachment to jobs such as mining and ranching—jobs that have sustained many families for generations.

Allen Freemyer, former senior staff member on the House Committee on Natural Resources, emphasizes the cultural dimension involved in envisioning a new future. "Part of the struggle is needing to build economies [in public lands counties], but [the citizens of those counties] not wanting their communities to change very much. There's a reason these people live there, right? It's because it's a small community with the values that these people want and desire, and the problem is that what comes with that quality of life is [that without change], your kids are going to have to leave town to find decent-paying jobs."

"When we talk economics in a rural context, we're talking culture," Ben Alexander, economist at the Resources Legacy Fund, says. "They are still making investments in, and supporting programs that support, an extractive culture, a culture of land use, understood historically. They are not thinking about and supporting economic development that is more culturally new, and urban in some ways."[7]

"What I see generally is that [rural logging counties] don't want to have those discussions," Lindsay Slater, chief of staff for Representative Mike Simpson (R-Idaho) comments. "They don't want to talk about their future. I think they'd love to have a whole different [future] but they don't want to think about change. It proves difficult when you try to come up with a solution to help them. They don't want to talk about solutions. Loggers and people who grew up in a logging family that still want to log, even though there are no logging jobs."

Brock Johansen, CEO of Emery Telcom, well knows the challenges of finding new paths toward a sustainable economic future. The remaining coal-fired power plants in Emery County are scheduled to cease operation between 2035 and 2040. Coal mining will no longer serve as a foundation for the local economy as the nation shifts from fossil fuels to renewables. Leaders in the community are working aggressively to explore paths toward a more diverse economic future. For example, Emery County is now home to the San Rafael Research Center, where the county and three major universities in Utah are collaborating in an effort to attract businesses or groups working on

7. See also Resources Legacy Fund (home page), accessed June 2, 2021, https://resourceslegacyfund.org/.

solar energy, thorium reactors, and coal-to-carbon fiber research.[8] However, many residents fear change, as jobs in the mines and at the power plants have paid well and sustained families for generations.

"The county commissioners, the lead business people, are [thinking about a different future], but the general public as a whole, they're coal miners," Johansen says. "They don't see another future. They see that their industry is dying. What makes it hard with Emery County is the push right now against coal: They've had one [power] plant shut down, and what's looming on the horizon is that the current plants [have] an end date on them. It's real hard for the community to have [what feels like] an end date on your community."

"[Counties] have to have the political will to want to change the way they think about their public lands," explains Ashley Korenblat, the managing director of Public Land Solutions. "We're involved with a lot of communities that are pivoting from dependence on resource extraction

8. Julie Johansen, "Emery County Commissioners Developing San Rafael Research Center," ETV News, June 26, 2019, https://etvnews.com/emery-county-commissioners-developing-san-rafael-research-center/.

Kayaking in red rock country. Photo courtesy of Whit Richardson, https://whitrichardson.com.

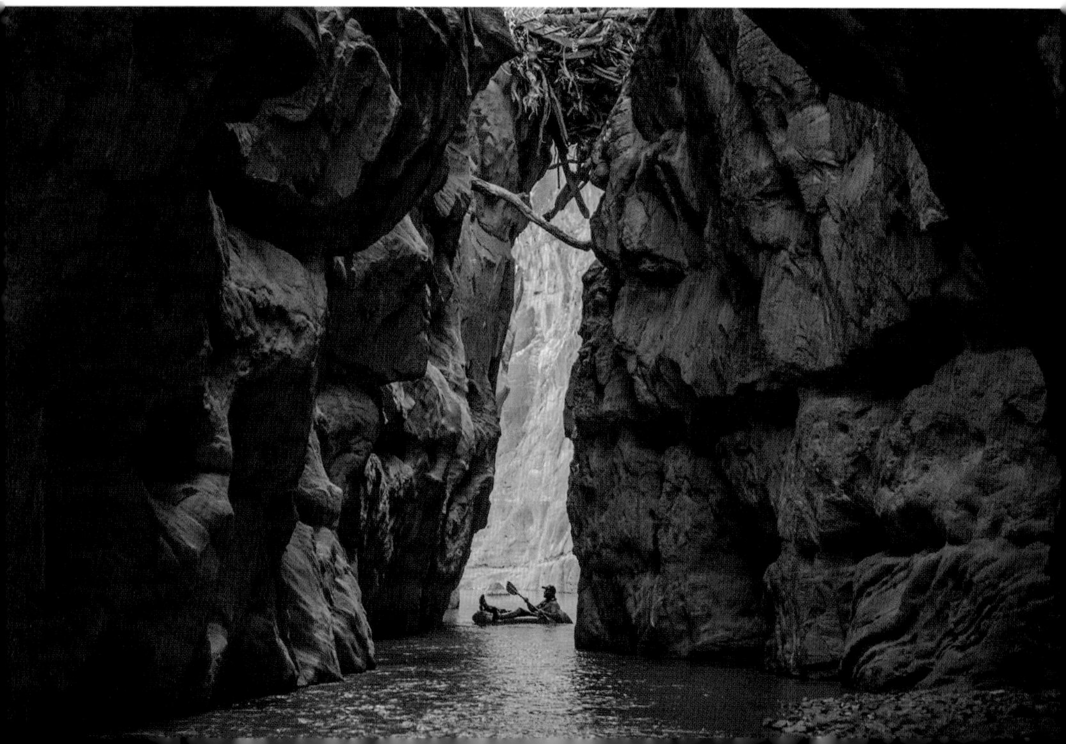

Coal combustion testing equipment arriving at the San Rafael Research Center in Emery County. Courtesy of ETV News.

to recreation. The first thing that has to happen is that they have to decide they want to do it. We're asking them to make a hard pivot from thinking that the most honest way to make a living is to pull something off the land, like being a farmer or a rancher or a miner, . . . to participating in the recreation economy."

Recreation offers one way to transition from economies based on resource extraction. Attracting recreationists and tourists not only provides immediate economic benefit, but may serve as a catalyst for attracting retirees (along with their retirement funds), entrepreneurs, and the infrastructure (new roads, hospitals, and schools) needed to support them.

What often overcomes what might be called "cultural inertia" and motivates planning for the future is an external event: the closing of a mine, or of a coal-fired power plant. That has been the case in Farmington, New Mexico, where Korenblat is currently working to help the town and surrounding communities envision a future in which recreation jobs begin to replace those that have been, or will be lost. "In Farmington, they are faced—and

Price, Utah, as well—they have a solid date, a certain date that their coal-fired power plant is going to close. That motivates the community to really start looking at what their other resources are, and when they [do that, they] decide that recreation wants to be a component of their future economic development."

Ben Alexander looks to rural public lands counties that have successfully initiated structured discussions about their future. "Those counties ask 'What are the human resources, technical and financial resources, the partnerships we need to develop?' Then you [can] start to build those relationships and resources, and as you do that you move towards execution. That's what I see in places that are successfully navigating the difficult transitions [and] including public lands as an asset in the mix of things that they're considering. It's really exciting to see it when [it happens]."

Former Idaho Conservation League executive director Rick Johnson believes that the public lands counties that see economics and conservation as intertwined will have sustainable futures. "I think you [initiate dialogue about sustainable futures] by linking these communities with conservation," Johnson says. "[You] do this by taking what is often the most volatile issue in that community [conservation versus jobs], and in the process of resolving that volatile issue you create a different future. That begins with a conversation. That begins with disparate interests stitching something together that they cannot do independently. I think conservation is an anchor to how we make democracy work in the rural West."

To reach a sustainable economic outcome, rural public lands communities will need not only local leadership and a commitment to grassroots collaborative processes to imagine a different future, but support from state and federal governments, nonprofit organizations, and conservation groups.

In Ben Alexander's mind, many individuals far removed from the challenges of rural public lands counties "[can sometimes] disparage people [from public lands counties] because they want to keep doing what they've been doing. They say, 'these people just don't have any adaptive capacity at all. Or these people just have no leadership. Or these people have no access to resources. They've just been passed by.' There's so much condescension out there."

If we aspire to have rural public lands counties be partners in conservation efforts, their citizens need—and deserve—a combination of respect and support for planning a future that in the fullness of time will benefit us all.

Provide Funding to Support Community Visioning and Planning Studies

Collaborative planning for a sustainable future depends on a combination of sound leadership and the participation of a wide range of stakeholders from the local community, the state, and the country.

According to Ben Alexander, once formed, collaborative groups need to ask themselves, "Do you have an underlying strategy for success here? Are you leading the way forward? Do you see how you can diversify the sources of wealth in your community? Are you starting to capitalize on larger market trends and changes locally? How are you preparing your kids for success? What are the infrastructure needs for tomorrow's economy? All those kinds of things are about taking control of your destiny."

Taking the next steps requires collaboration with individuals having experience in economic planning and, later, grant writers, followed by consultants who can work with counties to recruit or retain businesses, and to attract entrepreneurs as well as individuals looking to take advantage of the amenities offered by public lands counties. Counties with populations as small as Emery (10,000), Custer (4,200), and Owyhee (12,000) may lack the full range of expertise needed to plan and then grow their economies.[9]

"[Most rural public lands counties] don't have the resources to do the sort of planning and advertising, public outreach and so on, that would allow them to take the first step toward diversifying their economy," says Allen Freemyer. "Those challenges are faced by many rural counties of that size. The population base isn't large, [nor is] their economic base."

To carry out successful planning thus requires funding from some combination of federal, state, and private sources. Finding such funds can be a challenge—another impediment to initiating steps toward more diverse, sustainable economies.

"Emery County could really benefit from having funds for individuals who can help recruit small businesses and companies to come to the county," Emery Telcom CEO Brock Johansen says. "But Emery County can't do that alone."

Representative Mike Simpson (R-Idaho) remembers his time on the city council in Blackfoot, Idaho, and the difficulty in gaining access to individuals

9. All statistics from the Economic Profile System of Headwaters Economics: "Custer County, ID"; "Emery County, UT"; "Owyhee County, ID."

with the skills to locate opportunities, and to apply for funding. "Applying for anything federal is tough for rural counties," Simpson says. "Boise had a guy who did nothing but apply for grants and knew every grant that was available. In Blackfoot, we didn't have that kind of person. We had to rely on somebody else telling us that [a grant] was available."

Representative John Curtis (R-Utah) is keenly aware of the need to provide expert assistance to rural public lands counties ready to plan for a sustainable future. "In my opinion, there is a severe need for planning. I really think we need to see that as one of the steps still ahead of us, is to help these communities plan for a diverse economy, one that's not solely built on tourism, but handles tourism well, as a good component."

Brock Johansen hoped that funding for an economic development director might come from the state of Utah. However, he argues that the state has yet (even in 2021) to make a commitment at the level needed. "How is a rural commissioner going to go out to some company back east and talk them into coming out here? Especially when they can't afford to spend more than $50,000 or $60,000 for a rural economic development director. [The commissioner] isn't the guy that you can put in a room and recruit a business. That's where the state really should come in and help us."

Cody Stewart, who served as director of federal affairs for former governor Gary Herbert (R-Utah), believes that Utah needs to do more to help rural counties:

> I think that the state probably needs to reconfigure some of the incentives that they have in place now. They still seem to be giving a lot of incentives to corporations that are locating along Silicon Slopes (the corridor of high-tech industry located between Provo and Salt Lake City) or on the Wasatch Front—areas which don't really need new economic development—whereas these rural communities still have 8, 9, 10 percent unemployment and just don't have many prospects. The state needs to take a look at reconfiguring incentives to encourage more development off the Wasatch Front and into these rural areas. It wouldn't be too difficult to do that if the political will is there.

Former Emery County commissioner Randy Johnson hopes that the state will be more forthcoming with planning assistance. He notes that in 2017 "[Governor] Herbert challenged Utah businesses to create twenty-five thousand jobs throughout rural Utah by the end of 2021, demonstrating that he is very aware of [the situation in] southern Utah. [We are also fortunate to] have a very proactive state senator from Emery County, so I think there's a possibility we could do some lobbying for [someone like a planner or a recruiter]. It's hard [to work in] the financial/grants arena without people who know how to do those things. Having somebody that could do that for, say, the monies that might be available through the Farm Bill—I think would be . . . invaluable."[10]

Increase Federal Resources to Support Economic Development in Public Lands Counties

The federal government also supports programs to assist economic transformation and growth in some rural public lands communities. Most of these programs are housed in the U.S. Department of Agriculture and funded through appropriations made in the Agriculture Improvement Act of 2018 (commonly dubbed the "Farm Bill").[11] These programs provide opportunities for communities to apply for grants that can support a wide variety of initiatives, from improving broadband service and infrastructure to building community facilities.[12] Particular preference is given to proposals for projects relating to outdoor recreation, explicit recognition of the value of recreation to the economic future of rural public lands communities. Language in the Farm Bill also encourages coordination with the USFS to develop public-private partnerships that advance recreation opportunities in those communities.[13]

However, economic development funds through the Farm Bill are generally available to communities adjacent to Forest Service lands. No programs of analogous scale are available through the Department of the Interior for communities adjacent to BLM land.

10. See also "Building 25k Jobs: Supporting Rural Utah's Future," Utah Governor's Office of Economic Development, accessed June 2, 2021, https://business.utah.gov/25kjobs/.

11. "Farm Bill," U.S. Department of Agriculture, accessed June 2, 2021, https://www.usda.gov/farmbill.

12. U.S. Library of Congress, Congressional Research Service, *Rural Development Provisions in the 2018 Farm Bill (P.L. 115-334)*, by Alyssa R. Casey, R46235 (2020).

13. "Congress Recognizes Outdoor Recreation in Farm Bill," Outdoor Recreation Roundtable, accessed June 2, 2021, https://recreationroundtable.org/congress-recognizes-outdoor-recreation-in-farm-bill/.

"To my knowledge, ever since I've been in politics, it's always been the same way. BLM is kind of the poor stepchild in the funding chain," Ron Dean, who served as natural resources counsel to former senator Orrin Hatch (R-Utah), reflects. "The National Park Service is the fair-haired child. They get funded better than the Forest Service, which gets funded better than the BLM. The BLM kind of gets the leftovers. I'm not aware of any funding mechanisms like [those in the Farm Bill] on BLM ground. The public doesn't have that same appreciation for the kind of ground that BLM generally oversees. Honestly, I think that's what drives the funding equation, the public's perception of the value of the ground overseen by each agency."

Involve Nonprofits and Recreation Groups in Collaborative Programs

Outdoor recreation groups as well as conservation groups are beginning to work with both political leaders and businesses in rural public lands communities. Outdoor Recreation Roundtable executive director Jessica Wahl notes that "groups like Access Fund, [many of the groups in] the Outdoor Alliance, and Outdoor Alliance itself are getting involved in some of the planning that's happening."

Jason Keith of Access Fund and Public Land Solutions works with local municipalities "to help them develop their recreation economies. A typical project for us would be [represented by the contract we have with] Farmington, New Mexico, where their coal plant is scheduled to be decommissioned. They're casting about trying to figure out [how they will replace those coal jobs]. We come in there and we do what we call a recreation audit, which is basically like a SWOT [strength, weakness, opportunity, threat] analysis of their prospects for diversifying into the recreation economy sector."

Paul Spitler of the Wilderness Society cites an effort to work with a rural public lands county in Montana. "Close to my home here in Montana, we're working on another lands bill, (the Blackfoot Clearwater Stewardship Act), very similar to Emery in our approach. Prior to even getting to propose a lands bill in this place, we funded a local economic development plan. We raised funds for a sculpture park. We raised funds for new motorized and nonmotorized trails, and so on. [For the Wilderness Society] to have a viable

Blackfoot Pathways: Sculpture in the Wild encourages creation of artworks inspired by the environmental and industrial heritage of the Blackfoot Valley, about sixty miles east of Missoula, Montana. Pictured here is Chris Drury's *Ponderosa Whirlpool*, 2016. The Wilderness Society is a supporter of Blackfoot Pathways. Photos courtesy of Kevin O'Dwyer and Chris Drury.

business model, we have to make sure that we're paying attention to local economics."[14]

John Sterling, former executive director of the Conservation Alliance, suggests that the conservation and recreation communities may in future be willing to work more closely with rural public lands counties to provide expertise and funding for collaborative economic and conservation planning:

14. See also Office of Senator Jon Tester, "On the Banks of the Blackfoot River, Tester Introduces Blackfoot Clearwater Stewardship Act," press release, June 7, 2019, https://www.tester.senate.gov/?p=press_release&id=6813; Blackfoot Pathways: Sculpture in the Wild (home page), accessed June 2, 2021, http://www.sculptureinthewild.com/.

> I think they [public lands counties] would find willing participants from both the conservation and recreation community, whether it's providing marketing expertise or whether they want to better understand what recreation amenities they have in their county. I know that there's great climbing and bouldering in Emery County and great hiking. We have access to resources that can quantify exactly what's there. We could probably help them better understand what places within their county to promote for recreation because they may not be as aware of what current outdoor recreation enthusiasts are interested in doing on public lands.[15]

Better Match Federal Support Programs to the Needs of Public Lands Counties

Public lands counties face a major challenge in meeting budget needs: federal lands, which dominate the acreage in their counties, are not subject to taxation. County budgets benefit from royalties or fees associated with mineral extraction, logging, or ranching on federal lands. However, economic returns from these lands depend on the degree to which those activities are consistent with federal land designations and associated management protocols. For example, returns from activities carried out in wilderness areas and national parks will be minimal, while income from BLM and USFS land will depend on the kind and level of activities authorized in resource management plans (BLM) and land management plans (USFS). External market exigencies also influence the returns from commercial use of public land.

In 1976, Congress instituted a program to compensate counties for the nontaxable status of public lands: Payment in Lieu of Taxes (PILT).[16] In creating PILT, legislators hoped to provide a predictable payment that was tied to the amount of federal land in a county and the county's population, rather than to royalties from mineral extraction. In doing so, they hoped to diminish incentives to increase the level of commercial activities on federal lands. Under the terms of the 1976 legislation, counties containing USFS lands continued to receive revenue-sharing payments linked to receipts from timber harvesting on those lands. Over time, as income from timber

15. See also Conservation Alliance (home page), accessed June 2, 2021, http://www.conservationalliance.com/.

16. "Payment in Lieu of Taxes," U.S. Department of the Interior, accessed June 2, 2021, https://www.doi.gov/pilt.

harvesting dropped, Congress later provided for additional "temporary" payments under a program called Secure Rural Schools (SRS).[17]

Public lands counties receive annual payments from the federal government comprising a combination of PILT and SRS funds (in an amount determined by population, public land area, and the identity of the public lands administrator, USFS or BLM), along with royalty payments that depend on the yearly, fluctuating returns from mining, logging, and grazing fees.

The annual budgets of many rural public lands counties are relatively small. Three of our case-study counties—Custer, Emery, and Owyhee—have annual budgets of $12 million, $12.5 million, and $10 million in 2018 dollars, respectively. In these small counties, PILT and SRS payments represent on the order of 10 percent of their annual budgets.[18] These payments are typically used by county governments to carry out services such as construction of public schools and roads, firefighting, police protection, and search and rescue operations. Given their small, tight budgets, the cost of unexpected events—for example, the need to rescue hikers lost or injured in a remote canyon—can wreak havoc on a county's finances. PILT and SRS payments play a crucial role in a county's ability to meet these unpredictable challenges.

Rural public lands county commissions, along with their representatives in Congress, have long argued for PILT appropriations that match levels authorized by Congress, and for more certainty regarding the fate of the SRS program, which must be periodically reauthorized by Congress. Some have argued that counties that include public lands with high levels of protection (e.g., wilderness areas or national monuments, both of which have strict rules precluding commercial activities) should receive higher PILT payments, as royalties from these protected lands will be nil or negligible.

Allen Freemyer, former chief of staff for the House Committee on Natural Resources and now a lobbyist and legal consultant, captures both the

17. "Secure Rural Schools," Wilderness Society, accessed June 2, 2021, https://www.wilderness.org/articles/article/secure-rural-schools; Jonathan Shuffield, "Continue Revenue Sharing Payments to Forest Counties: Support the Secure Rural Schools (SRS) Program," National Association of Counties, August 19, 2020, https://www.naco.org/resources/continue-revenue-sharing-payments-forest-counties-support-secure-rural-schools-srs-program.

18. All statistics from the Economic Profile System of Headwaters Economics: "Custer County, ID"; "Emery County, UT"; "Owyhee County, ID."

importance of PILT and SRS payments to rural public lands counties, and the insufficiency of those payments: "I represent a couple of rural counties in Utah, so I fully understand how important PILT payments are and SRS payments are to these counties because they end up forming the base of their budgets to a large extent. There are those county commissioners who see conservation lands as nothing but a suck on their resources because they're [responsible for] conducting the rescues and picking up the trash and doing all those kinds of things."

Former Emery County commissioner Ray Peterson laments that receiving predictable PILT funds matched to county needs represents an ongoing challenge. "It seems like it's always a struggle to get funded. Every rural county believes that they [the PILT/SRS funds] need to be more consistent: just nail it down so they don't have to be approved every Congress. And [the payments] should be more. How you make that happen, that's been a struggle for as long as I can remember."

Representative Mike Simpson (R-Idaho) reflects on the difficulties he has faced over the years to draw attention to the importance of SRS and PILT payments to rural public lands counties:

> When I was the ranking member before I became chairman of the House Appropriations Subcommittee on Interior, Environment, and Related Agencies, a good Democratic friend of mine from the East was the chairman. Good guy. One day we started discussing Secure Rural Schools payments in committee. [He finally said] "My constituents want to know why they have to pay for their child's education and your child's too." And I said, "that's a hell of a good question."
>
> What I did was I gave him a map that showed where the public lands were and how much we tax ourselves for our schools versus what they tax themselves, and [showed him] how much of our land is taxable versus theirs. I said, "take this home and look it over." He came back the next day, and to his credit, he said, "you know, I didn't know what I was talking about." I said, "That's the issue. Trying to convince a lot of other people." We know this in the West because we have so much public land. [Public lands counties face] certain challenges that the rest of the nation sometimes doesn't understand.

Ron Dean believes that legislators representing the eastern half of the country are often unaware of the difficulties that small, rural public lands counties face in making ends meet. "If you don't live in a public lands state, if you're east of the hundredth meridian, people just really don't get it," Dean says. "That was a constant battle over twenty-five years that I was involved—to get members of Congress from non–public lands states to understand and care about how these kinds of things, PILT, and other things operate, and how tough it can be if you're living in rural America in a public lands state."

Former Emery County commissioner Randy Johnson echoed Dean's frustration:

> When they organized PILT originally it was recognized by Congress as something that was essential because of the impacts and demands that public lands put on resources of local counties. I've spent twenty years working to get PILT levels increased, and I am extremely angry and frustrated that you have to go back to Congress and beg for PILT money and be treated as though we're asking for a welfare payment. I can't even tell you how indignant that makes me feel. Because here we're sitting in Emery, and [it seems] every week we have volunteers search and rescue people. They're down there doing their job on public lands and risking their lives, and yet when we go ask [Congress] to increase our PILT and get it up to a [level], it's as though we're there with our hats in our hands begging for dimes.

The Wilderness Society's Brad Brooks suggests that Americans should recognize the importance of public lands not only to the nation, but to the individuals living closest to these lands. "We don't want counties to be dependent upon 25 percent payments from the timber industry, where they're incentivized to do large-scale clear-cut operations [to balance their budgets]."

Explore Alternative Policies for Providing Support to Public Lands Counties

Rural public lands counties containing large tracts of wilderness or other heavily protected public lands receive far lower federal payments than those with lands open to mining or logging, leading some to suggest that such counties should receive larger PILT or SRS payments.

Cody Stewart, former director of federal affairs for Utah governor Gary Herbert, believes that adopting such an approach would have two advantages: providing support for rural public lands counties most in need of increased payments and, in future, making other counties far more amenable to accepting restrictive designations such as wilderness. "I think there should eventually be a sliding scale, that the more restrictive the land use designation the more compensation there should be," Stewart says. "If you did that, then there actually might be a very different approach to wilderness designations if there was a PILT payment, say, three times as high as the standard payment. I think most communities would feel very different about it. But for whatever reason, that idea never really took off."

The Wilderness Society's Brad Brooks also supports increasing PILT payments to rural public lands counties containing protected public lands. "One of the ideas that we came up with is essentially like a premium, so changing the formula for SRS and PILT to put a premium payment on counties that have protected lands within their boundaries," Brooks says. "I think it's a great idea because it incentivizes counties to want to have protected lands. There are a lot of political challenges to that, but we absolutely support it."

At present, allocations of PILT funds are linked to a complex formula involving both the acreage of public lands within a county and its population. Applying this formula results in relatively large allocations to counties containing both metro areas and large acreages of public lands. The fractional contribution of PILT payments to these metro public lands counties is relatively small, but summed over all such counties in the country can be quite substantial. Some economists and political leaders suggest that the PILT allocation formula should be changed so that payments to metro public lands counties would be reduced, with the saved money reallocated to small rural counties.[19]

Economist Ben Alexander of the Resources Legacy Fund argues for a dual approach: increasing the level of PILT and SRS funding, and changing the allocation formulas. He says:

> One of the most effective things we could do right now to take the temperature down in these rural public lands counties is to give them full appropriation for

19. Mark Haggerty, "PILT Proposal Would Help Small-Population Counties," Headwaters Economics, December 18, 2019, https://headwaterseconomics.org/public-lands/county-payments/pilt-proposal/.

> PILT and SRS. The second thing we could do is listen to what they're telling us about adjusting the formulas so that we can actually meet more pressing needs and not send valuable dollars within the PILT and SRS allocations to major metro areas for whom these dollars are a rounding error and don't make any difference at all to their underlying budgets. So simple reforms: full appropriation [year to year] and formula changes. [That's] really doable and really important.

Representative Mike Simpson's (R-Idaho) chief of staff, Lindsay Slater, is quite direct in criticizing what he views as the inequities in the PILT allocation formula, but he is pessimistic about changing them in the near future. "The PILT formula itself is skewed. We look at Boise, and [its home of] Ada County gets so much money from the PILT funds, because of the population. But they're not going to change it. The large counties and [the National Organization of Counties] aren't going to allow it to be corrected."[20]

Some economists have proposed gradually replacing PILT, SRS, and royalty payments from mineral extraction and timber harvesting with what Ray Rasker of Headwaters Economics calls a national resource trust.[21] The trust would be seeded by a onetime, multibillion-dollar congressional allocation, and then populated over the years by royalties from mineral extraction and timber harvesting on public lands. This approach has the advantage of providing predictable income, no longer linked to year-to-year congressional allocations or fluctuating returns from commercial activities on public lands.

Consider Purchasing Public Land to Advance Rural Economies and Support Conservation Goals

Over his long Senate career, now-retired senator Harry Reid (D-Nev.) made extensive use of public land swaps and sales, which enabled urban growth in Nevada, provided protection for over a million acres as wilderness, and funded multiple conservation initiatives. The Southern Nevada Public Land

20. See also National Association of Counties (home page), accessed June 2, 2021, https://www.naco.org.

21. Headwaters Economics, *Rethinking Public Land Revenue Sharing: Utilizing a Natural Resources Trust to Address Volatility, Equity, and Incentives*, December 2014, https://headwaterseconomics.org/wp-content/uploads/whitepaper-natural-resources-trust.pdf.

Management Act (SNPLMA) and the Reid-Ensign White Pine Rider represent two examples of this strategy.[22] Proceeds generated by the land sales are used for conservation and recreation projects such as the development of parks, trails, and capital improvements on public lands. Over the years, funds raised by the SNPLMA have provided more than $1 billion for conservation and recreation.[23]

However, not everyone has been happy with the SNPLMA and the Reid-Ensign Rider. The sale of public lands and their attendant use to support urban growth have been met with varying levels of outrage by environmental groups.[24] Despite the protection afforded large swaths of land as wilderness, and significant funding for conservation, many objected not only to the specifics of land transfers and sales, but to the precedent of selling large tracts of public land whatever the motivation.

The Washington County land bill approached meeting the county's need to expand its metropolitan areas while simultaneously advancing conservation goals by following a much-scaled-down version of Reid's model. The bill empowered the federal government to sell or release environmentally nonsensitive lands to developers. In return, Washington County worked with federal agencies to establish a framework for conservation efforts, including protection for the endangered desert tortoise. Funds from public lands sales were used to subsidize these efforts.

Former Emery County commissioner Randy Johnson thinks that the Washington County approach could serve as a model for future conservation efforts. "Having some lands become available for designed growth seems to me benefits everybody," Johnson says. "[Plus], the sale of the land goes to enhance all kinds of conservation efforts. It was always a little bit of a puzzle to me that [you would be] somehow losing on the environmental side if you

22. Southern Nevada Public Land Management Act of 1998, Pub. L. No. 105-263, 112 Stat. 2343 (1998). On the rider, see "2013–2014 Interim Legislative Committee on Public Lands: White Pine County Update August 1st, 2014," Nevada Legislature, August 1, 2014, https://www.leg.state.nv.us/App/InterimCommittee/REL/Document/6871.

23. "Public Lands Management Act: Keep the Proceeds in Nevada," *Nevada Business Magazine*, July 1, 2005, https://www.nevadabusiness.com/2005/07/public-lands-management-act-keep-the-proceeds-in-nevada/.

24. Ralph Maughan, "Horrible News from the Congressional Wrap-Up . . . Nevada Ughh!," Wildlife News, December 10, 2006, http://www.thewildlifenews.com/2006/12/10/and-some-bad-news-from-congressional-wrap-up/.

convert some of that land to designed growth, and [use proceeds from land sales] for conservation purposes."

Cody Stewart is skeptical that bills balancing wilderness designation with public lands sales can happen in the near future. "[I don't think that could happen] unless you've got a situation where you had someone, and to be honest with you it would probably need to be a Democratic senator, take the lead. Senator Reid greased the skids for a lot of land exchanges and activity in Nevada."

It remains an open question, however, whether the advantages of such land sales outweigh the potential downside of setting a precedent that would result in wholesale sell-offs of public lands either to states or to the private sector. There is also the question of whether the BLM has the on-the-ground data necessary to determine what areas are nonsensitive. A rational discussion of the merits and liabilities of public lands sales for counties, states, and conservation interests probably awaits a time when ideological and partisan passions cool.

Reintroduce Earmarks to Support Rural Economies and Facilitate Conservation Efforts

Until the beginning of the 114th Congress, in 2015, it was possible for individual members of Congress to insert directed expenditures, better known as "earmarks," into appropriations bills.[25] Earmarks were generally used to enable or enhance projects in a member's district. To insert an earmark into an appropriations bill, a congressional member needed to find support from someone on the House or Senate Committee on Appropriations. A good deal of horse-trading often took place, with the member who was requesting an earmark agreeing to support legislation of importance to a committee chair or House or Senate leadership, or to support an earmark proposed by a member of the Committee on Appropriations. The near-universal need among members to attain results required a mutual willingness to trade and compromise with members within and outside one's party caucus.

Earmarks were eliminated owing to pressure both from groups—those who believe all expenditures should first be authorized and then appropriated, and those who viewed earmarks as an avatar for excessive government

25. "Earmarks," Ballotpedia, accessed June 2, 2021, https://ballotpedia.org/Earmarks.

Representative Mike Simpson (*third from left*) opens construction on the Redfish to Stanley Trail. Photo courtesy of the Office of Representative Simpson.

spending. For context, legislative earmarks typically represented on the order of 1 percent of the federal budget.[26]

Members who once could deliver earmarked funds often saw their standing in their district increase and, in many cases, were able to facilitate programs or projects that might otherwise have met resistance, had traditional channels and processes been followed.

The ability to earmark projects was one factor in gaining support for bills protecting wilderness among citizens and political leaders in Custer, Owyhee, and Washington Counties.

Representative Mike Simpson recalls that "earmarks made things work. That was how you got things done. It's a horrible thing to say, but they greased the wheel and not in a bad way. It just worked. Our view is that every member knows their district better than anybody else and that's how we were able to get things through. For Custer County, we did economic development earmarks. The Forest Service is building a bike trail from Redfish Lake to Stanley, a four-mile bike trail. That's going to be [good] for economic development. They're building a community center in Challis. We got money for roads [in the county]."

26. "Yes, Earmarks Can Be Part of Smart and Responsible Governing," Congressional Institute, March 26, 2018, https://www.congressionalinstitute.org/2018/03/26/yes-earmarks-can-be-part-of-smart-responsible-governing/.

The Owyhee County bill not only designated 517,000 acres of wilderness in and around the Owyhee Canyonlands in Idaho, but also released 199,000 acres of federal land initially classified as wilderness study areas for multiple uses, and provided ranchers with cash in exchange for private land along with adjustments in grazing rights. Many arrangements in the Owyhee County bill would have been difficult to implement were earmarks embargoed in 2009, when the bill was passed.

Ron Dean, who served in Senator Orrin Hatch's staff while earmarks were still allowed, was candid regarding the loss of earmarks as a legislative tool. "Earmarking [somehow] got turned into a boogeyman by political opportunists," Dean says. "I mean it had its bad examples, like everything, but I'll tell you what, Orrin could do a massive amount of good for his communities through earmarking. Most people wouldn't draw that conclusion, but the polarity of Congress as it currently sits, and how that polarity developed with the end of earmarking—they coincide. Earmarking helped Congress work together."

At some point in the future, Congress may reconsider the merits and liabilities of earmarking. If so, use of directed expenditures in conservation bills may offer another avenue for conveying funds to enhance the economies of rural public lands counties. Indeed, in late February 2021, the House Committee on Appropriators voted to reinstate earmarks provided total earmarks do not exceed 1 percent of the top-line federal budget. As of this writing, the Senate and House have not yet agreed on procedures and restrictions on congressionally directed expenditures.[27]

Find Influential Voices to Advocate for Rural Public Lands Counties

Over the decades, both national and local conservation groups have been remarkably effective in engaging citizens throughout the country in efforts to protect public lands having extraordinary scenic, scientific, cultural, and ecological value. Though relatively small in number and often lacking in financial clout, these organizations have appealed to that place in the American

27. Jennifer Shutt, "House Appropriators Officially Bring Back Earmarks, Ending Ban," Roll Call, February 26, 2021, https://www.rollcall.com/2021/02/26/house-appropriators-to-cap-earmarks-at-1-percent-of-topline/.

psyche that believes that wild, open spaces are a part of our heritage, a gift to be treasured and passed down to future generations. The persistence of conservation groups in battling special interests, and finding allies in Congress, has, over time, led to their gaining significant political influence.

More recently, recreation groups, representing a range of manufacturers and outfitters, have joined the fray. Their interests often, but not always, overlap with those of the conservation community. When the recreation and conservation communities join forces to seek protection of public lands, they represent a powerful lobbying force.

However, public lands counties lack the strong national influence of the conservation and recreation communities. They are small and don't have the financial resources or manpower to mount national campaigns to support their needs. This is not to say that they are without influence: their opposition to public lands protection, expressed through their local and state representatives, often counterbalances the efforts of conservation groups to protect public lands surrounding their communities. Moreover, they represent an important political constituency in rural states, which collectively wield considerable power, particularly in the U.S. Senate.

Nevertheless, while often able to block conservation efforts, these counties have been less successful in finding allies to support funding for a sustainable economic future: broadband, roads, and other infrastructure investments. They as well often lack access to capital to facilitate investments in amenities—hotels and restaurants—that would allow them to develop a robust tourism base, and become desirable destinations for young people eager to leave cities and work remotely. Attracting retirees, along with their nest eggs, is also a challenge, as many rural public lands counties lack nearby medical facilities.

Might there be a way for conservation groups and public lands counties to find common ground, to work together to advocate for protection of public lands and for funding initiatives to improve the economic health of the counties?

Anders Reynolds, formerly of the Pew Charitable Trusts and currently at the Southern Environmental Law Center, believes that such an alliance could be mutually beneficial. "It is in the interests of both counties and conservation groups to see the economic base of rural counties, particularly rural counties that are adjacent to public or conservation-worthy lands, to diversify away from resource extraction," Reynolds says. "Counties have to know that they need to diversify their economies, and conservation groups ought to want that. It seems like there should be common interests there even if the parties haven't figured out how to tackle it."[28]

Romel Nicholas, who worked closely with now-retired senator Orrin Hatch in forging the Emery County Land Bill, is blunt in urging conservation groups to work with public lands counties: "If conservation groups spent half the money they spend on advertising on constructive economic development in rural communities, I think they'd be amazed at the results."

"In the Farm Bill in 2018, we actually got some language in there speaking exactly to rural economic development," Outdoor Recreation Roundtable executive director Jessica Wahl shares. "There's now about a $300 million pot of money for rural economic development grants. We got language in the Farm Bill that allows [some of] that money to go to recreation."

Ron Dean encourages both citizens and organizations in urban areas to consider the needs of rural counties:

> I think rural America, not only in the public lands states, but rural America all over the United States, is really suffering and being taken for granted. [These areas provide] so much of the necessities of what make life in America so good, and they get so little credit. All the extractive minerals that are used in technology. All the food that we eat. The management of our watersheds. That's all primarily in rural places. If we start paying a heavy price for that negligence, that's probably when the realization will dawn on urban folks that they need to help these rural economies, as these rural economies provide us with so many of the necessities of life.

Involve Conservation Groups in a Coordinated Effort to Support Public Lands Counties

Many highly effective conservation groups work primarily at the local or state level rather than nationally. These groups are often small, and they are funded by contributors eager to see results: either protection of conservation-worthy lands, or highly visible efforts to resist development of commercial

28. See also Southern Environmental Law Center (home page), accessed June 2, 2021, https://www.southernenvironment.org/.

activities on these lands. Such groups generally lack the bandwidth or funding needed to develop long-term strategic plans in coordination with other local or national groups.

However, these groups, along with national conservation organizations, might well consider the potential value of participating in broad coalitions with the dual goals of protecting valuable public lands and advancing the economic prospects of rural public lands counties.

Drew McConville of the Wilderness Society believes that conservation groups should devote more energy to long-term strategic planning aimed at identifying national policy issues where a coordinated approach would prove effective. "Long-term strategic planning across conservation groups—I see it a lot campaign by campaign," McConville says. "I think our community probably has some work to do to organize themselves more effectively on those national policy issues and actually focus on some of those solutions that would help align conservation outcomes and economic outcomes of communities. It's certainly something that we have given thought to, and I think others have, but I don't know that we or anybody has broken through yet on a big national push."

"Some of that big-picture coordination does happen," the Wilderness Society's Brad Brooks says. "But it is very much to our [the conservation community's] detriment that we can't agree on bigger things all the time. I get it. There's only so much time you can spend trying to help other people and other groups, [even though] coordination is in their best interests."

Who might catalyze such discussions? Among the options might be the public policy schools of universities, or institutes that work in collaboration with those schools. One such example is the William D. Ruckelshaus Center at the University of Washington, whose focus is to "help parties involved in complex public policy challenges occurring in the Pacific Northwest tap university expertise to develop collaborative, durable, and effective solutions."[29] The Salazar Center for North American Conservation at Colorado State University and the Andrus Center for Public Policy at Boise State University are undertaking similar efforts in the Mountain West.[30]

---

29. "William D. Ruckelshaus Center," University of Washington, accessed June 2, 2021, https://www.washington.edu/research/research-centers/william-d-ruckelshaus-center/.

30. "Salazar Center for North American Conservation," Colorado State University, accessed June 2, 2021, https://salazarcenter.colostate.edu/; "Andrus Center for Public

Another option might be institutions analogous to the John S. McCain III National Center for Environmental Conflict Resolution, part of the Udall Foundation. The McCain Center serves as a nexus of "impartial collaboration, consensus-building, and conflict resolution [that aims to enhance] multiparty problem solving and decision-making . . . on a wide range of environmental, natural resources, and public lands issues involving the Federal Government."[31]

Concluding Remarks

Numerous steps can be taken to achieve conservation goals while ensuring the health of public lands counties and their communities. Perhaps the most important step is to build trust and mutual understanding through meeting face-to-face in cherished landscapes.

"Those interactions get you out of the office," former Idaho Conservation League executive director Rick Johnson says, "away from the computer and in front of the Rotary Clubs and in front of the Chambers of Commerce and in front of all the business leaders. You're talking about values and common interests as opposed to winning. Of course it's very hard, it takes a long time, but lo and behold, you become changed as well."

Policy," Boise State University, accessed June 2, 2021, https://www.boisestate.edu/sps-andruscenter/.

31. "John S. McCain III National Center for Environmental Conflict Resolution," Udall Foundation, accessed June 2, 2021, https://www.udall.gov/ourprograms/institute/institute.aspx; "About Us," Udall Foundation, accessed June 2, 2021, https://www.udall.gov/AboutUs/AboutUs.aspx.

Fremont granaries. Note the scattered corncobs, which have survived for hundreds of years. Photo by Jonathan T. Bailey.

Author Reflection

Jonathan T. Bailey

Like many in Emery County, I can trace my ancestry to the beginning of Mormon settlement in Castle Valley six generations back. On my mother's side, the Keisels raised sheep through Sevier County and the Henry Mountains, where they are said to have regularly encountered Butch Cassidy and members of his Wild Bunch in transit from Robbers Roost.

My mother's family eventually pushed northward into the San Rafael Swell. They traveled through iron-rich crimson cliffs in the swell's southwestern corner, where these landscapes—Keesle Country—now bear their name. In time, they made it as far as the Molen Reef, where they etched their names in a cliff overlooking a now-historical woolen mill.

My father's side has a similar story. The Baileys traveled to Emery County at Brigham Young's calling, managing to eke out a living as farmers and carpenters in the town of Molen, just to the east of Ferron. While their story is more incomplete, their legacy of "toughing it out" in the face of adversity certainly carried down to my grandfather.

My paternal grandfather contributed to the development of Emery County as a member of the Civilian Conservation Corps, and as an employee of the local Des Bee Dove coal mine. Many years later, he was partially paralyzed after his arm was pulled through a conveyor belt leading into the mine shaft. Despite the challenges that his injury presented to the family, my father followed in his footsteps, working at the coal-fired power plant in Castle Dale; he recently retired after working for forty years at the plant.

My own journey into the San Rafael Swell began shortly after I was born. In my younger years, I spent most of my time wandering canyons close to home, sometimes walking from my doorstep to thousand-year-old structures propped atop mesas just a few miles away. On many occasions, our parents would gather us into a single-cab truck, stop at the now-defunct Ferron Mercantile on Main Street in Ferron, and head to explore the canyons in the swell.

In the course of these travels, I became fascinated by the images carved into and painted on canyon walls, and wondered about the people who conceived such hauntingly beautiful imagery. I spent every dime I could gather on archaeological literature, including the works of Polly Schaafsma, Sally Cole, and Alfred Kidder, all working at various frontiers of southwestern archaeology. In compiling a veritable library, I stumbled on the works of photographers David Muench and Diane Orr, which would prove pivotal. Shortly thereafter, my parents gifted me with an old film camera, and a passion for photography took root.

As I entered my early teenage years, I ranged farther into southern Utah and adjacent states, usually forgoing gifts in order to fund travel to carry out small photography/conservation projects throughout the Southwest. After Internet forums came into being, I was able to find and connect with people who shared my passions. Two people, in particular, had a significant influence on my career. The first was Alan Cressler, a photographer from Georgia, who had amassed an unbelievable archive of photographs from around the world, featuring plants, archaeology, and beautiful, serpentine cave systems. He was extraordinarily generous with his support: granting me access to books and equipment, and providing the tools to better store and manage my by then hefty photograph collection. His contagious enthusiasm for the natural world heavily influenced my expansion into other areas of scientific and creative photography.

The other person was Connie Massingale, a storied canyon dweller who frequently ventured to Emery County to join me on extended travels through its canyons. We spent countless nights under bottomless night skies, sharing stories beside the faint glow of firelight. Somehow, she always managed to effortlessly weave together almost impenetrable scientific literature with the emotional, sacred qualities palpable in the presence of ancient places. The time I spent with her gifted me with a deeper commitment to honoring not only fine technical details, but also the spirit and character of place.

A few years after I met both Alan and Connie, I began studying architecture in a college course offered by the local high school. In a fateful encounter, my instructor—Jim Keele—asked his class whether anyone in attendance was interested in archaeology. Soon after, we became close friends, spending nearly a decade exploring some of the most remote places in Emery County. He unfortunately passed away in 2018. Without our shared companionship, I doubt that either of us would have been able to explore the wondrous—albeit precarious—places we managed to reach, deep in the heart of the San Rafael Swell.

A few months shy of my nineteenth birthday, I was critically injured in a climbing incident just beyond the western border of Emery County. An unusual, rapid snowmelt had destabilized cliffs above the steep talus on which I stood, causing part of its exposed rock to break free. Following the impact of the falling sandstone, it was clear to onlookers—and me—that my injuries might well be fatal. Miraculously, major arteries were spared by a few inches. While I somehow managed to evade boulder-inflicted decapitation by about an inch, parts of my leg were stripped to the muscle.

As luck would have it, shortly after the incident, I received a call from Diane Orr, the aforementioned photographer and member of the Utah Rock Art Research Association's preservation committee. Knowing that I had spent a good deal of time in the Molen Reef adjacent to Castle Valley, she asked me to examine the possible effects of oil and gas leases on sites in the area. Little did I imagine how this challenge would change my life, or that Diane, who influenced my becoming a photographer, would end up as one of my closest friends.

In the months after the injury, I was unable to walk, but once I became capable of hobbling through the desert, I got back to work. After compiling locations of rock art and cultural sites we had previously visited, and using these data to persuade the Bureau of Land Management to defer issuing the leases, we quickly began more intensive studies of the Molen Reef and other regions.

In the following years, more leases were offered for auction in the Molen Reef, as well as in the Mussentuchit Badlands and the San Rafael Desert. Diane and I quickly became involved in conservation efforts, meeting with oil executives, high-ranking state and federal officials, tribal leaders, conservation groups, and members of the Emery County Public Lands Council. For nearly a decade, we worked to provide on-the-ground data to support the protection of these sacred landscapes. During this time, I assembled the material for my first book, *Rock Art: A Vision of a Vanishing Cultural Landscape*, which featured testimonies from tribal leaders, archaeologists, and artists.[1] Our collective goal was to inspire preservation throughout Utah from the lessons I had learned in Emery County.

In 2016, the Utah Public Lands Initiative proposed expedited energy development in some areas despite our community-driven request to include protection for the Molen Reef.[2] After Congress failed to pass the Public Lands Initiative, we hoped that the Emery County Public Land Management Act would take cognizance of the need to protect sensitive sites in the Molen Reef; unfortunately, it did not. We were disappointed that we were not given an opportunity to participate in shaping the legislation, despite the years we had spent in collaborative efforts to explore avenues for protecting these sites. Although the Emery County legislation contains numerous positive outcomes for conservation, we are concerned that its passage may make it difficult to resume discussions aimed at protecting areas that are extremely susceptible to human impact.

Nonetheless, our optimism for finding collaborative solutions to enable protection of the rich cultural landscape in the county has not wavered. Over the years, we have sat down with people having beliefs nearly orthogonal to ours. What we have found is that emotion—fear of large, faceless entities taking something away in "the middle of the night"—precludes the opportunity to listen and find common ground. I, too, often find myself trapped at the crossroads of culture and conservation. I am a conservationist at heart—but I am a conservationist born and raised in Emery County, who comes from multiple generations of energy workers. While I am unwavering in my commitment to the land and climate, I am sympathetic to the struggles of energy-dependent employment. I have faith that over time, our seemingly irreconcilable differences can be overcome, and that progress can be had without making dangerous sacrifices to our quickly warming planet.

---

1. This book was originally published in 2016 by Johnson Books of Denver, Colorado, and was significantly updated in 2019 for its second edition.

2. The Molen Reef National Conservation Area proposal was hand delivered in Washington, D.C. to Fred Ferguson, chief of staff of then U.S. representative Jason Chaffetz, and then forwarded to U.S. representative Rob Bishop. It outlined a national conservation area that supported traditional, local uses while restricting future oil and gas development near archaeological sites. The proposal was accompanied by letters from local residents who supported further preservation of the region. Despite our community-driven request for preservation within the Utah Public Lands Initiative, the Molen Reef was proposed as an expedited energy zone within the final bill.

If my experience demonstrates nothing else, it is that fate has a tendency to bring people together—from the people who have been with me from the beginning, to the people I have met more recently. Shortly after I moved to Tucson with my boyfriend a few years ago, kismet led me to connect with Stephen E. Strom, who just happened to be assembling the material for a book about the San Rafael Swell. This book is the product of that serendipitous encounter. In a similar fashion, I hope that fate will in future lead to new encounters and to fruitful conversations about how these landscapes can be thoughtfully managed in service of generations to come.

San Rafael Reef and Caineville Reef. Aerial photo by Stephen E. Strom.

Author Reflection

Stephen E. Strom

My personal journey started in a Bronx box apartment in New York City. There, beneath bright and polluted New York skies, where the Milky Way was barely visible, I somehow developed an early passion for astronomy. I buried myself in popular-level science books, reveled in science fiction, and spent most of my early teenage years grinding and polishing telescope mirrors and listening to visiting astronomers kind enough to share their research results and professional journeys with young amateurs.

From the Bronx, I headed to Cambridge, Massachusetts, convinced in my monomania that the main, perhaps only, attraction of Harvard College was its astronomy department. I spent nearly a decade in Cambridge, marrying early, having four children in rapid succession, and in passing, earning my doctorate.

It was astronomy that brought me to the Southwest, first to the Davis Mountains in West Texas, then to Kitt Peak National Observatory, west of Tucson. My first reaction to the desert was to recoil, in fear of a landscape that seemed alien to someone eastern bred: an arid, treeless land teeming with creatures that were stealthily hiding behind cacti or in grass, waiting for an opportunity to strike. It took the better part of a decade, a move to Tucson, and the persistence of two good friends for me to venture out from behind my desk and hike in nearby Aravaipa Canyon.

Slowly, and with the help of my sometimes exasperated but always insistent wife, Karen, I began to embrace the desert. A burgeoning interest in photography cemented the connection, as the desert's sculptural and chromatic rhythms compelled a deeper and deeper bond. Our children, willing or not, became part of our ever-expanding expeditions. It was not uncommon for us to spend an unplanned week on the Navajo Reservation, or head to

Zion National Park on a search for orchids hidden in "gardens" hanging from the roofs of sandstone alcoves.

An unexpected exigency in our professional lives brought us back east, to the Pioneer Valley, where we took up residence in Amherst, Massachusetts. The desert continued to call, though, and during spring breaks, I was able to persuade (mostly willing) colleagues to arrange their teaching schedule so their department chair (me) could escape for two soul-enriching weeks to southeastern Utah. There, we would meet with two of our children and four of our grandchildren, introducing them to the lands around Bears Ears and the southern parts of the San Rafael Swell. Astronomy, too, brought us back periodically to the Southwest, where, after taking measurements with Kitt Peak's telescopes, we would always make time for hiking and photographing.

By then, my research, aimed at understanding how stars and planetary systems form, was complemented by a competing passion: using photography as a tool to express my emotional response to desert landscapes. Books followed—collaborations with Muscogee poet Joy Harjo, and Navajo poet, playwright, and librettist Laura Tohe.

Eventually, the lure of the desert proved too strong, and my wife and I left Amherst to return to a small town in the grasslands southeast of Tucson: Sonoita, Arizona, a perfect base for continuing our astronomical research, and for deepening our connection to Utah's red rock country. Our love for that landscape led naturally to a broader interest in conservation. We joined the Southern Utah Wilderness Association, and began to think of photography not only as a creative activity, but as one that offered the possibility of following the path of Ansel Adams and his acolytes—raising awareness of threatened landscapes worthy of protection. At the time, we viewed the world in Manichean terms: identifying with the side advocating for an unquestioned good (preservation of wilderness), and finding contemptible those whom I then perceived as viewing public lands simply as barren entities ripe for exploitation.

More books followed, some with an explicit conservation theme, others carrying a more subtle message about the value of wild places. Two life events altered my path: the first, a mild heart attack, which led to my retiring from my position at the National Optical Astronomy Observatory in Tucson; and the second, Karen's passing in 2013 after fifty-four years of marriage. The first afforded me time to fully embrace photographic and conservation-related pursuits. The second led to a compact with my eldest grandchild, Rebecca Robinson, then thirty and an accomplished journalist.

Together, while remembering my wife during a celebration on Cedar Mesa in Utah, Rebecca and I decided to collaborate on a book to honor her life, as well as her connections with Native communities in the Southwest. At the time, we conceived the book as one that would support ongoing efforts to advocate for a Greater Canyonlands National Monument—giving protection to lands that Stewart Udall and Bates Wilson believed in the early 1960s merited designation as a national park.

As fate would have it, our efforts began at nearly the same time that the Bears Ears Inter-Tribal Coalition was initiating its campaign to have 1.9 million acres in southeast Utah's San Juan County designated a national monument to be comanaged by tribes and the Bureau of Land Management. We quickly decided that following the efforts of the tribes, the leaders of San Juan County, Utah's political establishment, and conservation groups throughout the country should properly be the focus of our efforts.

We began what became a nearly four-year process, during which we interviewed more than seventy individuals: tribal members, San Juan County commissioners, and members of Utah's congressional delegation, as well as ranchers, recreationists, archaeologists, and members of the conservation community.

The experience of assembling the material for what turned out to be two books was for me transformative. In order to tell the full story of Bears Ears, I needed to open myself not only to the voices of those who advocate for public land protections, but to residents of San Juan County whose families have lived and worked in the county for five or six generations; and to tribal members who trace their connection to Bears Ears to "time immemorial."

We completed the book just before President Barack Obama, as one of his last acts in office, protected 1.35 million acres of public land in San Juan County as the Bears Ears National Monument. As much as the declaration was celebrated by the tribes and the conservation community, it elicited a furious response from many residents of San Juan County and from Utah's political leadership.

A year later, President Donald Trump rescinded all but 15 percent of the monument. Tribes, conservationists, and recreation organizations challenged the president's executive order, and as of this writing, his action is still being litigated.

While the rescission of Bears Ears was personally disheartening, the acrimony both preceding the initial monument declaration and following President Trump's action was equally distressing. The resulting internal unease, combined with curiosity whetted by some of our interviews for the Bears Ears books, led me to wonder what might have led to a viable compromise solution, rather than an acrimonious legal battle that may take years to resolve.

In the course of our research for the Bears Ears book, Rebecca and I interviewed a former county commissioner in nearby Emery County, Ray Peterson. Ray provided background on Emery County's then two-decade-long effort to find a compromise solution that would shape the future of public lands management in the county in ways that would satisfy the interests of a broad range of stakeholders.

Those efforts were still ongoing in 2018 when we finished the Bears Ears books. As Karen and I had spent a fair amount of time in the San Rafael Swell from 1980 onward, it seemed natural to look to Emery County to see how its efforts to shape the future of its public lands compared with those that ultimately led to irreconcilable differences in San Juan.

I once again began to travel to Emery County, first to familiarize myself with landscapes in areas where I had not yet had time to explore. Working on the ground, from a Cessna, and with a drone, I began an effort to complement my earlier ground-based photography with images that might provide readers with a sense of the complex and compelling landscapes in the county.

In March 2019, Emery County's twenty-five-year effort to reach certainty regarding the fate of its public lands came to fruition with the passage of the Emery County Public Land Management Act. It was a welcome surprise, given the rancor surrounding Bears Ears, and the extreme ideological divisions that have in these times precluded bipartisan cooperation on most pieces of major legislation.

In light of the Emery County bill's passing, I accelerated my efforts to understand how Emery County had been successful in reaching the compromises needed to pass the bill. Conversations with more than forty individuals involved in Emery County's efforts, as well as similar efforts Washington County in Utah and Owyhee and Custer Counties in Idaho, completed my transformation from a strict conservationist, to someone who tries to see public lands through the eyes of those who live closest to those lands.

I still consider myself an advocate for conservation, but I now believe firmly that protecting land must be tied intimately with ensuring that the economic needs and cultural attachments of rural communities are addressed and honored. Thus, this book—dedicated to catalyzing civil conversation about processes and policies that will achieve both conservation and community goals.

Largeflower onion (*Allium macropetalum*). Photo by Jonathan T. Bailey.

Acknowledgments

Jonathan Bailey wishes to thank the following individuals and organizations for the contributions that made this project possible:

Five people—R. E. Burrillo, archaeologist for SWCA Environmental Consultants; Kenneth Carpenter, director of the Utah State University (USU) Eastern Prehistoric Museum; Daryn Melvin, member of the Navajo and Hopi Nations; Steve Simms, USU professor emeritus of anthropology; and Alan Titus, paleontologist for the Bureau of Land Management—were hugely helpful in their feedback on the Indigenous peoples and paleontology/geology chapters.

The Hopi Cultural Preservation Office, particularly Troy Honanie Jr. and Clark Tenakhongva, provided so much support over the years, from meetings on the ground to discuss land management issues to frequent check-ins just to make sure all is well. It was sincerely appreciated.

The people who joined me on travels through the San Rafael Swell or in areas for the purpose of this publication, often helping transport gear or acquire more technical photographs, include the Bailey family, Keeley Criswell, Ryan Hermansen, Jerry and Lisa Otto, and David Schwartz.

The people who dedicated a great deal of their time meeting with me, either in office or on-site, to seek common ground on public lands were: Lowell Braxton, Utah representative, Western Energy Alliance; Jim Dabakis, Utah state senator; David Hinkins, Utah state senator; Ray Peterson, Emery County public lands director; Fred Ferguson, former chief of staff for U.S. representative Jason Chaffetz; too many current and past local, state, and federal employees of the Bureau of Land Management to mention individually; and members of the Utah Trust Lands Administration.

The nonprofits that have provided support, feedback, and access to people and resources that contributed significantly to this publication include

Archaeology Southwest, Ecoflight, Grand Canyon Trust, Southern Utah Wilderness Alliance, and Utah Rock Art Research Association.

The people who provided their expertise, either by identifying species, or by supplying insight for more in-depth issues regarding their given field, include Michael Bogan, biology professor at the University of Arizona; Austin Hess, bird specialist; Dwight Hoxie, retired U.S. Geological Survey hydrologist; Kevin Madalena, geologist and paleontologist with Jemez Pueblo; Jody Patterson, archaeologist for Montgomery Archaeological Consultants; and Kent Williams, geographic information system (GIS) specialist.

The artists that generously provided their talents to vividly portray Emery County's environment, both past and present, were Steve O'Connor, John Olsen, Kevin Wellard, and Emily Willoughby.

Utah State University Eastern Prehistoric Museum graciously brought me in to photograph a few artifacts in its collections (which were used herein). Likewise, rock art researcher Layne Miller let me into his home to photograph his holster.

Alan Cressler has supported my photographic endeavors for well over a decade. He has also accompanied me on many travels through the San Rafael Swell, Grand Staircase-Escalante, Bears Ears, Nevada, New Mexico, and Arizona. He has also provided his expertise for a variety of natural resources.

Aaron Goldtooth has been my companion in life and the outdoors for over five years. While his contributions are far too numerous to name individually, he has been one of my most faithful supporters. His family, too, has been incredibly kind with their love and support.

Jim Keele was an incredibly skilled and adventurous hiking companion for nearly a decade, traveling into some of the most remote areas of Emery County. Unfortunately, Jim passed away in 2018. He is deeply missed.

Connie Massingale has shared so many stories and travels with me over the years, venturing into the canyons of Emery County, the Glen Canyon area, the Moab area, and Bears Ears. She has provided valuable insight into the sacred nature of these tortuous landscapes.

Diane Orr has accompanied me in preservation battles for nearly a decade. In this time, we have hiked countless canyons, traveled to many meetings, and cherished many victories. She has provided so much assistance, support, and conservation experience that has proven essential in my life moving forward.

Finally, although he has been mentioned previously, R. E. Burrillo has provided so much assistance in shaping this publication—not only in sharing his archaeological experience but also in offering feedback and insight on almost every component of this book.

To everyone who has been mentioned, and many more who are far too numerous to name individually, your contributions are deeply appreciated.

Stephen Strom wishes to thank the following individuals for spending the time to provide critical background information, as well as a range of perspectives on issues related to public land use and rural public lands counties in the West:

Ben Alexander, economist, Resource Legacy Fund; Ray Bloxham, Southern Utah Wilderness Alliance (SUWA); Robert Bonnie, former undersecretary for Natural Resources and Environment, U.S. Department of Agriculture, now Rubenstein Fellow, Duke University; Brandon Bragato, staff director, House Subcommittee on National Parks, Forests, and Public Lands; Brad Brooks, the Wilderness Society; David Brooks, Democratic counsel, U.S. Senate Committee on Energy and Natural Resources; Adriana Chimaris, travel, tourism, and museum director, Emery County, Utah; Lorie Fowlke, district director, Office of Congressman John Curtis; Allen Freemyer, former staff director and counsel to the U.S. House of Representatives Subcommittee on National Parks, Forests, and Public Lands; Edward Geary, professor of history (retired), Brigham Young University; Stuart Gosswein, Speed Equipment Manufacturing Association (SEMA); Scott Groene, executive director, SUWA; Carrie Hamblen, Green Chamber of Commerce, Las Cruces, New Mexico; Brock Johansen, CEO of Emery Telcom; Ashley Korenblat, managing director, Public Land Solutions; Athan Manuel, director of the Lands Protection Program of the Sierra Club; Drew McConville, the Wilderness Society; Ray Rasker, executive director, Headwaters Economics; Anders Reynolds, federal legislative director, Southern Environmental Law Center; Adam Sarvana, communications director, U.S. House of Representatives Committee on Natural Resources; John Seebach, Pew Charitable Trusts; Karen Simms, natural resources division manager, Pima County, Arizona; Eric Snyder, SEMA; John Sterling, the Conservation Alliance; Gary Tabor, Center for Large Landscape Conservation; Jessica Wahl, executive director, Outdoor Recreation Roundtable; Kent Wilson, Emery County commissioner; and Dan Van Wagoner, mayor of Castle Dale, Utah.

Andrea Keller Helsel, program officer for western conservation at the Hewlett Foundation, not only provided insight and critical commentary but was instrumental in connecting me to individuals involved in collaborative conservation efforts throughout the West.

John Leshy, emeritus professor at the University of California Hastings College of Law, provided invaluable comments that, I hope, significantly elevated my discussion of the role of public lands throughout American history. Many thanks.

Jason Keith of the Access Fund shared his perspectives both on the elements he considered critical to passing the Emery County Public Land Management Act and on the role of the conservation and recreation communities in shaping the contours of the bill.

Paul Spitler of the Wilderness Society was extraordinarily generous with his time in discussing the role played by his organization in the Emery County bill's passage, and he provided insight into current thinking in the conservation community regarding how to approach public lands issues in the future. His critical comments on the manuscript were also invaluable.

Randy Johnson and Ray Peterson together spent many hours with me, discussing the challenges they faced in working with the citizens of Emery County; representatives from the state of Utah and from federal agencies responsible for managing public lands in the county; a broad range of stakeholders from outside the county; and political leaders in Congress. Their persistence in seeking viable compromises regarding the use of public lands in Emery County over nearly a quarter century has earned my admiration and enormous respect.

Randy also deserves thanks for introducing me to the genesis of the effort that led to the passage of the Washington County Land Bill.

Rick Johnson, former director of the Idaho Conservation League, was extraordinarily generous with his time, providing his perspective both on the efforts that led to the Owyhee Canyonlands and Boulder–White Clouds Wilderness Areas, and on the increasing role that conservation collaboratives are playing in catalyzing constructive discussion regarding public lands in the West.

Rick introduced me to Lindsay Slater, chief of staff for U.S. Representative Mike Simpson, and to Representative Simpson. Discussions with Lindsay and Representative Simpson by phone and in Washington offered insights into the complexities of bringing together stakeholders and negotiating the political compromises that were essential to creating the wilderness areas.

My conversations with Tyler Owens by phone and in Washington provided essential insight into the multiyear effort that led to the compromise that created wilderness and national conservation areas in Washington County while also providing land needed to accommodate the expansion of St. George, Utah.

The late senator Robert Bennett (R-Utah) also contributed his thoughts regarding the factors that led to the successful passage of the Washington County Land Bill, as well as the challenges faced in enacting public lands legislation in this era of extreme polarization.

I owe a great debt of gratitude to the staff members on the House and Senate side who worked tirelessly to forge the compromises needed to bring the Emery County Public Lands Management Act across the finish line.

Ron Dean, who served on Senator Orrin Hatch's staff for over two decades, was patient with my questioning and candid with his insights into the factors that led to the successful passage of the Emery County bill. Romel Nicholas, also of Senator Hatch's staff, provided candid, colorful, and insightful analysis of how the "sausage" that became the Emery County bill was made.

I owe a particular debt of gratitude to Jake Bornstein, who serves on U.S. Representative John Curtis's staff. Jake was an essential source of background information, and was always willing to answer questions and clarify my thinking as well as my prose. His linking me to many of the individuals listed above was essential to shaping and rounding out the story of the Emery County bill.

A heartfelt thanks to Representative John Curtis. His willingness to make his staff available, and to speak candidly about the Emery County bill and other public lands issues—whether by phone, in Washington, or in Emery County—was beyond valuable. In our conversations, he spoke with passion about his love for public lands, and expressed deep commitment to exploring policies aimed at supporting the people who live closest to them. Muchas gracias, Representative Curtis!

Nate Rydman once again served as pilot for an overflight of Emery County in May 2017. His knowledge of the landscape—both from the air and on the ground—proved invaluable.

My deepest thanks and appreciation to Kathy Huntington and Rebecca Robinson Schlessinger, whose help in editing multiple drafts of the manuscript has been critical. Their comments have kept me (and the text) from wandering too far off logical paths, and their candor reigned in my tendency to indulge my passions for an issue at the expense of more reasonable exposition. Thanks, daughter and granddaughter!

Finally, I would be remiss were I not to mention Gwyn Enright, my traveling companion during the period when much of the background research and aerial photography for this book was carried out. Gwyn attempted, and sometimes managed, to modulate my tendencies to "get out over my skis" whether on a hike or in evaluating whether my Toyota 4Runner could navigate a particularly challenging bit of terrain. She tried, often with little success, to remind me that there was more to life than work, and to at least attempt to be in the moment once in a while. Gwyn passed away in January 2020. I do and will continue to miss her.

The authors are grateful for support provided by the Center for Large Landscape Conservation.

Appendix A

Lands Proposed for Additional Protection

In 1989, Utah Representative Wayne Owens (D-Utah) introduced America's Red Rock Wilderness Act (ARRWA). The act, supported by the Southern Utah Wilderness Alliance (SUWA), the Sierra Club, and over two hundred conservation organizations, advocated for congressional action to protect large tracts of public lands in the Intermountain West as wilderness. In 1997, Senator Richard Durbin (D-Ill.) introduced a version of the bill in the U.S. Senate. Despite having gained a significant number of cosponsors in the House and Senate over the past two decades, the bill has yet (as of 2021) to receive majority support in either chamber.

Among the iconic lands identified as meriting wilderness protection in the ARRWA are the Molen Reef, Mussentuchit Badlands, San Rafael Desert, and Price River Basin. SUWA in particular continues to spearhead efforts to obtain wilderness designations for these regions.

In June 2015, the Utah Rock Art Research Association (URARA) forwarded a proposal via then representative Jason Chaffetz (R-Utah) to Representative Rob Bishop (R-Utah), at that time chair of the House Committee on Natural Resources, to have the area around the Molen Reef declared a national conservation area. This proposal, based on a survey of Native American cultural sites, argued for protecting a somewhat larger area around the reef than was originally identified in the ARRWA.[1]

In the next sections, we outline the rationale for seeking some form of protection for each of these four areas. Later, we summarize the threats to the areas, along with the concerns raised by Emery County residents should these areas gain protections and possibly constrain future economic uses

1. Proposed Molen Reef National Conservation Area, submitted to the House Energy and Natural Resources Committee by the Utah Rock Art Research Association in June 2015.

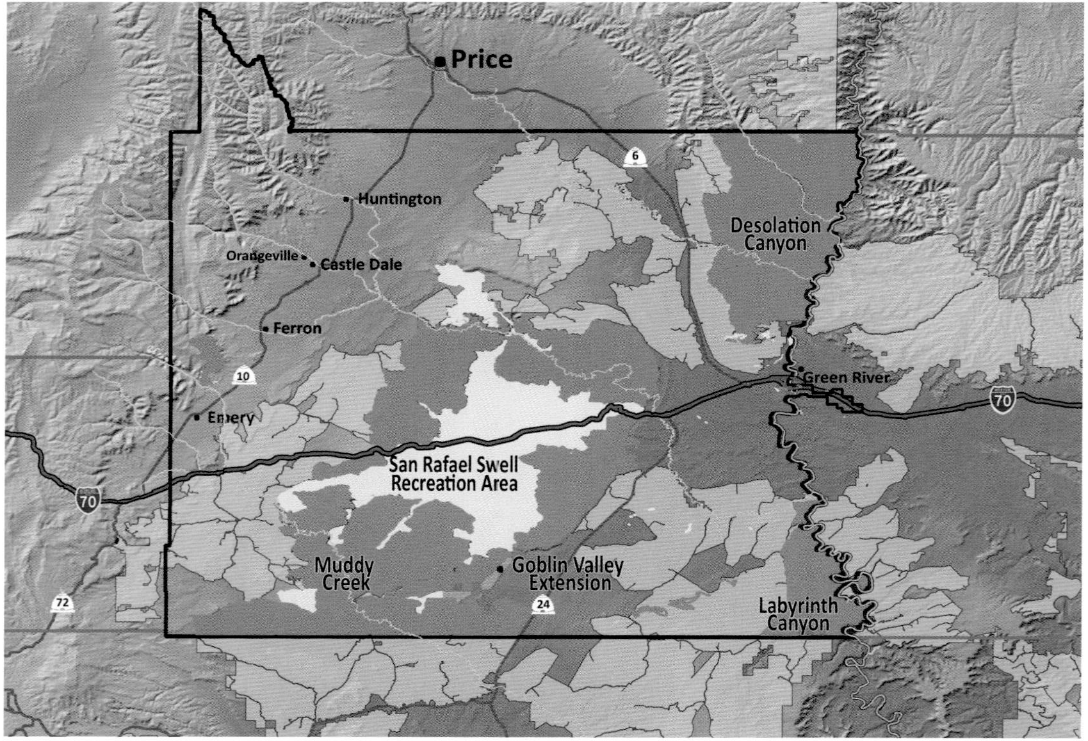

Map of Emery County with protected lands and potential protected lands indicated. Areas protected by the Emery County Public Land Management Act include Muddy Creek, Labyrinth Canyon, and Desolation Wilderness Areas (*brown*); the San Rafael Swell Recreation Area (*light blue*); and the Goblin Valley Extension (*green*). The map also indicates lands included in the proposed America's Red Rock Wilderness Act (*butterscotch yellow*) and the area proposed by the Utah Rock Art Research Association for designation as the Molen Reef National Conservation Area (*light purple, superimposed onto the yellow*). These potential protected lands include the San Rafael Desert (*yellow*), to the west of Labyrinth Canyon; Price River drainage (*yellow*), to the west of Desolation Canyon; and the Mussentuchit Badlands, to the south of Interstate 70 and west of Muddy Creek Wilderness (*yellow/purple*).

or traditional access. We end by suggesting possible options for balancing arguments for conservation with the needs of Emery County citizens.

Rationale for Seeking Protection for Four Regions

The four areas for which additional protections are currently sought by URARA, SUWA, and other organizations are described in some detail in the first chapter, "Emery County: Its Land and People." Here we summarize the key arguments that motivate these ongoing efforts.

Molen Reef

The Molen Reef possesses a unique combination of paleontological richness, cultural resources, and geological diversity. The landscapes of the region are as dramatic as they are austere, inviting contemplation of deep time. The history of Indigenous cultures spanning ten millennia is written along and adjacent to the reef. Without protection, that history may be lost should

The Molen Reef stretches across the landscape east of Castle Valley (tall mesas starting in the upper part of the photograph). The reddish badlands toward the center of the photo are densely fossiliferous. Aerial photo by Stephen E. Strom.

Fremont petroglyphs, Molen Reef. Photo by Jonathan T. Bailey.

mines, oil and gas exploration, and associated road usage inadvertently damage the land.

Mussentuchit Badlands

The landscapes of the badlands region—ranging from rolling gray-blue lands, to colorful, rugged badlands threaded by an intricate web of washes, gullies, and ravines, to volcanic dikes and boulders—evoke wonder, and invite silent reverence. Indigenous peoples who once occupied these spaces left haunting rock art that record history and stories that span millennia. Other historical places are found throughout the region: ranch sites, stock tanks, and small clay, selenite, and gypsum mines. URARA, SUWA, and their supporters believe it important that the area be protected, lest its rich cultural history fall victim to industrialism.

San Rafael Desert

The stark, windswept landscape of the San Rafael Desert is threaded by the San Rafael, Green, and Dirty Devil Rivers, which over eons have carved ser-

Chromatic and sculptural rhythms in the Mussentuchit Badlands landscape. Aerial image by Stephen E. Strom.

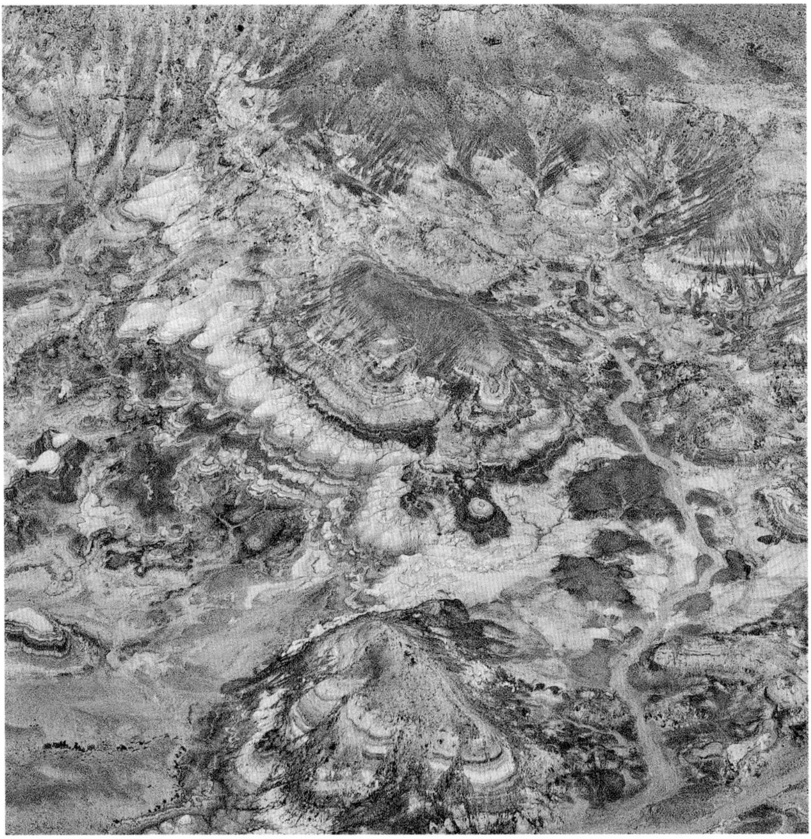

Badlands, northern San Rafael Desert. Aerial photo by Stephen E. Strom.

pentine slot canyons and red rock canyons now bounded by towering walls. The region has been occupied for more than ten thousand years. Rock art from the Archaic period and Fremont complex, as well as from more recent Ute occupation, is found throughout the landscape. The region's Native artifacts and compelling geology argue for consideration of additional protection.

Price River Drainage

Originating in the Wasatch Plateau, the Price River winds its way through Carbon County, into Emery County, and to its confluence with the Green River in the Book Cliffs. Scenic cliffs and rugged terrain surround this remote river,

Slot canyon tributary to the San Rafael River in the northern San Rafael Desert. Photo by Jonathan T. Bailey.

Examples of rock art in the Mussentuchit Badlands, San Rafael Desert, and Price River Basin: Fremont (*upper left*), Fremont / Archaic period transition (*upper right*), Barrier Canyon Style (*lower left*), and Fremont (*lower right*). Photos by Jonathan T. Bailey. Locations omitted to protect the sites.

and harbor the cultural history of Indigenous peoples who once depended on the river for sustenance. The extent of these cultural resources is barely known and, without protection, may be lost.

Threats to the Four Regions

All of these regions are threatened by vandalism and looting of cultural and historical sites; irresponsible off-highway vehicle (OHV) usage, which can destroy sensitive desert landscapes; and oil and gas developments, whose management protocols often fail to protect sensitive sites and landscapes.

At present, most of these lands are managed by the Bureau of Land Management (BLM). The agency, as currently configured and funded, lacks the resources and people needed either to survey the cultural resources in the area, or to protect known important sites. Typically, a BLM ranger working out of the Price Field Office is responsible for patrolling several million acres in Emery County: an impossible task. Moreover, there are but two archaeologists assigned to the field office. Even with their work supplemented by collaborative efforts with university-based and other groups, the archaeologists face the nearly impossible task of identifying and gaining a comprehensive understanding of cultural resources in Emery County's public lands.

OHV enthusiasts find the landscape both compelling and challenging. Many Utahns and visitors make use of OHVs to explore the geological, historical, and cultural wonders of the region. The majority respect designated travel routes and recreate in a responsible manner. However, a subset of OHV users believe that there should be little constraint on their "freedom" to travel anywhere on public lands, even in areas with the barest hint of a two-track "road." The irresponsible actions of a few can have long-lasting, destructive effects on sensitive landscapes.

To different degrees, all four regions are believed to contain oil and gas resources. At present, parcels of public lands deemed suitable are offered publicly for leasing. Individuals or corporate entities granted leases are then charged with making a good-faith effort to assess the viability of leased land for mineral extraction. In many cases, the areas surrounding lands offered for auction have not been thoroughly evaluated for the presence of nearby cultural resources, and as a result, such resources may well be damaged in the course of exploratory drilling.

Concerns of Emery County Citizens

In 2012, Emery County adopted a county plan that outlined policies, objectives, and proposed implementation steps agreed to by county residents in the course of open public meetings.[2] The plan details concerns regarding selected regions of the county, including parts or all of the Molen Reef, Mussentuchit Badlands, San Rafael Desert, and Price River region.

2. "Emery County General Plan: County Policies, Objectives and Action Steps," Emery County, Utah (government website), accessed June 2, 2021, http://www.emerycounty.com/b&z/2012-general-plan-final-draft.pdf.

The plan's recommendations for managing each region express the county's desire to ensure a robust economic future and continued access to public lands within the county. Specifically, the plan calls for:

(1) Achieving and maintaining a continuing yield of mineral resources, with emphasis on oil and gas extraction where possible.
(2) Achieving and maintaining livestock grazing at the highest sustainable levels.
(3) Maintaining and keeping open all roads, and developing new access roads as needed.
(4) Achieving and maintaining traditional access to outdoor recreational opportunities. Here the county is specific in stating that recreational access should avoid favoring any one mode of recreation to the exclusion of others. "Traditionally, outdoor recreational opportunities in the Molen Reef Region have been open and accessible to working class families, to families with small children, to the sick and persons with disabilities, to the middle aged and elderly, to persons of different cultures for whom a primitive solitary hike may not be the preferred form of recreating."[3]
(5) Opposing wilderness designations, or managing lands within these regions for wilderness characteristics.
(6) Opposing designation of areas of critical environmental concern (ACECs) by the BLM absent demonstration that a proposed ACEC meets the criteria for such designations as outlined by the Federal Land Policy and Management Act (FLPMA).
(7) Managing the regions so as to protect precontact rock art, three-dimensional structures, and other artifacts and sites recognized as culturally important and significant by the state of Utah.

Another key section of the plan affirms county support for protecting "an abundance of prehistoric and archaeological resources as well as a strong cultural heritage," and adds that "the preservation of their heritage and cultural resources, including access to the sites and settings of local history has great significance for the citizens of Emery County."[4]

3. "Emery County General Plan," 47.
4. "Emery County General Plan," 6.

The challenge facing the residents of Emery County—and indeed all American citizens—as stewards of public land is how to balance economic needs and cultural perspectives with conservation goals.

The context for initiating dialogue aimed at achieving such a balance is embodied in the opening sections of the plan:

> Emery County recognizes the need to protect and preserve the public lands for present and future generations. It is the stated position and belief of Emery County that there are many land-management tools available that provide protection to public land and its resources in Emery County. Emery County desires to explore all available options and tools for public land management and apply those options that best fit the needs of local public lands on a case-by-case, area-by-area basis. By utilizing a broad array of options, and by allowing local involvement in the decision-making processes, Emery County is confident that the natural values of the lands can be protected without endangering the economic and cultural future of our communities.[5]

Evidence of the county's commitment to these principles is manifest in the compromises that led to the adoption of the Emery County Public Land Management Act.

Possible Paths Forward

In our view, collaborative discussions aimed at exploring creative management approaches for these areas should start at the local level, mirroring the approach of the Emery County Public Lands Council in shaping the Emery County bill.

Actions that would establish a favorable context for successful conversations are: suspending or mitigating potentially damaging activities in selected areas in the county while discussions are underway; seeking funding to enforce extant regulations on public lands in service of protecting those sites; and stipulating that the ultimate goal of the discussion is to protect specific areas of cultural, scientific, and historical interest.

Options worth exploring include: identifying mutually agreed-on ACECs that meet criteria outlined in the FLPMA; working collaboratively to change

5. "Emery County General Plan," 9.

the BLM resource management plan for the regions; and engaging with the county to discuss a mix of possible alternative designations appropriate to land use in specific regions.[6]

The San Rafael Swell Recreation Area Advisory Council and the Emery County Public Lands Council represent two possible forums for initiating such collaborative discussions.

6. "Areas of Critical Environmental Concern," Bureau of Land Management, accessed June 2, 2021, https://www.blm.gov/programs/planning-and-nepa/planning-101/special-planning-designations/acec.

Appendix B

Public Lands Primer

History of Public Lands

Public lands are a uniquely American idea. Nearly a third of our nation's land is held in trust for us by the federal government. All of us, no matter our status in life, have access to a panoply of treasures: national parks, national forests, national monuments, national grasslands, wild and scenic rivers, national recreation areas, national historic sites, and land where humans have yet to significantly alter its natural state: wilderness.

Today, public lands provide expansive habitats for plants and wildlife, stores of minerals and timber, and abundant acreage for grazing, along with opportunities for recreation, solitude, and contemplation of the people and events that shaped our nation. In our fast-paced, largely urbanized life, these lands are a balm for the soul and an essential reminder that America's future can be as wide open with possibility as the past. These lands are truly ours: we the people collectively determine how these lands are to be used or protected.

There might not have been a United States had our Founding Fathers failed to agree to the concept of publicly held lands. Many of the original thirteen colonies claimed lands stretching from their coastal enclaves to an indefinite and little explored "West." Often, colonial claims conflicted. Following the end of the Revolutionary War, as the colonies were faced with the challenge of forming a union, the disposition of these lands became a point of significant controversy. These conflicts were resolved just a year prior to the signing of the Constitution by the Continental Congress.[1]

1. John Leshy, *Debunking Creation Myths About America's Public Lands* (Salt Lake City: University of Utah Press, 2018), 4.

After considerable debate, Congress passed the Northwest Ordinance, in which the colonies agreed that a national government would take ownership of the lands of the Northwest Territory (encompassing much of today's upper Midwest), and laid out a process for admitting states to the nascent union.[2] The status of these publicly owned and federally administered lands was further clarified in the "property clause" of article 4 of the Constitution, which gave Congress authority to "make all needful rules and regulations regarding" these lands and other property "belonging to the United States."[3]

As the country expanded westward, "lands belonging to the United States" increased, first through the Louisiana Purchase, and later through acquisition of Spanish Territory. At one time the amount of public land administered by the federal government totaled 1.5 billion acres.[4]

As each state joined the union, a fraction of the lands within its boundaries was kept as nationally owned and administered public land. For each newly admitted state, the federal government granted a subset of these public lands to be held in trust by the state in order to fund public education.

Early in our history, these public lands were used primarily to generate wealth from livestock grazing, logging, and mineral extraction. The states admitted to the union during the first several decades of the nineteenth century were granted authority to dispose of these public lands. In the latter half of the century, laws regarding the disposition of public lands by newly admitted states became far stricter. As a result, most of the remaining 970,000 square miles (640 million acres) of public land currently held in trust by the federal government is located in the West, while the amount of publicly held land east of the Mississippi now represents only 4 percent of the total.[5]

Public lands played a major role in western expansion. In order to encourage building of transportation infrastructure, Congress passed the Pacific Railway Act of 1862, which provided grants of federal lands to railroads with

2. "The Northwest Ordinance of 1787," History, Art and Archives, U.S. House of Representatives, accessed June 2, 2021, https://history.house.gov/Historical-Highlights/1700s/Northwest-Ordinance-1787/.

3. Leshy, *Debunking Creation Myths*, 5.

4. Leshy, 6.

5. For an excellent map of public lands in the United States, see Quoctrung Bui and Margot Sanger-Katz, "Why the Government Owns So Much Land in the West," *New York Times*, January 5, 2016, https://www.nytimes.com/2016/01/06/upshot/why-the-government-owns-so-much-land-in-the-west.html.

the stipulation that they build tracks to specified locations.[6] The expectation was that people would follow the railroads, establish communities, and increase the value of public lands granted to rail companies.

Higher education was also the beneficiary of public lands. The Morrill Act of 1862 granted federal land to the states in order that profits from sale of those donated lands be used to endow land-grant colleges.[7] The initial mission of these colleges was to teach practical skills: agriculture, mining, science, and engineering. Most of those land-grant colleges evolved into today's public universities, many of them world-class centers of learning.

At the height of the Civil War, Congress passed the Homestead Act, which provided 160-acre lots of public land to citizens who would improve the lot, build a dwelling, and cultivate the land.[8] The completion of railroads and roads, along with the Homestead Act and the hope of starting a new, prosperous life in "virgin" land, spurred a flood of migration westward. The ready availability of vast tracts of public lands provided a base for grazing stock, harvesting timber, and mining minerals. The cost of expansion was high: the tragic loss of lands that long sustained America's Indigenous population, and the deaths—corporeal and spiritual—of Native Americans that followed.

In the 1860s, the first steps were taken to reserve public land for other than economic purposes. In 1864, President Abraham Lincoln signed a bill that granted a large tract of public land around Yosemite, California, to the state, with the purpose of protecting the area in perpetuity for public enjoyment of its beauty and inspirational qualities. In 1872, two million acres of land was set aside as Yellowstone National Park, the first such park in the world. In the 1890s, Yosemite was officially named a national park, as was Sequoia to the south, also in California.[9]

---

6. "Landmark Legislation: The Pacific Railway Act of 1862," U.S. Senate, accessed June 2, 2021, https://www.senate.gov/artandhistory/history/common/generic/PacificRailwayActof1862.htm; Maury Klein, "Financing the Transcontinental Railroad," Gilder Lehrman Institute of American History, accessed June 2, 2021, https://ap.gilderlehrman.org/essays/financing-transcontinental-railroad.

7. Committee on the Future of the Colleges of Agriculture in the Land Grant University System, *Colleges of Agriculture at the Land Grant Universities: A Profile* (Washington, D.C.: National Academies Press, 1995), chap. 1, https://www.nap.edu/read/4980/chapter/2.

8. "About the Homestead Act," National Park Service, last updated June 16, 2021, https://www.nps.gov/home/learn/historyculture/abouthomesteadactlaw.htm.

9. Leshy, *Debunking Creation Myths*, 11–12.

In the relentless quest for wealth in a rapidly growing nation, public lands often became degraded as a result of overgrazing, clear-cutting, and mineral extraction that scarred the lands. In response, a movement to protect and conserve these lands took root and flourished. In 1891, Congress passed the Forest Reserve Act, which gave the president power to reserve public lands to protect watersheds.[10] The act also established forest preserves, the precursors to our current system of national forests. And in 1906, in reaction to desecration of Native American archaeological and cultural sites, Congress passed the Antiquities Act, granting the president the authority to preserve features "of historic or scientific interest that are situated upon the lands owned or controlled by the Government of the United States [as] national monuments."[11]

For more than a century, there has been tension—perhaps inevitable—between those wishing to use public lands to support local, state, and national economic growth, and citizens desiring to conserve those lands for their aesthetic, scientific, cultural, and spiritual values. During the latter half of the twentieth century, efforts to conserve public lands for recreation and wilderness and to sustain a healthy environment have developed powerful constituencies. Their influence is manifest in the 1970 establishment of the Environmental Protection Agency, the passage of foundational environmental legislation including the National Environmental Protection Act of 1970 and the Endangered Species Act of 1973, and the establishment of an ever-increasing number of protected areas: wilderness, national parks, monuments, and recreation areas, among others.

In 1976, passage of the Federal Land Policy and Management Act (FLPMA) brought the tension between use and conservation to a head.[12] FLPMA changed the character of the Bureau of Land Management (BLM, which oversees the largest fraction of public lands in the United States) from one that favored ranching, logging, and mining, to one that seeks a balance among multiple uses including conservation.

---

10. Gerald W. Williams, *The USDA Forest Service: The First Century* (Washington, D.C.: Forest Service, 2005), https://www.fs.usda.gov/sites/default/files/media/2015/06/The_USDA_Forest_Service_TheFirstCentury.pdf.

11. "General Antiquities Act," U.S. Department of Justice, last updated July 15, 2020, https://www.justice.gov/enrd/general-antiquities-act.

12. "BLM and FLPMA," Public Lands Foundation, accessed June 2, 2021, https://publicland.org/about/blm-flpma/.

Neil Kornze, who headed the BLM during the second Obama administration, succinctly summarizes the goals of FLPMA: "FLPMA defines our mission as one of multiple use and sustained yield. This means thoughtful development in the right places to drive economic opportunities for local communities. It also means protecting natural, cultural, and historical resources that are simply too special to develop. And above all, it means working with a changing nation to make decisions that are balanced and forward looking."[13]

In reaction to FLPMA, ranchers, miners, loggers, and some citizens in the West who harbor skepticism toward regulation by the federal government formed a countermovement: the Sagebrush Rebellion.[14] Both the movement and its emotional resonance with many citizens in the West have pervaded land use politics from the mid-1970s to the present.

Nowhere is the tension between economic needs or desires and conservation goals greater than in western public lands counties: counties dominated by public lands. Many citizens in these counties are animated by the spirit behind the Sagebrush Rebellion. Debates about the future uses of these lands are existential. The livelihood of citizens living in these counties is heavily dependent on public land, either directly from employment associated with mineral extraction, ranching, or logging, or indirectly from funds spent by tourists or recreationists. Moreover, residents of many public lands counties have lived among these lands for generations, and formed strong bonds in their communities, with the land, and with the jobs the land provides. Any changes in public land policy affect them economically and culturally.

The conflict between conservation and economic uses has smoldered for generations in some areas, and it permeates discussion of public lands in many rural counties to this day. In others, citizens and conservationists have increasingly begun to develop collaborative approaches aimed at achieving an equitable balance between seemingly incompatible goals. "The most

13. U.S. Department of the Interior, comp., *The Federal Land Policy and Management Act of 1976, as Amended* (Washington, D.C.: Bureau of Land Management, 2016), https://www.blm.gov/sites/blm.gov/files/AboutUs_LawsandRegs_FLPMA.pdf.

14. Jonathan Thompson, "The First Sagebrush Rebellion: What Sparked It and How It Ended," *High Country News* (Paonia, Colo.), January 14, 2016, https://www.hcn.org/articles/a-look-back-at-the-first-sagebrush-rebellion; Florence Williams, "Sagebrush Rebellion II," *High Country News* (Paonia, Colo.), February 24, 1992, https://s3.amazonaws.com/hcn-media/archive-pdf/1992_02_24_Catron.pdf.

successful collaborative processes are . . . community-driven, occur at the scale of the conservation problem, and involve diverse stakeholders who are willing to seek common ground together, share resources and co-create solutions that provide equal benefit to people and place."[15]

A Guide to Public Land Designations and Management

Federally Managed Public Lands

Agencies of the federal government administer 640 million acres on behalf of all U.S. citizens—this land is held in trust for, and open to, all of us. "There are many glories inherent to our federal public lands, but perhaps the most profound is this: they comprise a magnificent assemblage worth trillions of dollars in ecological goods and services and immeasurably more in aesthetic, spiritual, cultural, historic, and psychological benefits and they belong equally to each and every one of us from the homeless person to the dishwasher to the home health aide to the hedge fund manager. Federal lands represent the best remaining strands holding together the web of life."[16]

The fraction of public land is highest in the Mountain West, with federal holdings ranging from 30 percent of the total land area in Colorado to 81 percent in Nevada. In Utah, 63 percent of the land is administered by agencies of the federal government.[17]

The primary agencies responsible for overseeing and caring for these lands are the BLM, the National Park Service (NPS), and the Fish and Wildlife Service (FWS), all housed in the U.S. Department of the Interior,

15. Center for Collaborative Conservation, *Building Capacity for Collaborative Conservation*, May 2017, http://naturalresourcespolicy.org/docs/Final-Needs-Assessment-External-Report-071020175b15d.pdf; Robin S. Reid et al., "Collaborative Conservation in Practice: Current State and Future Directions," Center for Collaborative Conservation, accessed July 10, 2021, https://collaborativeconservation.org/media/sites/142/2018/02/LEE collaborative_conservation_in_practice.pdf.

16. Steven Davis, "Democracy, Collective Values, and Public Lands," Headwaters Economics, May 7, 2019, https://headwaterseconomics.org/public-lands/papl-davis/.

17. U.S. Library of Congress, Congressional Research Service, *Federal Land Ownership: Overview and Data*, by Carol Hardy Vincent, Laura A. Hanson, and Lucas F. Bermejo, R42346 (2020).

and the U.S. Forest Service (USFS), housed within the U.S. Department of Agriculture.[18]

LANDS HELD BY THE BUREAU OF LAND MANAGEMENT

The BLM manages 245 million acres of surface public land in the United States—more land than any federal agency, and nearly all in the western United States. The BLM also manages 700 million acres of underground minerals such as oil and gas, and it oversees the National Landscape Conservation System (NLCS). The NLCS was created in June 2000 to "conserve, protect and restore the BLM's nationally significant resources for future generations." The system now has nearly nine hundred units encompassing twenty-seven million acres of wilderness areas, wilderness study areas, national conservation areas, national monuments, wild and scenic rivers, and national scenic and historic trails. In 2009, President Barack Obama signed the Omnibus Public Land Management Act, which included legislation that provided permanent status to the NLCS.[19]

BLM land is generally managed for "multiple uses": recreation; grazing, timber harvesting, and mineral extraction; protection of watersheds, wildlife, and fish; protection of natural and cultural resources; and protection of wilderness.[20] BLM land lacking additional levels of protection (e.g., an entity such as a national park, national monument, or national recreation

18. "National History," Bureau of Land Management, accessed June 2, 2021, https://www.blm.gov/about/history/timeline; "Quick History of the National Park Service," National Park Service, last updated May 14, 2018, https://www.nps.gov/articles/quick-nps-history.htm; "About the U.S. Fish and Wildlife Service," Fish and Wildlife Service, last updated February 12, 2021, https://www.fws.gov/help/about_us.html; Nancy C. Nye, "Recreation and the U.S. Forest Service," Forest History Society, accessed June 2, 2021, https://foresthistory.org/research-explore/us-forest-service-history/policy-and-law/recreation-u-s-forest-service/.

19. "National Landscape Conservation System Celebrates 10th Birthday," U.S. Department of the Interior, press release, March 24, 2010, https://www.doi.gov/news/pressreleases/National-Landscape-Conservation-System-10th-Birthday-Celebration; Bruce Babbitt, "The National Landscape Conservation System—The Next Ten Years," Center of the American West, April 15, 2010, https://www.centerwest.org/archives/1045.

20. "Multiple Use Lands," U.S. Department of Justice, updated May 12, 2015, https://www.justice.gov/enrd/multiple-use-lands; "Who We Are, What We Do," Bureau of Land Management, accessed June 2, 2021, https://www.blm.gov/about/our-mission.

area) must still be governed subject to applicable environmental statutes and the stipulations of resource management plans unique to each unit of the agency.

LANDS HELD BY THE U.S. FISH AND WILDLIFE SERVICE

The FWS is responsible for the conservation, protection, and enhancement of fish, wildlife, plants, and their ecosystems.[21] The service is charged with implementing the Endangered Species Act, the North American Wetlands Conservation Act, and the Marine Mammal Protection Act. As part of its mission, it protects and attempts to recover endangered species, restores fisheries, conserves wetland habitats, and supports international conservation efforts. FWS manages 95 million land acres, 760 million submerged lands and waters, 567 national wildlife refuges, 5 marine national monuments, and 63 refuges containing wilderness areas.[22]

LANDS HELD BY THE U.S. FOREST SERVICE

The USFS is part of the U.S. Department of Agriculture.[23] The USFS oversees 193 million acres of public land and is charged with managing national forests and national grasslands.[24] There are 154 national forests located throughout the United States, and twenty national grasslands, all but four of which are located in or on the edge of the Great Plains.[25] The USFS regularly develops land management plans that provide the legal context for balancing multiple uses: conservation, timber harvesting, livestock grazing, watershed protection, fish and wildlife protection, land restoration, and recreation.

---

21. U.S. Library of Congress, Congressional Research Service, *U.S. Fish and Wildlife Service: An Overview*, author redacted, R45265 (2018).

22. "Public Lands and Waters," U.S. Fish and Wildlife Service, last updated June 8, 2021, https://www.fws.gov/refuges/about/public-lands-waters/.

23. "Our History," Forest Service, accessed June 2, 2021, https://www.fs.usda.gov/learn/our-history.

24. "Forests and Grasslands," Forest Service, accessed June 2, 2021, https://www.fs.usda.gov/managing-land/national-forests-grasslands.

25. "The National Grassland Story," Forest Service, accessed June 2, 2021, https://www.fs.fed.us/grasslands/aboutus/index.shtml; Francis Moul, "National Grasslands," Encyclopedia of the Great Plains, University of Nebraska, Lincoln, accessed June 2, 2021, http://plainshumanities.unl.edu/encyclopedia/doc/egp.sr.039.

Missions of Federal Agencies Responsible for Managing Public Lands

NATIONAL PARK SERVICE

The NPS was established in 1916 as a new bureau within the U.S. Department of the Interior. It is charged with administering and preserving all elements of the national park system: national parks, monuments, battlefields, historic sites, lakeshores, seashores, recreation areas, and scenic rivers. Together, these areas cover more than eighty-four million acres. The mission of the NPS is "to conserve the scenery and natural and historic objects and wildlife therein and to provide for the enjoyment of the same in such manner and by such means as will leave them unimpaired for the enjoyment of this and future generations."[26]

BUREAU OF LAND MANAGEMENT

The BLM is also located within the U.S. Department of the Interior. The agency is the bureaucratic descendant of two entities, the General Land Office and the U.S. Grazing Service, which merged in 1946.

In 1976, Congress passed the FLPMA, which established the term "multiple use management" to clarify the BLM's dual role of using public lands for their economic benefits as well their natural beauty and other conservation values. At present, the BLM describes its mission as "sustaining the health, diversity and productivity of America's public lands for the use and enjoyment of present and future generations."[27]

U.S. FISH AND WILDLIFE SERVICE

The FWS, along with the NPS and BLM, is located within the U.S. Department of the Interior. The agency oversees programs aimed at ensuring the viability of coastal ecosystems and bird habitats, and the health of freshwater and saltwater bodies of water that support a variety of fish species.

The FWS was created in 1940 when two agencies merged: the Commission on Fish and Fisheries, established in 1871; and the Division of Economic Ornithology and Mammalogy, established in 1885.

---

26. "About the National Park Service," National Park Service, last updated March 30, 2016, https://www.nps.gov/aboutus/aboutus.htm.

27. "Our Mission," Bureau of Land Management, accessed June 2, 2021, https://www.blm.gov/about/our-mission.

Since 1973, the FWS has been charged with administering the Endangered Species Act, which provides for conservation of species that are in danger of extinction, and for preservation of the ecosystems on which they depend.

The FWS views its mission as "working with others to conserve, protect and enhance fish, wildlife, plants and their habitats for the continuing benefit of the American people."[28]

U.S. FOREST SERVICE

The USFS is part of the U.S. Department of Agriculture and is responsible for managing lands designated as national forests or national grasslands. The agency carries out a number of functions including fighting forest fires, protecting wilderness and wildlife, managing timber production, carrying out scientific research, supporting recreation, and stewarding broad ecosystems.[29]

The USFS is a descendant of the Department of Agriculture's Division of Forestry, formed in 1881. As is the case with the BLM, the USFS manages land for multiple uses: ensuring productivity of the land and protecting the quality of the environment.

The USFS views its mission as "to sustain the health, diversity, and productivity of the nation's forests and grasslands to meet the needs of present and future generations." Its motto is "Caring for the land and serving people."[30]

Public Lands Having Additional Layers of Protection

Most Americans are familiar with national parks and national monuments, but less well known are national conservation areas, national recreation areas, wilderness study areas, wilderness areas, national recreation areas, and wild and scenic rivers. All these designations have been made with the goal of providing enhanced levels of protection of federal land already in the public domain.

28. "FWS Fundamentals," U.S. Fish and Wildlife Service, last updated July 16, 2013, https://www.fws.gov/info/pocketguide/fundamentals.html.

29. "Managing the Land," Forest Service, accessed June 2, 2021, https://www.fs.usda.gov/managing-land.

30. "Meet the Forest Service," Forest Service, accessed June 2, 2021, https://www.fs.usda.gov/about-agency/meet-forest-service.

NATIONAL PARKS

National parks are "spacious land . . . areas essentially in their primeval condition and so outstandingly superior in beauty to average examples of their several types as to demand preservation intact and in their entirety for the enjoyment, education and inspiration of all the people for all time."[31] They are designated as parks by acts of Congress and managed by the NPS to ensure that activities within the park do not cause impairment of natural resources, and to preserve the park ecosystem as well as individual plant and animal species.[32]

NATIONAL MONUMENTS

National monuments protect public lands most often via proclamation by the president of the United States, under executive powers granted by the Antiquities Act of 1906, but they are also occasionally named by act of Congress. The Antiquities Act was enacted in response to rampant looting of Native artifacts and archaeological sites, and it empowers a president to set aside monuments to protect "historic landmarks, historic and prehistoric structures, and other objects of historic or scientific interest."[33] Monuments can be administered by the NPS, BLM, USFS, and FWS, individually or jointly.[34] The level of protection offered by a monument varies. In most monuments, livestock grazing is permitted, though often with significant restrictions. Mining activities may be permitted depending on the language of the enabling legislation, so long as such activities do not cause significant degradation to the landscape or affect protected cultural resources. No new mining claims can be issued once a monument is declared. The framework

31. Devereux Butcher, *Exploring Our National Parks and Monuments*, 6th ed. (Boston: Houghton Mifflin, 1969), 356.

32. "Brief History of the National Parks," Library of Congress, accessed June 2, 2021, https://www.loc.gov/collections/national-parks-maps/articles-and-essays/brief-history-of-the-national-parks/; Dave Harmon and Jeff Jarvis, "The National Landscape Conservation System: A Model for Conservation of Significant Landscapes," in *Science and Stewardship to Protect and Sustain Wilderness Values*, comp. Alan Watson, Joaquin Murrieta-Salvidar, and Brooke McBride (Fort Collins, Colo.: Rocky Mountain Research Station), 185–89, https://www.fs.usda.gov/treesearch/pubs/38793.

33. U.S. Library of Congress, Congressional Research Service, *National Monuments and the Antiquities Act*, by Carol Hardy Vincent, R41330 (2018).

34. "How We Designate National Monuments," Wilderness Society, accessed June 2, 2021, https://www.wilderness.org/articles/article/how-we-designate-monuments.

for managing a monument is set either by the president's declaration, or—if it was declared by Congress—by its enabling legislation. The detailed management plan for a monument is typically developed by the federal agency responsible for overseeing it.

NATIONAL CONSERVATION AREAS

National conservation areas are designated by Congress to conserve, protect, and manage public lands for the benefit of current and future generations. Factors that enter into consideration when deciding to establish a national conservation area include cultural, ecological, historical, scientific, and recreational values.[35]

The level of protection offered by national conservation areas varies. Typically, management plans are developed over a period of years via consultation with the public at large and key stakeholders. Livestock grazing and mining can usually continue, subject to the regulations spelled out in either the enabling legislation or the management plan. The BLM is the agency most frequently charged with managing national conservation areas.

NATIONAL RECREATION AREAS

National recreation areas are designated by Congress. The majority are located near large reservoirs or other bodies of water that offer water-based recreational activities: kayaking, fishing, and boating. One well-known example is the first national recreation area to be established by legislative statute: Lake Mead National Recreation Area, on the Arizona/Nevada border. National recreation areas may also protect nearby natural or cultural resources, and the designation has also been used for natural areas proximate to urban centers. National recreation areas can be managed by the NPS, USFS, or BLM.

WILDERNESS STUDY AREAS

A provision of the 1976 FLPMA directed the BLM to evaluate all lands under its jurisdiction for wilderness qualities. The survey resulted in the designa-

---

35. "Monuments, Conservation Areas and Similar Designations," Bureau of Land Management, accessed June 2, 2021, https://www.blm.gov/programs/national-conservation-lands/monuments-ncas; "America's Public Lands Explained," U.S. Department of the Interior, June 13, 2016, https://www.doi.gov/blog/americas-public-lands-explained.

tion of wilderness study areas (WSAs), areas of federal land deemed to have wilderness characteristics in terms of size (roadless areas of at least five thousand acres) and primitive natural qualities (appearance affected primarily by natural rather than human activity), along with opportunities for primitive recreation and/or solitude.[36] Each WSA is managed by the BLM as part of the NLCS in a manner that ensures that the area is preserved as wilderness until Congress either designates it as wilderness or releases it from WSA status. Released WSAs continue to be managed in a manner that minimizes impairment of wilderness characteristics.[37]

WILDERNESS AREAS

Wilderness areas, according to the Wilderness Act of 1964, "are area(s) where the earth and community of life are untrammeled by man, where man himself is a visitor who does not remain."[38] Public lands having those characteristics can be designated as wilderness areas by Congress and, upon recognition as wilderness, become part of National Wilderness Preservation System.[39] Wilderness designation provides the strongest protection of public lands: logging, mining, and motorized vehicles are not permitted, although in some areas, livestock grazing and mining are allowed if they antedate the declaration of wilderness. Some areas permit regulated hunting.

WILD AND SCENIC RIVERS

Wild and scenic rivers are areas designated by Congress or the secretary of the interior in order to "preserve certain rivers with outstanding natural, cultural, and recreational values in a free-flowing condition for the enjoyment of present and future generations." As of 2019, the National System of Wild and Scenic Rivers protects more than 13,000 miles of 226 rivers in forty-one

---

36. "Wilderness and Wilderness Study Areas," Bureau of Land Management, accessed June 2, 2021, https://www.blm.gov/programs/national-conservation-lands/wilderness.

37. "What Is a Wilderness Study Area?," Wilderness Study Area Management Module 1, National Conservation Lands, Wyoming County Commissioners Association, accessed June 1, 2021, http://www.wyo-wcca.org/~wcca/files/2714/9445/7104/What_is_a_Wilderness_Study_Area.pdf.

38. "The Wilderness Act of 1964," U.S. Department of Justice, updated May 12, 2015, https://www.justice.gov/enrd/wilderness-act-1964.

39. "Wilderness and Wilderness Study Areas," Bureau of Land Management.

states and Puerto Rico.[40] Administration of designated rivers is carried out by the BLM, USFS, and FWS, with coordination among agencies effected by the NPS.

NATIONAL SCENIC AND HISTORIC TRAILS

National scenic and historic trails are designated by Congress for protection of trails that follow historic routes of exploration, migration, trade, and military battles. They provide a way of placing these historic events in the landscape context in which they took place. The BLM administers and manages eighteen designated trails in fifteen states as part of the NCLS.[41]

State Trust Lands

In 1787, the Northwest Ordinance was passed by the Congress of the Confederation of the United States.[42] It anticipated that new states would emerge from the Northwest Territories (now the upper Midwest) and required that part of the lands within the boundaries of any newly admitted state would be administered by the federal government as public land. Under the terms of the ordinance, Congress established a policy of granting a subset of those public lands to the states, with the goal of providing the states with an asset to be held in trust to generate funds for support of public education.[43] Examining land use maps in many western states reveals vast tracts of public lands, which include within their boundaries a checkerboard pattern of one-mile-square (640-acre) "sections" of school trust lands. The most common revenue return from these lands in the West comes from resource extraction: minerals, oil and gas, and timber. In Utah,

---

40. "About the WSR Act," National Wild and Scenic Rivers System, March 2019, https://www.rivers.gov/wsr-act.php.

41. "National Scenic and Historic Trails," Bureau of Land Management, accessed June 2, 2021, https://www.blm.gov/programs/national-conservation-lands/national-scenic-and-historic-trails.

42. "The Northwest Ordinance of 1787," History, Art and Archives, U.S. House of Representatives, accessed June 2, 2021, https://history.house.gov/Historical-Highlights/1700s/Northwest-Ordinance-1787/.

43. Andy Laurenzi, "State Trust Lands: Balancing Public Value and Fiduciary Responsibility," Lincoln Institute of Land Policy, July 2004, https://www.lincolninst.edu/publications/articles/state-trust-lands.

state lands are administered by the School and Institutional Trust Lands Administration (SITLA).[44]

Additional Resources

Durrant, Jeffrey O. *Struggle Over Utah's San Rafael Swell: Wilderness, National Conservation Areas, and National Monuments* (Tucson: University of Arizona Press, 2007).

Johnson, Rick. "'Endless Pressure, Endlessly Applied': Idaho's Boulder–White Clouds Wilderness Bill." EDR Blog, University of Utah, June 20, 2016, https://law.utah.edu/endless-pressure-endlessly-applied-idahos-boulder-white-clouds-wilderness-bill/.

Schultz, Erik B. "A New Approach to Idaho Wilderness: History and Politics of the Boulder–White Clouds." Master's thesis, Prescott College in Environmental Studies, 2006. ProQuest 304718155 (open access).

44. "Trust Lands Administration (SITLA)," Utah Division of State History, accessed June 2, 2021, https://history.utah.gov/repository-item/trust-lands-administration-sitla/.

INDEX

Note: Pages in *italic type* refer to illustrative matter.

ABOUT THE AUTHORS

Stephen E. Strom is a retired astronomer who has served in numerous positions including chair of the Galactic and Extragalactic Program at Kitt Peak National Observatory, chairman of the Five College Astronomy Department, and staff member at the National Optical Astronomy Observatory in Tucson, Arizona. He received his PhD in astronomy from Harvard University. He is also a photographer and is a part of several permanent collections at the Center for Creative Photography at the University of Arizona, the Fred Jones Jr. Museum of Art at the University of Oklahoma, the Mead Art Museum in Amherst, Massachusetts, and the Boston Museum of Fine Arts. His photography has appeared alongside poems and essays in several books, including *Secrets from the Center of the World* (1989), *Sonoita Plain* (2005), *Tseyi / Deep in the Rock* (2005), *Otero Mesa* (2008), *Earth and Mars: A Reflection* (2015), and *Voices from Bears Ears: Seeking Common Ground on Sacred Land* (2018). His website is https://www.stephenstrom.com/.

Jonathan T. Bailey is a conservation photographer with a background in cultural resources. He has directed or participated in various conservation projects seeking protections for thousands of tribal heritage sites, numerous federally listed endangered species, and millions of acres of public lands; and he has worked with tribal leaders, politicians ranging from rural commissioners to congressional representatives, conservation groups, energy executives, archaeological organizations, ranchers, and individual stakeholders. His work has appeared in books including *Rock Art: A Vision of a Vanishing Cultural Landscape* (2009) and *When I Was Red Clay* (2022) and numerous places such as *Archaeology Southwest, Salt Lake Tribune, Landscape Photography Magazine, NBC News*, and *Indian Country Today*. His website is https://www.baileyimages.com/.